The English/ Language Arts Handbook

Classroom Strategies for Teachers

Stephen N. Tchudi
Susan J. Tchudi

Department of English
University of Nevada
Reno, Nevada

Boynton/Cook Publishers
Heinemann
Portsmouth, New Hampshire

Boynton/Cook Publishers, Inc.
A Subsidiary of Reed Publishing (USA) Inc.
361 Hanover Street, Portsmouth, NH 03801-3912
Offices and agents throughout the world

© 1991 by Stephen N. Tchudi and Susan J. Tchudi. Portions originally © 1979 by Winthrop Publishers, Inc., under the title *The English Teacher's Handbook: Ideas and Resources for Teaching English*. All rights reserved.

Every effort has been made to contact copyright holders for permission to reprint borrowed material where necessary, but if any oversights have occurred, we would be happy to rectify them in future printings of this work.

Library of Congress Cataloging-in-Publication Data

Tchudi, Stephen, 1942–
    The English/language arts handbook : classroom strategies for
teachers / Stephen N. Tchudi and Susan J. Tchudi.
       p. cm.
    Rev. ed. of: The English teacher's handbook. c 1979.
    Includes bibliographical references (p.) and index.
    ISBN 0-86709-288-2
    1. Language arts.   2. English language—Study and teaching.
I. Tchudi, Susan J. (Susan Jane), 1945– . II. Tchudi, Stephen,
1942–   English teacher's handbook. III. Title.
LB1576.T358   1991
428'.007–dc20   91-11034
                                      CIP

Designed by Maria Szmauz.

Printed in the United States of America.

   93 94 95   9 8 7 6 5 4 3

Contents

f o u r ○ Ideas for Teaching Language   161

f i v e ○ The Profession of Teaching   207

Preface

This new edition of *The English/Language Arts Handbook* (formerly *The English Teacher's Handbook*) comes to you with a long and winding history. That history began in the mid-1970s with the publication of *The Inkwell,* a monthly newsletter for English/language arts teachers. Your entrepreneurial authors believed that a practical, classroom-oriented newsletter would provide a service for teachers in the field and possibly bring us modest fortune. We had sensed in our university classes and at professional meetings a strong interest in how-to-do-it materials, and we found in *The Inkwell* a way of getting teaching ideas into the hands of a number of elementary and secondary teachers in the United States as well as the United Kingdom, Canada, New Zealand, and Australia.

Our entrepreneurial and writing energies were less than we had imagined, however, and after two years we discovered that we couldn't keep up writing, typing, and licking the stamps for *The Inkwell* by ourselves. Nor was our circulation great enough to warrant hiring others to do the dirty work (whether toiling at the typewriter or sorting newsletters by zip code). We condensed and reorganized the material into a book, which was subsequently published by Winthrop Publishers, then headed by Paul O'Connell.

We hope it wasn't causal, but shortly afterward Winthrop Publishers was absorbed by Little, Brown, and not too long after that, we received word that Little, Brown (and *The English Teacher's Handbook*) had become the catch of a still bigger fish: Scott, Foresman. When asked by colleagues who published our book or how they could obtain copies, we as often as not replied "Who knows?"

We're now delighted that the book, thoroughly revised, is being published by Boynton/Cook–Heinemann, which has, in our judgment, become the premier publisher of books in the field of English education. We hope that Boynton/Cook–Heinemann and *The English/Language Arts Handbook* have a long and happy publishing life together.

If you're familiar with the first edition, you'll see we've retained the earlier format, which proved popular and useful for both experienced teachers and prospective teachers in English methods classes. Each chapter begins with a concise overview of current theory regarding a particular aspect of English education, which is then followed by numerous practical teaching ideas that grow from that philosophy. We want to reemphasize that this isn't simply a grab bag of ideas or an eclectic smorgasbord. We're committed to a philosophy of English/language arts education that's variously and synonymously labeled *student centered, holistic, whole language, experience centered,* or *personal growth.* We believe you'll find our various activities consistent with that view of the teaching and learning of language.

As in the first edition, each section of the book concludes with a "Summary and Troubleshooting" chapter, in which we recap the main ideas of the section, and more important, discuss some of the problems that may emerge when you move from the printed pages of this book to your own classroom.

Those of you familiar with the first edition will also detect some rearranging of materials and ideas in this edition, and we've added a great deal of new stuff, in particular material reflecting the growing professional interest in electronic media, diversity in education, pluralism in society, and language as the core of learning in all disciplines.

Some of you may puzzle why, if we're committed to whole language, our chapter divisions follow the older "tripod" model of literature, composition, and language. In reply we note first that in each section of the *Handbook* we liberally cross-reference to show how the various components of the language arts intersect, and second that realistically, most of you still shift your focus among components of the tripod rather than trying to teach all aspects of language at once.

We readily admit that by no means did we dream up every last teaching idea or strategy that appears in these pages. Many come from the common stock or "lore" of bright ideas that are in circulation in our profession; many have been shared with us by our students in methods classes, in-service days, and summer workshops. We want to express our gratitude to those who've swapped ideas with us, even as we regret that we aren't able in every case to acknowledge the source of those ideas.

At the suggestion of our new publisher, we've changed the title of the book to reflect our increasing recognition that there isn't a great gap between theory and practice of teaching "English" at the secondary level and "language arts" in the middle schools, junior high schools, and elementary grades. We'll use the terms interchangeably (and often simultaneously, as the linked hybrid *English/language arts*) throughout the book, even as we urge you to adapt these ideas and strategies to the unique teaching situations in which you find yourselves.

We contemplated one other title for this second edition. In the first edition we noted that teaching English/language arts is potentially and fundamentally a positive, joyful act. Two popular books, *The Joy of Cooking* and *The Joy of Sex* (still best-sellers in new editions), are how-to books that combine discussion of naturally pleasurable activities with techniques and resources for making that pleasure greater. Perhaps we should have titled this edition *The Joy of Teaching English/Language Arts.*

Introduction

Do Not Remove
Under Penalty of Law

ou recall those labels, no doubt. They appear on pillows and mattresses and tell the consumer that an item is made from fresh filling, not recycled newspapers or old socks. If you were like us as a child, you probably wondered just what would happen if you removed that tag. The bolder among you probably *removed* the tag and waited for the consequences. (Steve confesses to having once removed a tag on a camp companion's sleeping bag just to see what would happen—to somebody else.)

There is no penalty if you skip the introduction of this book, as many readers may be tempted to do. You may feel an urge to plunge directly into the chapters most directly related to your current teaching interests: teaching writing, say, or helping students with correctness.

The COPS—Curriculum Overseeing and Protection Service—won't haul you out of bed in the middle of the night if you bypass the introduction (though, who knows, they may want to check the tags on your mattress and pillows!).

Nevertheless, we urge you not to "remove" the introduction from your reading list, and we ask you to spend a few minutes as we give you an orientation to our approach. We're especially concerned that *The English/Language Arts Handbook* not be perceived as a random collection of teaching strategies that "seem to work" for somebody or other. We've worked hard to give the book an intellectual center along with an orientation to classroom practice. We've included teaching ideas that hang together around a research- and practice-based approach to English/language arts instruction.

This book is necessary because we teach in dramatic, exciting, controversial times, and good teachers must be able to link their day-to-day practices consistently and defensibly to a coherent theory of instruction.

The teaching of English/language arts has undergone extraordinary changes in the past two and a half decades. It's easy to oversimplify, but in general, until the 1960s, English/language arts were taught by bits and pieces of knowledge: knowledge about spelling, grammar, authors' names, book titles, patterns of paragraph development.

1

"So what has changed?" you ask. "That's precisely how *I* was taught and how kids in my neighborhood are *being* taught."

Despite the persistence of older practices, it's fair to say that since the 1960s we have developed an approach to learning language arts that is centered in a deeper understanding of how language is acquired, how it is employed, and how people learn to use it successfully. There has been a shift in teaching emphasis away from mastery of knowledge toward actual use of language. In schools where the newer philosophy is practiced, students spend more time reading and writing, less time learning rules of writing and syntax. The set list of "classics" (led by the beleaguered *Silas Marner*) has been broadened to include a much wider range of literature for children, young adults, and adults. The former obsession with correct writing has been replaced by an interest in teaching students the processes of composing so they can solve writing problems on their own. Narrow absorption with the printed word has been replaced by recognition that our subject is *language,* not just print literacy, and that in today's world students must be able to talk and discuss intelligently, to communicate with and through computers, and to interpret and critique visual images.

Most important, we think, is that in recent years the teaching of English/language arts has progressed from being atheoretical—a collection of content and pedagogy loosely linked under the heading *English* — to being based on a deepening body of knowledge accurately describing how people go about mastering language.

All these changes have created new roles for teachers. Teaching language was once a matter of simply following the course outline or grammar or spelling book in sequences that were obvious, if dull: sounding out syllables preceded reading whole words and whole texts; "the sentence" always followed "parts of speech"; "organizing a composition" followed "paragraphs." Methodology consisted largely of lecture or discussion, the latter with the teacher's doing most of the talking. Literature was mostly explication for the students; language study meant grammar; composition meant having your errors in spelling, mechanics, and usage pointed out with a brightly colored (usually red) pencil.

Now we hear of "writing workshop" and "reading workshop" classes, where even the youngest children read whole texts of their own choice and write original compositions that are published and illustrated by the authors. We read of an interest in "response" to literature, in which kids' reactions to their reading are valued as contributing to literary knowledge rather than being an aberration from accepted critical interpretation. We see language study expanded beyond the sentence diagram to include discussion of the use and misuse of language in society, to the point of having youngsters call their elders to task for their obfuscation and pettifoggery.

This sort of teaching is neither universal nor without controversy. Yet there is enough consensus at national and international professional meetings, at in-service workshops and gatherings, and in the hallways and teachers' lounges of elementary and secondary schools that we can safely and accurately describe a "new English," born in the late 1960s, developed and tested in the 1970s and 1980s, and providing a professional core of knowledge as we approach the twenty-first century.

The new English is unquestionably exciting. It allows us to take a constantly new look at what we are doing, to take fresh approaches to teaching—using new books, drawing on current media, looking for alternate directions in composition, and, above all, examining the learning styles and patterns and personalities of learners.

But contemporary English teaching is also terribly demanding, for its very diversity (and the diversity of the students) creates a drain on material resources and on our energy, originality, and creativity. Whereas we could once plan on teaching the same courses, books, and units over and over (stories about teachers who had *memorized* the textbook are not exaggerated), today we are constantly reading new texts, surveying fresh paperbacks, and planning new units and activities for students.

And the schools themselves are not always conducive to this sort of teaching. At the secondary level, despite fifty years of lobbying by the National Council of Teachers of English, class size often remains at 30 students or more, and teachers often see over 150 students a day. ("Why don't you teach more writing?" asks a critical administrator who will, next September, add two or two dozen students to the load of every English/language arts teacher because of "fiscal constraints.")

At the elementary level, teachers are snowed under with paperwork and expected to include more and more in the curriculum, sometimes leading them to question where "home" ends and "school" begins, certainly creating a fragmentation of what they would like to teach as "whole" language and learning. At both levels there are cumbersome structures and traditions that make teaching difficult: bell schedules, grades, permissions slips and ephemeral forms to complete, and public address interruptions. In our time, too, innovative or progressive teaching is often viewed with suspicion. Growing unrest over the quality of schooling leads parents and administrators to call for a return to patterns of teaching remembered from their youth, even when those patterns may be part of the problem of education.

In such a milieu, it's easy for teachers to burn out. After a brief fling with contemporary techniques, many retreat in the direction of grammar books and plump anthologies. Some quit and go into real estate or law; others stay in the profession and simply become pessimists: unhappy with their teaching, their students, themselves.

Yet a great many English/language arts teachers not only survive, but thrive. We're amazed by the commitment and resilience of teachers we meet—of enthusiastic newcomers to the profession who know they could make more in business but choose not to, of gray-headed experienced teachers who bubble over with enthusiasm at professional meetings, happy with their students, themselves, and their profession.

But even if you're this kind of teacher, you need support, and you'll get it from spouses and friends, from colleagues, from administrators, and, just possibly, from a helpful handbook of teaching ideas.

It's in support of such teachers that *The English/Language Arts Handbook* has been prepared. Whether you're an undergraduate in a methods course getting ready for your student teaching or an experienced professional who occasionally feels overwhelmed by the job, we figure you need all the help you can get. At the same time, we feel it important to enter two cautionary notes:

1. *The teaching ideas presented here are meant to be catalysts to your own thinking, not surefire gimmicks.* Adapt them to your needs, to your students, to your classes. Don't simply pull ideas from here and there and expect them to work without modification. In our college classes, we frequently have students write a *Handbook* based on their *own* ideas, and those ideas are the ones that will truly bring success in their classrooms.

2. *Don't use this book as a cookbook.* The ideas aren't recipes, and the book is intended to supplement your course planning, not replace it. Further, don't pick ideas just because they are unusual or because they have shock value. Students can be tricked, manipulated, and "gimmicked" only so many times before the novelty wears off. The book begins with an intensive section on classroom planning, and we urge you to plan the broad dimensions of your work before selecting individual activities.

From time to time we've heard people say, "Well, *any* idea or method can work at some time in the hands of the right teacher."

We don't buy that idea, and we think such a philosophy leads to eclecticism of a very dangerous sort. So we've been highly selective in presenting ideas. The practices we recommend show internal consistency with what we interpret contemporary language arts philosophy and research to mean. Thus, we *won't* present ideas on "101 New Approaches to the Book Report," but we *will* discuss a variety of ways of helping students extend their responses to literature. We *won't* show you ways of "Making Grammar Fun!" but we *will* explore some ideas about engaging students profitably and with occasional laughter in thinking about the English language and their use of it. We *won't* offer you "The Five Paragraph Theme" or the "Power Paragraph" or the "Formula Paragraph" or the "Keyhole Theme," but we *will* suggest dozens of ways of helping students write well-organized compositions.

Underlying all our discussion is the belief that *teachers* are at the heart of solving classroom teaching problems. We don't believe formulas can be applied to teaching, whether mandated by a curriculum guide or suggested by a book like this. Growth in the ability to teach evolves from within, from teachers who are willing to explore and experiment with new ideas and techniques and possibilities.

o·n·e

Planning for English/ Language Arts Teaching

This first section of the *Handbook* takes a look at some general concerns and practices in teaching: setting aims, planning units, organizing for individualized instruction, and grading and assessment. We could just as easily have placed this section at the end of the book, after our presentation of specific practices for teaching reading, writing, composition, and language. Indeed, some of you may want to follow that order. However, we think it's important to keep the larger picture in mind, and thus we've organized the text from the general to the particular. In our in-service workshops and undergraduate classes, we often have people develop a general plan for a course or a unit as they read Part 1, then fill in more detailed activities as they read Parts 2 through 4.

Chapter One

Aims and Priorities

Why do we "teach" English/language arts anyway? Virtually all babies learn the hardest part of language—its basic syntax and vocabulary—on their own, without any meddling on the part of teachers. They learn all they need to know from their parents, older brothers and sisters, and friends through a number of methods: imitation, trial and error, and, above all, *using language to accomplish something:* to get a bottle, get a diaper change, get attention. Would such language learning come to an end if youngsters didn't have language arts teachers in the grades, English teachers further up?

As a matter of fact, there's a good deal of evidence to suggest that naturalistic learning of language *does* take place outside school, and it may be that some of the most significant learning happens there as people use language to engage with their world, to shape it, to control their corner of it. We know people even learn some of the print code—reading and writing—outside school: from signs, television, magazines, instructions.

Yet schooling can and obviously does affect the learning of language, and we'll argue vigorously that English/language arts deserves its place in the curriculum as the most widely taught school subject, from kindergarten through freshman composition. At its best, school instruction produces students who have confidence in their ability to tackle new language situations, who have pretty good control of the mechanics and correctness items, who have read widely and intend to keep on reading after school—both the school day and their last graduation. At its worst—well, we don't really have to describe for you what happens when language arts instruction goes awry; you can read the next batch of angry letters about functional illiteracy and inadequate schooling that appears in your local paper.

There's a lot of talk these days about "effective schooling." To many legislators, parents, and administrators this phrase has positive connotations based on business and industry, where (at least in myth) everything is tightly organized, goal directed, and efficient, leading to the highest quality product created at the lowest possible cost.

Daniel Stashower (1990) reports that the father of American science fiction, Hugo Gernsback (after whom the "Hugo" sci fi awards are named), once envisioned assembly line medical practice, where patients on conveyor belts would pass by specialized physicians who would work on particular ailments. We suppose Gernsback's vision could be called "effective medicine," but to anyone who has ever been treated in "take a number" fashion at a large hospital or an emergency room, the vision is a forbidding one indeed.

In English/language arts, "effective schooling" also has an ominous sound. Language learning, like medical practice, is not something that can be rushed, mechanized, or treated as an assembly line project. Language is one of the most highly individual learning enterprises, growing from unique experiences with words and the world.

Some basic premises about English/language arts

To us, "effective" English/language arts teaching is not so much *efficient* as it is *focused,* and that means having a clear idea of what you want to achieve and how you can go about it. This often requires that you avoid show-biz teaching practices and instead consider ways to achieve long-range, *slow* growth and development.

It further requires that you be willing and able to state your philosophy of English/language arts instruction clearly and concisely. At this point we will offer ours—a *credo* of sorts, a list of our fundamental beliefs, developed through teaching, sharing and debating issues with other teachers, and reading in the professional literature.

1. *Reading, writing, listening, and speaking are learned by doing, not principally by studying abstractions or completing exercises.* More and more it seems clear that English is a learn-by-doing skill, that our most important role as a teacher is not telling students about language but encouraging them to use it. To this end, *The English/Language Arts Handbook* is aimed at helping you develop a language-centered classroom, a place in which students use language constantly, in a rich variety of ways. (If you're a propaganda analyst, you may have noted the waffle words, "not principally," in this premise. We don't claim that language is learned without teacher intervention or occasional exercises or drills. However, decades of research into language learning demonstrate persuasively that such study must be peripheral to actual language use.)

[handwritten margin note: most skills are]

[handwritten note at bottom: most have teaching intervention + place for drills & exercises]

2. *Language growth is bound up with the broader dimensions of human growth and development.* We are "children" of the Anglo American Seminar on the Teaching of English, part of the Dartmouth Conference held in 1966. Whenever we reread the report of that seminar (Dixon, 1976) we are consistently impressed with the seminar's assertion that language grows in response to the human need to communicate. As people grow, their language expands. The implication is that English/language arts classes need to focus on children's lives—what they do and have done, what they are thinking about or have thought about.

3. *English/language arts should broaden the range of discourse that students can employ, both as "consumers" (listeners and readers) and as "producers" (speakers and writers).* "Effective schooling" programs tend to stress business language or practical language. ("After all, business executives write memorandums and reports, not poems.") We think such a view is extremely narrow and, in the long run, potentially incapacitating to people who find themselves trained in a limited range of language skills. We don't claim that writing a poem or a short story will get students good jobs, but we do feel that one of the differences between learning language in an English/language arts classroom and on the street is that within the schoolroom we can offer students the opportunity to extend the dimensions of literacy beyond the merely pragmatic. Similarly, the reading/literature part of the program should set as its goal helping students come in contact with the widest possible range of reading materials.

4. *"Literacy" involves more than print.* In recent years, we've heard about a range of "literacies": scientific, mathematical, computer, media, even religious. We need to resist allowing *literacy* to become synonymous with *competence,* but it's clear that today's "literate" person is master of a wide range of language forms.

5. *Language study is naturally interdisciplinary.* For a long time, English limited itself to literature, but developments in the "language across the curriculum" movement in the past two decades have forged links with math, science, the arts, social studies, and history. English/language arts programs increasingly draw on materials that go beyond the limits of traditional literature to include nonfiction and fiction on a variety of topics in many fields.

6. *Language teaching begins "where the student is" and moves him or her as far as possible.* We have little patience with professional finger pointing that argues that students ought to have learned something or other at an earlier time in their lives. Maybe a case could be made that more should have been done sooner, but we must work with

must know the students - be flexible

students as they come to us. This calls for highly individualized instruction and for acceptance—even celebration—of students who have widely different experiences and abilities.

7. *Meeting student needs is not incompatible with the values of traditional English/language arts classes.* There is much public worry about the values expressed in premises 1 through 6. The argument runs something like this: "If we just let students 'grow from experience' and if we just 'take them where they are,' they will never learn the difficult, classic material." To the contrary, a balanced English/language arts program will draw on classic as well as contemporary literature; it will challenge the advanced student as well as support those who are not up to speed; it will place a concern for correctness within the perspective of a broader goal: the concise, precise, imaginative use of language.

combine tradition learning with the newer approach

8. *The teaching and learning of language is a natural, pleasurable, invigorating experience.* We're distressed by the way language arts classes have become feared, dreaded, or seen as sites of boredom by so many students, mostly because these classes overemphasize correctness and the standard literature. Using language is, above all, a delightful experience, and that delight is shared equally by the babbling two-year-old, the punning nine-year-old, the hip-talking high school student, the joking or lovemaking adult. To capitalize on the natural pleasure in language, one need not create a classroom that is a circus or use a teaching approach that involves gimmicks, fun, and games. Many years ago, Alfred North Whitehead argued in *The Aims of Education* (1929) that serious learning could also involve romance and disciplined play. We think that sort of attitude should flourish in today's classrooms.

should be

A philosophy of one's own

The above premises don't exhaust our philosophy; nor are these ideas set in stone. In the first edition of this book we had seven premises. Of those, four have been dropped, amalgamated, and/or reconceptualized as we developed the eight for this edition. We hope you will see this not as wishy-washy, but as a reflection of our own critical evolution as teachers. A credo for most of us begins with the way we were taught (for good or ill) and evolves over many years. Here are some ways of forging yours:

- Critique our list, point by point. Which ideas mesh directly with your own views of learning? Which differ in whole or part? What items would you add to the list? Which would you delete?

- Create your own list, a "This I Believe" about teaching English/language arts. Put this in a safe place, or create a file on your word processor, and revise or amplify it throughout your career.

- Become a reader. We have provided an extensive bibliography at the close of this book, presenting what we see as the most significant books of the past twenty-five years (plus a few older classics). Although *nobody* seems to have enough time to read *everything,* we encourage you to make a reading list from this bibliography. Acquire the books you see as most significant, and begin developing your personal library. Alternatively, urge your school, college, or public library to build up its English education collection.

- Become a joiner. Become a member of the National Council of Teachers of English and join your local or state English teaching affiliate. Some of you may also want to join the International Reading Association and become active in one of its chapters. (The addresses of these and other organizations that may be of interest to you are included under Professional Resources.)

- Become a talker. Find some colleagues who are willing to exchange ideas freely, supportively. (One of the best "methods" classes Stephen took was a car pool with fellow student teachers. Going to and coming from school each day they talked, tested ideas, critiqued one another's plans, celebrated victories, and supported one another when things went less than well.)

The faculty and its aims

Teaching is often a solitary activity, but it is done in concert (or cacophony) with a group of people called "the faculty." Although you can accomplish a great deal with the classroom door closed—the classroom-as-castle metaphor—language growth and development for students will be a great deal richer if your faculty has a degree of congruence in its aims. The word we think most satisfactorily describes a good language arts faculty is *community*—a group of people who work (and sometimes play) together, who are united in a common cause, who function under a common set of guidelines and constraints. A community of teachers will grant freedom to its members to teach as they wish, yet it will also discuss mutual concerns and seek solutions to problems.

The faculty-as-community needs to spend time discussing basic issues and fundamental questions to discover its own nature and the skills of its members. Whether or not your faculty can fully agree on answers, spend time discussing such questions as the following (if you're not yet a member of a faculty, find a group of people who share your interest in teaching English/language arts—fellow students in a methods class, for example):

- What is our subject, whether we call it English, language arts, communication arts, communications skills, or just plain "literacy"?
- What is the role of teachers beyond presenting the fundamentals of spelling, penmanship, and basic reading?
- Should language arts be required in virtually every grade, kindergarten through college composition? What would happen if it were no longer required?
- What skills and abilities do youngsters bring to us at various grade levels? To what extent are students already literate? What seem to be their major needs?
- What are English/language arts teachers doing right? Where is there room for improvement?
- What is our faculty's strength as a community? What are the talents of individual members and how can we draw on those talents?

In far too many schools, faculties get together so infrequently that there's no coherence, no unity. Too often, as well, faculties don't meet to discuss their *own* problems—it's always an agenda set by the principal or triggered by the latest crisis. Some projects for the faculty-as-community:

- Have a session called "This Works for Me." Price of admission: copies of a handout describing a teaching technique you're willing to give away.
- Create a "handout exchange" and make the sharing of ideas a tradition among faculty members. You may have trouble overcoming past bad experiences with this one, since many teachers jealously guard their ideas for fear someone will steal them. To help solve that problem, create ground rules about the use and misuse of people's ideas. Certainly you don't want to have next year's students walk into your class having already experienced some of your best teaching strategies.
- Schedule regular meetings; rotate the faculty members responsible for the discussion topics.
- Have a "Problems and Pleasures" session at which you talk over the aspects of your teaching that are most satisfying and those that present recurring problems.
- Find out about summer workshops and institutes for teachers and lobby with the principal or the school district to enable some of your members to attend.

- Fight for control of book and textbook budgets and selection processes so you can obtain the best possible materials to use with your students.

- Explore the possibility of a week-long teacher exchange between schools. This brings in fresh ideas and costs nothing.

- Do the same thing with a nearby college or university. Have the college supply an instructor for your course while you work with the prospective teachers.

- Poll students, teachers, parents, and other concerned community members about their wishes and dreams for the school. Consolidate these and share them with the principal and the district language arts coordinator.

- Hold articulation meetings among senior high, junior high, middle school, and elementary school faculties. Ground rule: No finger pointing or accusations. Suggestion: Start with the elementary teachers and work your way up: don't fall in with the traditional approach of having senior high teachers dictate their needs first.

Setting priorities

We can't do everything at once; human energies and financial resources won't permit it. But we can plan—as individuals and as faculties—to establish and order our priorities and concerns so that changes come about systematically, rather than willy-nilly. Appendix 1–A is a survey that can be used by a faculty to create an informal rank ordering of possible techniques, approaches, and methods for teaching (or by a college methods instructor to determine topics for class discussion). (We want to thank Bob Graham, now at Wayne State University, for sharing this model of priority analysis.)

Appendix 1–A: A survey of priorities

Go through the list that follows and *circle* on a scale of one (high) to five (low) whether you think an item is an important part of English/language arts teaching today. This is an idealized list—what you think is important regardless of whether or not it is "practical."

Example: Teacher salaries match those of professional baseball players.

(1)   2   3   4   5

Then go through the list a second time and mark with an X whether you feel this item is widely practiced (or whether you feel competent to do it). This is your "realities" list.

Example: Teacher salaries match those of professional baseball players.

① 2 3 4 X

Look for discrepancies on your and other people's lists. If there's a great gap between your ideal and real scores (and, especially, if other faculty members have a similar gap), this is an item you may want to make a high priority for discussion.

This list is by no means exhaustive, so we've left blank items at the end for you to enter items of your own.

1. Literacy is taught in all content areas, not just as part of English/language arts.

   1   2   3   4   5

2. Every classroom has its own library.

   1   2   3   4   5

3. Letter grades are replaced by other forms of assessment and evaluation.

   1   2   3   4   5

4. The teaching of oral language (speaking and listening) receives equal attention with written language (writing and reading).

   1   2   3   4   5

5. Students are required to pass standardized competency examinations at various points during their elementary and/or secondary school years.

   1   2   3   4   5

6. Children's and/or other literature is taught by topical subjects or themes, e.g., "Dinosaurs," "Cities," "War and Peace," "Who Am I?"

   1   2   3   4   5

7. Grade-level minimum objectives for literacy are established.

   1   2   3   4   5

8. Students are involved in free or guided individual reading programs.

   1   2   3   4   5

9. Creative dramatics and role playing are incorporated in language arts classes.

   1   2   3   4   5

10. Student writing is treated as "literature" and young writers are respected as "authors."

    1   2   3   4   5

11. Personal and creative writing are taught to all students.

    1   2   3   4   5

12. Students learn basic principles of literary criticism like form, style, versification, biography, and analysis.

    1 2 3 4 5

13. Teachers allow students to use the dialect of their regional, racial, ethnic, or social background in speech and writing.

    1 2 3 4 5

14. Literature study provides students with an understanding of their cultural heritage.

    1 2 3 4 5

15. The materials of popular culture—films, recordings, video, radio, television—are given a prominent place in the language arts curriculum.

    1 2 3 4 5

16. Students who are speakers of nonstandard dialects are encouraged not to use those in school.

    1 2 3 4 5

17. Students read a common core of classic children's and adult literature in their K–12 schooling.

    1 2 3 4 5

18. Grammar is mastered in the elementary grades.

    1 2 3 4 5

19. Grammar is mastered in the junior high/middle school years.

    1 2 3 4 5

20. Grammar is mastered in the senior high years.

    1 2 3 4 5

21. Students use "spelling checkers" and "grammar checkers" to achieve correctness.

    1 2 3 4 5

22. Television replaces reading as the literature of our age.

    1 2 3 4 5

23. Teachers follow a set curriculum or set of agreed-on course outlines.

    1 2 3 4 5

24. Students whose first language is not English are taught apart from the rest of the language arts classes.

    1 2 3 4 5

25. Literature instruction focuses primarily on the student's own reaction.

    1 2 3 4 5

26. English language arts teachers are held accountable for the successes and failures of their students.

    1 2 3 4 5

Others (add you own): _____

_____

    1 2 3 4 5

Chapter Two

Planning for Successful Teaching

n *Emile* (1961), Jean Jacques Rousseau describes an idyllic teaching situation in which a teacher works one-to-one with the individual child, helping him or her discover new ideas, in nature or in books. In this sort of teaching, planning is done in direct response to a young person's needs and interests.

But most of us teach students in larger groups, occasionally as small as fifteen or twenty, more often twenty-five to thirty-five, pupil quantities dictated by the economics of mass education and by contract negotiations.

Many disadvantages are inherent in this "class" system. For one thing, a group of twenty-five to thirty-five students is anything but ideal for easily managed whole-class (or even subgroup) discussion. For another, it becomes extremely difficult for us to think of students as *individuals,* and that, in turn, forces us to adopt common textbooks, to set generic goals and standards, and to resort to mass measures for evaluation and assessment. The ideal of individualizing instruction—meeting students' needs as they come up—seems far removed from the reality of classroom possibilities.

In Chapter 3 we take up the topic of individualizing, with particular emphasis on the diversity of students we meet in schools nowadays. In this chapter we want to discuss some ways in which one can design blocks of instruction—we'll call these *units* of work—in ways that make it possible for English/language arts teachers to enrich the dimensions of their instruction for larger than Rousseau-esque numbers. By a unit, we mean something as brief as a week or two of concentrated study on a topic like "The Environment," to a semester-long high school course in British literature. A unit, then, is a teachable "chunk."

What makes a good unit?

Think back through the myriad courses and classes you've taken in your school life and identify the ones that seemed most successful. (If you're

19

an experienced teacher, recall some of the best units you've taught.) From your perspective as teacher and student, what made these special?

Probably the first thing that comes to mind is the instructor and his or her teaching style. Some teachers could probably teach anything from parts of speech to nuclear physics and hold our attention because of the force of their personality. And there are teachers from whom we would (and did) learn most anything simply because we trusted them and assumed that they had our best interests in mind.

Teaching is not solely a matter of personality and certainly should not become cultish, with students mesmerized by the teacher's magnetism. As we think about our best teachers—including Steve's fourth-grade year with Celia Reynolds and Susan's introduction to graduate English study with Joel Gold—as we review those experiences and some of our own good teaching units, we see the following common traits:

1. *A good unit interests and engages the teacher.* We *won't* go to the extreme of saying, "Teach only what interests you," but we *will* argue, "Teach what you know and love best." We've found that even when we're teaching under a set syllabus or course design, there's plenty of room for us to bring in our own particular interests—the books we like to read, the kind of writing we prefer to do. In that way, we think, students get a strong sense of the importance of what is happening in the classroom. Teaching what interests and excites you is also a way of teaching your*self.*

2. As a corollary, we'd like to offer that *a good unit allows the teacher to participate as a learner.* Recent composition theory, in particular, stresses the need for teachers to participate in the instruction they offer their students: to put pen to paper and write along with the students. We've found that our own teaching improves considerably if we constantly bring in fresh texts, new assignments, previously unexplored avenues of inquiry so that we can join in learning with our students.

3. *A good unit deals with a topic that somehow piques curiosity or meets student's need.* The notion that "teacher knows best" leads to instruction that fails to engage the learners. We think students often know best—or, at least, better—and have a pretty solid intuitive sense of whether or not a bit of instruction is valuable. We're not calling for easy relevance or a curriculum centered around Saturday morning cartoon characters. We do, however, feel that the curriculum has to prove itself anew with each student.

4. Thus, we believe that *a good unit involves students in the selection of topics.* More important than persuading students that a unit of work is valuable is to engage students themselves in choosing some

or all of the material to be discussed. In recent years we've learned much about the "negotiated" curriculum (Boomer, 1985), in which students are told some of the core aims of study and are allowed and encouraged to add goals of their own.

5. *A good unit offers a rich variety of materials for study.* We hope that the age of the textbook is waning. During the past two decades, English/language arts teachers have learned a great deal about individualizing reading and about the use of a rich variety of print and nonprint materials in their work. Teachers needn't rely on a single textbook as the source of instruction. However, even in schools where a common text is required, there is ample opportunity to use young adult and adult literature, newspapers, magazines, films, and videos to enlarge the range of instruction.

6. *A good unit makes its aims and expectations clear.* We've all suffered through classes in which a teacher or professor never made it clear what was wanted or required, or seemed to make assignments at random. A good unit will make its purpose and direction clear from the start. It will let students know how they can participate in the instruction and what they have to do to complete the work successfully.

7. *A good unit has a payoff for the individual student.* This is not to say that every unit must be "practical" or teach a skill like shoelace tying or omelet cooking. However, students must be able to make connections between the work and their lives.

8. *A good unit is organized.* Well, of course. That's obvious, isn't it? Yet when we asked you to think through courses and classes and units that succeeded and failed, you no doubt recalled times when the instructor had a sense of direction and purpose, conveyed that to you, and proceeded systematically in achieving the class aims. At the same time, one must be cautious about *over*organizing. You've probably had bad experiences in classes that were lifeless because excessive structure got in the way.

With those criteria in mind, we offer a seven-stage process for planning units and courses. It's a scheme we've used with both experienced and inexperienced teachers, planning units from the primary grades through college. The stages are:

1. Describing the students.
2. Choosing topics.
3. Setting goals.
4. Selecting materials.

5. Designing activities.
6. Creating sequence and structure.
7. Evaluating and following up.

In developing this plan, we were inspired by a presentation on planning "world famous" courses given at a national meeting by Robert Beck, an English teacher at John Swett High School, Crockett, California. We've also been strongly influenced by J. W. Patrick Creber, who, in his book *Sense and Sensitivity* (1965), argues powerfully for developing courses, classes, and units of work based on the needs and interests of students, rather than arbitrarily imposing the structures and knowledge of literary disciplines.

Describing the student

As the school year progresses, you get to know your students better, so you're able more confidently to predict their interests and to focus instruction to meet their needs. At the beginning of the year, especially, you're facing a group of unknowns—youngsters you've probably never met or have heard about only by reputation or through the teacher grapevine. The interests, concerns, and abilities of those kids are largely a mystery.

Further, children and adolescents are loath to be predictable and are skilled at defying stereotypes, so the quest for describing students is a year-round task. You can avoid a good deal of misdirection in your work by taking time to find out who is sitting in those seats in front of you.

What do you know about your students' likes, dislikes, and interests? What can you learn about their reading, writing, listening, and speaking backgrounds? What kinds of writing can you expect from them? School records can supply some information, as can teachers' lounge gossip, but we recommend proceeding cautiously with both of those data sources. We think it's terribly important to make your own judgments as you size up the student body.

Further, we think it's important to avoid all statements that begin with the phrase "Kids nowadays are/are not." For eons, adults have made generalizations about youngsters, often negative, often portraying child-hood (and the future of the world) locked into irreversible decline. "Why in my day, we _____." "You'd think kids today could at least _____, but, no, they insist on _____."

As Robert Pattison (1982) has observed, that students (and their language) are *different* than formerly is undeniable; whether they are *worse* is not provable. Young people of any generation differ in many ways from their parents and grandparents (though they are growing up in a culture created by those same ancestors). It's important to put these kinds of changes into perspective and to resist the grand generalizations.

What do we mean, then, by "describing the students"? Figure 2–1 provides a sample description of expected students by a teacher planning a ninth-grade general English course. It is brief, and teacher surveys of students can be *much* longer and more detailed. You might consider collecting some of the following kinds of information:

- What television programs are most popular with the students? Conduct a poll or survey. (Your students will enjoy this and talk about it freely, giving you a chance to assess their oral language as well. What skills do you detect as they speak on subjects close to their interests?) What films and videos do they watch? What does this information tell you about their interests and values?

- Collect some writing samples—preferably *not* the clichéd "My Summer Vacation." Set aside time for journal writing at the beginning of the class and allow students to choose their own topics, perhaps with a few promptings from you: sports, fashion, trends, coming school/social/entertainment events. Analyze these self-selected topics; then look at the writing itself for evidence of language skills.

- Take your class to the library and invite each student to identify five books he or she would like to see on a class reading list.

- Have students write about an imaginary "really good book for a reader like me."

- Flip through the subject index of the library jotting down questions you think might interest these students. Poll the class about the strength of their interests. For example:
  Does Nevada glow in the dark from nuclear testing?
  High Interest   5   4   3   2   1   Low Interest

- Assess students' interests by having them speculate about the future. What do they expect to be doing ten, fifteen, fifty years from now? What careers presently interest them? What do they see as the crucial problems the world must solve in their lifetimes?

- Create a literacy inventory in which you ask students to describe their interests and skills in reading and writing. What is the all-time best book they have read (or had read aloud to them by parent or teacher)? What's the worst book? What can they remember about learning to read? What is their day-by-day reading, including

As I plan for this course, I suspect this will be the most heterogeneous group of students I've ever taught. Since we don't group freshmen by abilities, the students will not be prescreened in any way. I imagine I will have some generally competent writers and some who are barely at or well below the basic skill level. In addition, given the makeup of the school district, I can anticipate that at least 15% of my students won't have spoken English as a first language. There will probably also be a wide range of dialects as well. My work will be cut out for me! This will be the students first year in high school, so they will probably be both intimidated and boisterous, especially the boys (not to be sexist, but they do act out --the girls are usually culturally conditioned to behave like more-or-less proper schoolgirls). This course will have to be really diverse, then. I think I'll need to proceed slowly with their writing in order not to scare them off, and I'll need to keep it pretty straightforward until I'm certain all the basic skills are under control.

Figure 2–1 ○ Students expected in a ninth-grade general English class

newspapers, television commercials, leisure reading, etc.? *Where* do they like to read? At what time of day or night? What school composition topics have been most fun to write about? What do they see as their strongest skills as writers? Do they think writing will disappear in the electronic twenty-first century? Would that be a good thing or not?

Choosing topics

We have a strong bias toward teaching language arts through *thematic* or *topical* units such as "Frontiers," "Dinosaurs," "The Harlem Renaissance," "Utopias." We greatly prefer such topics to units that center on elements of rhetoric or literary criticism—"The Paragraph," "Expository Writing," "The Short Story." A list of unit themes and topics that we have gleaned from the professional literature and developed for our own teaching is provided in Figure 2–2. It suggests the range of ideas and issues that can provide a framework for teaching English/language arts, K–12.

However, often units are dictated by the district curriculum guide or the adopted textbook. We have our doubts about textbook topics such as "The Golden Age of Literature in New England" or elementary or middle school units on "The Pleasure of Poetry," both of which seem to describe teacherly pleasures rather than student interests.

Still, even prescribed units like those can be subdivided and treated in a thematic or topical way. We'd work the "Golden Age" unit (which traditionally focuses on Emerson, Thoreau, Hawthorne, Whitman, et al.) into one of "Freedom and Individual Choice," with the writing of these usual nineteenth century New Englanders enriched by the writing of contemporary (and neglected) women and minorities. For the "Pleasure of Poetry" unit (which, we fear, puts poetry in peril by perpetuating the propensity to parse poems by poetic paraphernalia), we'd look for poems that touch on themes or topics identified as interesting by kids: animal poems, poems of the bizarre and satirically gruesome (in the manner of Shel Silverstein), poems about things that go bump in the night.

The selection of topics also presents opportunities to engage students in the planning process. Perhaps you know your students well enough to invite them to propose a direction for study. More commonly, you'll have a general topic or subject you want to cover, but you can still spend part of a class session asking students to brainstorm about ways in which it could be imaginatively and engagingly approached.

Some ideas to explore:

Detectives and Detecting
Poetry on Modern Themes
Minority Literatures:
  African American
  Asian American
  Jewish American
  Native American
  Eskimo
  Hispanic
Rebellion
Survival
Cities
Law
Women in/and Literature
People in Crisis
Hero(ine)/Antihero(ine)
War and Peace
The Environment
Comic Literature
Interdisciplinary Topics:
  Science
  History
  Math
  Arts and Humanities

Science Fiction
The Magazine Rack
Folklore
Fantasy
Romance
Conflict
People for/against Nature
Frontiers
Bridges
Sports
The Quality of Mercy
The Country
Humor
Regional Literature
Decision Time
Nightmares
Defining Humankind
Nuclear (Im)Possibilities
Supernatural Literature
Death and Dying
The Good Life
Languages
Careers
Stranger Than Fiction

Figure 2–2 ○ Unit themes and topics

- From the various interest inventories and assessments we have described, compile a list of themes and topics you'd be interested in teaching. Compare these with the chapter headings in your textbook or the assigned units in the curriculum guide. See which of the high-interest topics could be used to explore the core curriculum.
- Comb the newspaper for possible topics and subjects—bring headlines, articles, cartoons to class to see whether they can be used to lead into language work.
- Look for linking themes in any required literature in your text-book. Search for ways to link one unit to another.

Setting goals

English/language arts teachers are often (and sometimes rightly) faulted for having vague goals. Where the math teacher aims precisely at teaching students the tables from 1×1 to 12×12, the language arts teacher speaks more broadly of helping students appreciate literature or become more confident of themselves as writers. Specificity of objectives is important, although in our age of accountability and testing, it can be taken to extremes. A vaguish objective, say, "to teach students the pleasure of poetry," could be broken into specific objectives that have little to do with the original intention: Students will be able to identify the four major rhythmic patterns of poetry. Students will be able to distinguish metaphor from simile.

We believe that good goals and objectives answer a very simple question: *Why should anyone study or learn this?* Objectives can be written in many different forms, including:

- A letter to the students explaining what is to happen in coming weeks.
- A description of what the student will be able to do at the conclusion of this unit.
- A description of what the student will know at the conclusion of this unit.
- An advance copy of any exams or quizzes the students will be asked to pass.
- A list of the books or other materials students will be expected to read.
- A description of the writing and speaking that will be done as part of the unit.

English 9 has three main goals:
1. To provide students with a solid background in basic writing that they will use in high school:
    a. Students will write at least five papers during the first semester, ranging from personal narratives (storytelling) to school writing (preparing a short essay about their favorite school subject).
    b. Students will become familiar with the stages of the writing process -- planning, drafting, editing, proofreading -- and become responsible for managing their own writing process.
2. To build on and strengthen students' personal and academic reading skills:
    a. Each student will read at least five self-selected books and write journal entries describing each.
    b. The class will have weekly common readings of poems, plays, or short stories; the instructor will help them to see how to read these genres.

Figure 2–3 ○ Course goals for ninth-grade general English

c. The class will have several sessions
devoted to "how to read" textbooks in other
fields, including science, math and history.
3. To help students better understand the
nature of language and how it functions in
society and in their own lives.
   a. Students will keep a notebook of clippings
   from newspapers and magazines
   showing language in use in advertising,
   editorials, and letters to the editor.
   b. Students will create an "editing notebook"
   containing common usage errors
   from their writing, along with standard
   English versions of the same material.

Note: Most statements of goals and objectives
can be expanded to almost any level of detail
and specificity. Here the major goals and
subobjectives could be further subdivided and
amplified. Specific evaluation criteria for
student writing and reading could be stated;
each of the writing tasks could be described
in more detail; the nature of the language
projects could be amplified. The question for
the teacher (sometimes answered by supervisors)
is: Are these stated in enough detail that an
outsider would know what I'm attempting to
accomplish?

Figure 2–3 ○ (continued)

Figure 2–3 offers a set of goals for the general ninth-grade English course mentioned in Figure 2–1.

For any set of goals, you might want to ask the following questions to keep yourself on track:

- Are the objectives consistent with one another? That is, do they fit a coherent pattern, or are you teaching more than you can fit in or items that conflict with one another?

- Are your goals consistent with a supportable philosophy of teaching language arts? Can you back each one of them with an explanation of how a whole language philosophy makes this something valuable to do?

- Do the goals meet the real needs of students? (Here we go back to the need to describe your students carefully.)

A great many units seem to have goals centered more on what someone thinks kids need or ought to have than on what will actually move their language skills ahead.

Selecting materials

Finding materials for a course, class, or unit, is, to us, one of the most enjoyable parts of the planning process, especially if begun well in advance rather than the night before. As a starting point, look for resources in novels, nonfiction, magazines, articles, poems, short stories, public radio, recorded literature, recorded music, painting, sculpture, plays, films and videos, and information bureaus.

As you start your unit, spend half an afternoon browsing in the bookstore. Take additional time in the public library. Turn your unit title over to the school librarian and ask for a list of resources available within the school. You'll soon come up with a list of dozens of titles that can be of help. As you compile this bibliography, we suggest that you code items, using a symbol system such as this:

W = appropriate for use by the *whole class*.

S = best with *small groups* of students.

I = most useful for *individual* study.

Some additional questions to ask about your materials list:

- Do you have a wide range of literature—poems, plays, stories, non-fiction?
- Are ethnic and other minorities represented?
- Have you included works from countries around the globe, not limiting yourself to the literature of the Western world?
- Are any classic works for children or young adults appropriate?
- Have you found materials from popular or contemporary culture?
- Do the materials allow for various levels of language skill?

Designing unit activities

You have a set of objectives. You have a list of materials. Now brainstorm for the substance of your course, linking your objectives and materials by developing actual reading/writing/speaking activities for your students. (The remainder of this book is dedicated to helping you generate more and more possibilities.) As before, code the activities according to appropriateness for the whole class (W), small groups (S), or individual work (I). As you proceed, consider:

- What writing assignments are appropriate to this course?
- In what ways can the reading selections stimulate writing?
- Have you provided a variety of ways for students to react to their reading?
- Are your assignments such that students can seek out reading material and project work appropriate to their ability levels?
- How might this course evoke writing for some audiences other than the teacher?
- How can students take control over finding writing projects and reading materials for the course?
- What kinds of oral language and/or dramatic activities can you develop?
- How can you use the media—film, video, recordings, radio, newspapers, magazines—as the starting point for activities?
- What connections can you make across the disciplines?

- Can you imagine possibilities for work outside the school, perhaps field trips or individual travel?
- Can you bring the world to your classroom through speakers, demonstrations, guests?

Creating sequence

This is the hard part—and the fun part: how to get from here to there, from A to Z, from beginning to end, from objective to fulfillment. Every teacher/student group has its own rhythm for teaching and learning. Some like a lot of structure and a detailed plan that tells exactly what will happen; others prefer to have some slack so that as a unit develops, students and teacher can take advantage of ideas that are generated along the way. Our general practice is to start out with a fairly specific set of plans and activities, including those in which we try to figure out the interests and needs of students we're working with. Then the unit starts to open up, particularly through the use of small groups and individual projects. Thus in our teaching, we're most satisfied with units that move:

- From whole-class to individualized activities.
- From teacher-initiated to student-developed projects.
- From core or common to individualized readings.
- From basic or introductory tasks to the more difficult ones.
- From where we perceive the students to be to where we think they probably should go.
- From where the students see themselves to where they want to be.

Of course, any structure you design before you actually teach the unit is tentative—a scenario, a sketch—not a blueprint to be followed to the last shingle. Although some teachers feel that typing out a syllabus or unit plan is unduly restrictive, in all of our teaching, kindergarten through college, we write out at least a tentative plan so the students will have a sense of where they're going.

Figure 2–4 shows a rough sketch of the ninth-grade English course we've been describing. You can see that the teacher has worked out a series of "phases" through which the course will progress. This outline could easily be expanded into a full syllabus or unit plan, with reading and writing activities spelled out in detail.

Part I (2 weeks). Getting acquainted. Use interest inventories to get to know students. Teacher reading aloud and student reading silently of high interest short stories, followed by journal responses. Students begin collecting examples of language use from newspapers.

Part II (6 weeks). Personal reading and writing. Students will write at least two personal narratives about important events in their lives. Time will be provided for free reading from the classroom library, with books mostly chosen from adolescent literature. Students start file folder of common usage errors, spelling problems etc. Teacher presents lessons on "how to read a poem," "how to read a play," etc.

Part III (6 weeks). Reading and writing about the larger world. Students write two papers reacting to issues and problems they see going on around them, in school, in the state, in the world at large. Newspapers-in-education program will provide us with copies of the daily paper for four weeks. Students read at least two books from the classroom library emphasizing nonfiction titles, mostly books written for adolescents.

Part IV (4 weeks). High school reading and writing. Students write one paper about a favorite subject, after reading at least one nonfiction book in that area. Instructor will help students see ways of applying their reading and writing skills in other school courses.

Figure 2–4 ○ Sequence for English 9

In our own work, we like to lay out a grid with a box for each day, Monday through Friday, and each week, one through infinity. We then fill each box with descriptions of specific activities. Checking the boxes keeps us on track day by day, while a glance at the grid gives the larger picture of scope and sequence.

Evaluating and following up

We discuss evaluation in more detail in Chapter 4, where we also take up the topic of *grading*. Suffice it to say here that evaluating a unit involves more than slapping a letter grade on student work. A number of alternative forms of evaluation exist, including conferences, teacher feedback, student self-assessment, and examination of student work. Any evaluation scheme needs to take into account the objectives of the unit and should convey to the students a sense of whether or not they have accomplished what they and you set out for them to do. In designing your evaluation plan, consider some of the following possibilities:

- Keep a teacher journal during the unit, spending just a few minutes each day describing your perception of what is happening.

- Have students do occasional "freewrites" during the unit, telling you what they think has been accomplished so far, what they understand about the material being covered, and what, if anything, leaves them feeling in the dark.

- Systematically collect samples of student work, perhaps photocopying a representative range, from best to worst or from most successful to marginal. Review these for evidence of how your unit is proceeding.

- Have students keep records of their achievement: what they read, what they write, what activities they complete.

- Carefully consider whether your tests and examinations (if any) really get at the core learnings you have in mind.

In addition, we like to treat *follow-up activities* as an integral part of the evaluation of a unit. "OK, we've gotten this far. What next?" We often engage students in this discussion, since it encourages them to offer suggestions for subsequent activities. Even if you're losing students at the end of a unit because it's also the end of a semester or school year, you may want to think about follow-up activities. You can hold discussions with students about what they can expect from other teachers and suggest ways they can apply the learning from your class in their next language arts class as well as other classes in the school or district.

A footnote on lesson planning

The seven-step unit plan we have described provides you with a skeleton or outline, but it does not delve into the details of day-to-day teaching. The term *lesson plan* is anathema to many teachers, and a lot of old pros in the business claim they never use one. We're old pros, too, and happily confess that we still write lesson plans, feeling that it's important to go into class having a guide down on paper. (We also confess that our lesson plans are shorter and a good deal less formal than they were in our student-teaching days, when we were required to turn in typed plans.)

For new teachers and experienced veterans both, we suggest a lesson planning form that is a microcosm of the seven-step unit plan, beginning with objectives and moving toward evaluation. Given our earlier discussion of unit planning, we think the lesson plan given in Figure 2–5 is self-explanatory.

---

1. **Objectives**
   In two or three sentences, describe the major objectives of the lesson: what the students will read, discuss, write, think about—and *why* Focus on what students will actually accomplish in the lesson. Your objectives may also show how this lesson builds on whatever preceded it.

2. **Materials**
   List the basic resources: texts, records, speakers (even pencils, scissors, glue, so you don't forget).

3. **Procedures**
   Outline what you plan to do in as much detail as is required for clarity and your own understanding. Don't lock yourself into a script the students won't follow. We usually break our "procedures" into the classic "beginning, middle, and end."

Figure 2–5 ○ A short form for lesson planning

---

4. Evaluation and Follow-Up

Note how you propose to assess the lesson, even if this simply means your own subjective judgment about whether the class "got it." Assessment may include tests or evaluations of student writing as well. It is quite important to show how this lesson leads to whatever comes next. Lessons take place in the context of a larger unit of work. A good (or even an unsuccessful) lesson leads to another.

5. In Retrospect

Leave this blank at first. After you have finished your teaching, spend a minute or two writing up your own reactions. How did it go? What would you change in your teaching if you were doing the same lesson tomorrow?

6. You might also write an **In Prospect** section discussing how what you and the students learned from this experience can be applied in the future.

Figure 2–5 ○ **(continued)**

Chapter Three

Diversifying and Individualizing

here's little disagreement among English/language arts teachers about the need to meet students' individual needs and interests. "Meeting kids' needs" is virtually a cliché in our profession. We know that students come to us with varying backgrounds and skills in language. Some seem to have been born speaking fluent, articulate, socioeconomically "correct" language. Others struggle with language, particularly the forms that are generally accepted and promoted by the schools. We realize, too, that unlike some subjects and disciplines in which goals are common for all students and the sequence of instruction clear, language study is by its very nature less precise and predictable.

Yet when it comes to *creating* a classroom responsive to these varying individual interests, learning styles, language abilities, reading levels, listening/speaking competencies, and writing skills, overwhelmed teachers often prefer a less effective—but less chaotic and more time honored—"shotgun" approach: teaching a bit of everything, aiming in the general direction of the class, and hoping that most of the students are hit by one linguistic pellet or another.

Further, individualizing is made difficult by large classes. Paying attention to diversity would be a lot simpler if we could see kids one at a time or in small groups.

Nevertheless, individualizing is possible even under less than ideal conditions. If you're truly committed to the philosophy of "teaching kids where they are," and if you're willing to explore alternative ways of structuring and organizing the class—everything from text selection to how you spend your time in the classroom—there are a number of approaches and strategies that can work for you.

Characteristics of the individualized classroom

1. *Your role as a teacher is widely varied.* Sometimes you will be at the center of the classroom, providing instruction or directions for a

project in which the whole class is involved. At other times, you act as a resource person, moving from student to student, group to group, helping students make decisions about how they want to approach their work. You may also act as a librarian, assisting students in finding materials, and this, in turn, requires that you know a wider range of literature than the usual classics. You must be alert to techniques and approaches that will involve many different kinds of students. Which kids seem to need highly structured activities rather than independent projects? Which students function best in small groups? Which ones are loners who prefer to be by themselves? Are there students whose language background prevents them from participating fully in class or in groups? Are there kids who are sufficiently bored or alienated by school that they need particular attention to get back on track?

2. *The roles of students vary and often are different from classroom to classroom.* Students often become accustomed to lockstep assignments about which they don't have to make very many decisions. *Independence* for the learner is an important component of the individualized classroom, and students often must receive instruction before they can work successfully. In fact, they sometimes rebel, initially, when forced to figure out things for themselves. They don't know what's important to learn, because they haven't been asked to think about it before. Students may not have worked in small groups, and they may not have experienced self-selected projects. Rather than lamenting these problems, you as an individualizing teacher must see this learner dependency as an opportunity to help students function in a wider range of learning/self-teaching ways.

3. *The individualized classroom requires a variety of ways of assessing students' progress and keeping records.* Perhaps the biggest objection we've heard to the individualized classroom centers on record keeping. "It's tough enough to monitor thirty kids doing the same thing. How am I supposed to keep track of the same bunch doing thirty different things at once?" Although there are no easy answers to this objection, individualized classrooms have been around long enough that we know some concrete ways of doing the record keeping (or having the students do it themselves).

4. *Individualization requires a lot of materials and organization.* A second common objection we hear involves the raw amount of material required: more books, more recordings or tapes, a wider range of activities. It's understandably easier to select a chapter from the text and give everybody the same assignment. However, the world is full

of useful and engaging materials, many of them available in your school or community at very low cost. The trick is, first, to have the commitment to individualize and, second, to become aggressive in moving your classroom beyond the limitations of the textbook.

5. *Individualized classrooms require flexible use of furniture and space.* Wait. We'll modify that to say *at best*, individualized classrooms are furnished helpfully. We've dreamed about an ideal classroom for years: one with a variety of comfortable chairs and tables, a publishing center, a reading cubicle, small-group meeting space, private carrels for individual work, and a cabinet filled with electronic devices ready to plug in. Yet our own teaching has more often than not been in barren conventional classrooms, including some with desks bolted to the floor. Despite those limitations, we find it possible to individualize.

In this chapter, we offer some ways of getting started in creating an individualized classroom (keeping in mind the reality that most of you will *not* teach in idyllic conditions with unlimited supplies). Then we review some ways of structuring and organizing the individualized classroom, and conclude with a potpourri of ideas for introducing even greater range and diversity into your English/language arts class.

Some first steps

It's important to remember that individualizing *takes time*. Don't try to individualize all your classes at once, and don't try to do it every day of the year. Further, don't abandon the cause when your early attempts to reach difficult students fail or when kids sit around doing nothing rather than thanking you through action for the opportunity to take control of their own learning. Here are some ways to get started gradually:

- Set up a corner or cabinet in your classroom to be used by students who have completed their regular class work. Stock it with magazines, current newspapers, a paperback book rack, a file of crossword puzzles, some word games.
- Establish freereading and freewriting days, times when the *only* assignment is for students to engage themselves productively in *their choice* of language activities. Many teachers who start this sort of program eventually use the approach for entire classes. If *free* bothers you or sounds too unstructured, call these "reading/writing workshops."

- Use workshop or freereading/writing days for conferences. Talk with students individually about their favorite assignments, books, or projects. Help them with reading and writing assignments. Discuss what they might like to do in the future.

- Identify the most difficult or least motivated students in your class and concentrate on bringing in books they might especially enjoy.

- Expand the number of options you give in assignments. If you've been giving students one topic to write about, let them have a choice of three. If everybody has been reading the same novel, experiment with offering two or three choices.

- Start a file for each student and keep the folders in a box or crate in the classroom. Make it the student's responsibility to include (organized) copies of written work completed for the class, along with lists of books, stories, and poems read. Get your students used to bringing the file when you hold conferences.

- Begin a journal writing project. Journals are near-universal favorites among students. Even ten minutes a day given over to journal writing can get students started pursuing individual interests in writing.

- Send half your class to the library with the assignment to come back with a book they want to read. Meet with the other half to discuss the kinds of books they enjoy reading.

- Assign more small-group work. Only when you get yourself away from center stage can true individualizing take place. As kids work in groups, you'll find you are freed to begin working with them one-to-one.

- Use your responses to student writing as an opportunity to help students get to know you better, rather than as an opportunity to correct their syntax. That is, see your writing back to students as being closely tied to the process of individualizing.

A catalog of structures for individualizing instruction

The project method

This technique dates back to the 1920s, when progressive education was experimenting with new approaches. The class (or a group of students), with the assistance and advice of the teacher, selects a topic or project for study. Projects can range from the handy/practical (building birdhouses, planting a community garden) to the abstract and/or political (getting out the vote, lobbying for better after-school child care). Literary, historical, even philosophical topics can be investigated as well. The individualizing comes about as students break the project or task into manageable portions for individual or small-group work.

Britisher Geoffrey Summerfield wrote what is perhaps the best book on topic selection, *Topics in English* (1965). (It's unfortunately now out of print.) His topics for work with junior-high-aged children include "Reptiles," "Fire and Ice," "The Antarctic," and "Home and Family." For each topic he lists literature for the teacher to read aloud to the students, literature for individual reading, and ideas for individual study. The projects he suggests range from "hands on" research (such as observing a snake in a terrarium and reporting on its habits) to imaginative writing (a short story about being terrified by a snake). If you can find a copy of Summerfield's book, read it.

If you can't obtain one, Stephen also discusses the history and technique of project teaching in *Travels Through the Curriculum* (Tchudi, 1991). Another difficult-to-obtain but useful reference is Geoff Ward's *I've Got a Project On ...* (1989). Ward provides ideas for selecting projects (with student input), linking projects to the curriculum, helping children develop the necessary research and independent learning skills, managing the process, and assessing student work.

Project teaching is still done in a great many elementary schools in Great Britain, Australia, and New Zealand. It has never caught on fully in the United States. More's the pity, we say.

Teaching by themes

A variation of the project method better known in the United States involves teaching by themes. (The unit design plan we present in Chapter 2 reveals our personal interest in this style of teaching, which we rely on heavily in both our school and college classes.) The steps in thematic teaching are these:

1. *Choose a theme or topic to provide focus for the class.* (A list of sample themes is provided in Figure 2–2.)

2. *Identify core or common readings for the whole class.* This might be a single text, even a required novel. More often, the core reading will be short stories or poems or plays, either read by the teacher or found in classroom anthologies or collections.

3. *Create possibilities for individual and/or small-group reading and writing on the theme.* Frequently these can grow from initial

discussion of the core readings, so students themselves are identifying the books they would like to read, the writing they want to complete.

4. *Provide time for individual and small-group work.*

5. *Provide time for coming together and sharing reading and writing.*

The pattern, then, is one of starting from a common point, branching out into individual work, and returning to the center.

The workshop approach

The enormous growth of interest in teaching writing "as process" in the United States has helped teachers learn about the workshop approach to teaching. Of course, the workshop is an old and respected model for teaching in many fields and disciplines, from theater to woodshop. It is project centered, hands on, and places the teacher in a tutor/tutee or master/apprentice relationship with students.

In the writing workshop, writers work on their own papers, developing their work from idea to draft to final copy. Students sometimes work in small groups, but they spend much of their time alone. The teacher may circulate throughout the class, chatting with the students individually, or may sit at a desk or table serving as a consultant for students who want to discuss particular problems or get a response to their most recent draft.

The writing workshop approach seems so comfortable and productive that many teachers, have launched their own reading workshops, in which students read on their own, completing books at their own pace and turning in appropriate reports at the end.

Nancie Atwell's book *In the Middle* (1987) describes the workshop approach in considerable detail for middle school classes, and most of her strategies are adaptable at higher and lower levels.

The essence of the workshop method is, ironically and possibly uncomfortably, to abandon the notion of a common curriculum. The teacher helps students identify topics to write about through interest inventories and journal writings and assists them in finding books to read, either in the library or from book carts brought to the room. The students are shown that they can work at their own pace, as long as they are productive, and the teacher, freed from the common or core curriculum, has plenty of time for individual conferences and assistance.

Of course, a pure workshop approach—five days a week, 180 days a year—may seem excessive, and workshopping can be combined with other possibilities. Many teachers are comfortable doing common activities two or three days a week and conducting class workshop the rest of the time.

Many teachers have reservations about workshop teaching—it seems unstructured, it doesn't guarantee common learnings. We invite you to consider that properly carried out, a workshop guarantees that kids will concentrate on self-chosen reading and writing topics much of the time they are in the language arts class. Given the amount of time spent over the years flogging students through grammar, spelling, organization, and literature-appreciation lessons, we see the hands-on, time-on-task focus of workshopping decidedly superior.

Small-group work and student-to-student teaching

A key to individualized learning is for you as the teacher to abandon the traditional role of lecturer/information dispenser and become a kind of classroom administrator or manager: one who guides students into language and encourages them to take responsibility for their learning. Having kids learn from each other is a very effective way of accomplishing this change of role. Some possibilities:

- Cross-age teaching. Many schools have experimented with using students to work with pupils of other ages. Second-grade children read books to kindergartners. Tenth-grade students read to senior citizens. Junior high kids put on a puppet show for fourth graders. College education students teach senior high writing. In these settings "teachers" seem to learn as much as or more than "students."

- Peer tutoring. Equals can learn an astonishing amount from one another. Although some teachers worry about "shared ignorance," peer tutoring more frequently turns out to be sharing of growth. Let students tutor students in reading, writing, literature. They can read to one another, work out common solutions to problems, edit one another's writing, teach difficult spelling words or usage items.

- Small groups. Group work is a mainstay of individualized teaching. Instead of asking questions about the meaning of a poem, give it to a small group and ask them to present an analysis. To add authenticity to the writing process, create writer-response groups, in which students are charged with giving one another feedback on their drafts. Use groups to subdivide and explore thematic topics or class projects; ask groups to locate reading materials for the class; allow groups to prepare and dramatize scripts or readings of student writing.

- Student assistants. Using students as teacher aides is an exciting concept, provided you make aiding a positive experience, not just a way of handling routine classroom tasks like filing papers or dusting the erasers (does anybody dust erasers anymore?). At Thunderbird Elementary School in Vancouver, Canada, Stephen saw aides helping the librarian put together collections of reading materials for in-class libraries that were rotated twice monthly. We know of fourth-grade aides in Grand Rapids, Michigan, who put together tape recorded book reviews so that children choosing new books could listen to a taped commentary by a peer before confirming a selection.

- Sharing skills. We are continually astonished by the range of skills and knowledge that students bring to our classes, and we often ask them: "What do you know about that people never ask you in school?" We discover students who are skilled in sports, crafts, and hobbies; students who are involved in community service and clubs; and, not infrequently, students who like to read and write on the sly, outside the watchful eyes of teachers. Have your students share their skills and interests. In doing so, they'll create a great deal of interesting and lively language.

Activity centers

In activity centers, *materials* do the work of structuring and individualizing. You collect ideas and materials beforehand, place them in a particular area of the class, and provide necessary instructions for students to be able to work on their own. Some possibilities for centers include:

- Reading (with a rich supply of books and magazines).
- Responding (a "coffee house" for discussion of books).
- Writing (well stocked with writing utensils, lap boards, a computer or typewriter).
- Editing/copyediting (set up with reference books to help students polish their writing).
- Graphics (for production of books, magazines, posters, slides, transparencies—ideally, equipped with a computer that has both desktop publishing and drawing/drafting programs).
- Listening (recorded literature).
- Language games (*Scrabble,* crosswords, hangman, word jumbles).

Activity cards

An activity-center approach obviously requires a permanent classroom of your own, something not always available to secondary school teachers. A "peripatetic alternative" we've used is to create activity cards. We do these on eight-and-a-half-by-eleven-inch pieces of poster board, with glued on graphics, instructions, photographs. In simpler form, activity cards can be some instructions typed or handwritten on an index card.

Each activity card contains a task or assignment, plus instructions on how to complete it. You can construct activity cards for:

- Writing assignments.
- Study questions for literary works.
- Individual projects done in conjunction with thematic teaching.
- Library assignments.
- Individualized reading.

Whether or not you have a permanent classroom, you might construct sets of cards for particular units you're teaching. At appropriate points, open up your box of cards and allow students to select the ones on which they want to work. You'll achieve instant individualization (backed up with a good deal of preparation).

With the aid of a computer, you can simplify your work by filing away ideas in a databank or hypertext program, adding to your collection year by year, sorting through the cards electronically, and printing out fresh copies of the ones you need for a given class.

Several examples of activity cards are given in Figure 3–1.

Contract learning

In contract learning, students design or "contract for" the work they will complete in order to satisfy a class requirement. Contracts can be written for just about any component of a language arts class: reading, literature, writing, drama, speech. Generally a contract, designed by the student and approved by the teacher, will include:

1. *The topic or title,* plus a one-sentence description of what's to be done.
2. *The student's aims* in completing the contract: what does he/she want to learn?
3. *A specific plan:* books to be read, writing to be completed, scripts to be created.
4. *A timetable* for completion of the project.
5. *A set of criteria for evaluation* showing both teacher and student whether the contract has been fulfilled.

Activity card on a large sheet of
cardboard or construction paper

(FRONT)   (BACK)

Activity card on two sides of a
4" x 6" index card

Activity card made of a file folder

Figure 3–1 ○ Sample activity cards

Malcolm Knowles's book, *Using Learning Contracts* (1986), provides a particularly comprehensive look at the design of contracts, although his focus is primarily on adult education and fields other than language arts. You can learn a great deal, however, by analogy from the contracts his students have designed in such fields as nursing, psychology, and higher education. (We also take up contracts as a useful method of *grading* in the next chapter.)

Independent study

Independent study is one of the most traditional forms of individualized learning, one often overlooked in the schools. A problem with independent study is that students often don't know how to handle it. We'd like to see schools offer instruction in independent study at all levels. If kids had some experience working on projects of their own from kindergarten on, by the time they reached secondary school the curriculum could consist primarily of self-directed work.

Putting it all together

There's no fixed or obligatory pattern for individualizing class instruction. The very word suggests flexibility rather than a master plan. As we suggest in Chapter 2, our own teaching usually begins with common or core activities that set the tone and content of a unit. We then increase the amount of small-group work in the class, helping students become more and more skilled at working independently of their teacher. Eventually (or perhaps concurrently) we encourage students to think about individual topics, projects, or readings, sometimes as a spinoff from whole-class or small-group activities, at other times simply growing from students' own interests. We then draw this all back together through reports, presentations, and performances based on small-group or individual work. This pattern, incorporating the various approaches to individualization discussed in this chapter, is presented in Figure 3–2.

Additional ideas for individualizing and diversifying

- Search through the holdings of your school or district media center for materials that will add diversity to your teaching.
- Systematically videotape programs that make connections with your teaching.

Whole Class

Announcements, Requirements, Common Readings
Discussion of Central Theme, Brainstorming for Projects
Lectures (as needed), Whole-Class Discussion
Common Writing Assignments, Films and Videos

Small Groups

Literature Discussions, Peer Editing, Scripting
Investigating Theme Subtopics, Planning Presentations
Reading Special-Interest Books
Working in Activity Centers

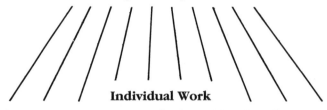

Individual Work

Contract Work, Independent Study, Individualized Reading
Special-Interest Writing, Completing Activity Cards
Tutoring and Being Tutored, Reading/Writing Center
Student-Teacher Conferences
Solo Work in Activity Centers
Personal Evaluation, Record Keeping, and Assessment

Whole Class

Shared Writing, Book Reviews and Reports
Small-Group Reports and Presentations
Individual Reports and Presentations
Discussion and Evaluation of Whole-Class Performance

Figure 3–2 ○ **Patterns of individualizing class instruction**

- Work with your school librarian to build up the children's and young adult collections in the school. Read *The English Journal* and *Language Arts* regularly, looking for reviews of titles that your library should acquire.

- Invite parents to read and review books for you. (This is also a useful way to head off censorship problems.) Parents might also volunteer to go to your local public library and look up appropriate titles *and call numbers* to help students find individualized reading materials.

- Campaign to get a paperback bookstore established in your school, with proceeds to benefit whoever does the work: the student council, the PTO.

- Start a class newsletter, with most of the work done by the students, as a regular publishing venture. Send this home with explanations of what you are doing in your class.

- Form special-interest clubs in your class: a poetry club, a mystery readers' club, a writers' club, the journalists' club.

- Write the drama department of a nearby college or university and invite them to present plays for your kids.

- Learn the address of your state council for the arts and/or humanities and learn about their "writers in the schools" program.

- Find a book on sources of free and inexpensive things (most paperback bookstores carry several such titles). Engage your students in a campaign to write off for pamphlets, brochures, and posters that would be of use in your teaching. Also write to the U.S. government asking for its consumer catalog, which lists many free and inexpensive materials you'll find helpful in a variety of ways.

- Campaign for a school-wide reading/writing tutorial center, where kids with particular problems can get help.

- Cast about for businesses in your community that might be able to enrich your teaching by supplying materials or speakers.

- Tap the expertise of your students' parents. Find out what those parents have as special skills and invite them to come into your classroom to meet with the students.

- Look for volunteers to come into your class on a regular basis: parents, university students, senior citizens. Use these folks to help you break down the class into smaller and smaller groups.

Chapter Four

Assessment, Evaluation, and Grading

Teachers are often afflicted by the "end of term blues." Not only do they have papers and projects stacked up to read, but they must translate student work into a grade as well. Students must be sorted and categorized to find their place in an A,B,C or E,G,F or 4.0–0.0 or 100–0 scale. The problem is one of reducing the complexity of a student's growth and development to a single abstract symbol. Should we grade on interest and involvement? Cooperation? Overall growth? Competency? Work effort? Actual output? What do we do about the student who comes in with few language skills and works hard throughout the term, but who still performs less well than peers? Or the student who is very competent to begin with and produces uninvolved but acceptable work all term? (Figure 4–1 is Charles Schulz's slant on this particular problem.)

Regardless of the problems experienced by the teacher in reaching the final grade, we know too well the reactions of students and parents. The A's and 4.0's are prized; the B's and 3.0's are seen as measures of second-rateness (the great sin in the United States of finishing other-than-first); and the C's and 2.0's are interpreted as indicators of outright mediocrity. Grades often divert attention from true language development; they induce false competitiveness in students; they force students and teachers to focus on narrow, "countable" aims and objectives.

In the field of English/language arts, grades are extraordinarily subjective. Assemble a dozen English teachers and ask them to come up with a concrete list of criteria for "good" writing, or ask them to place letter grades on some themes read in common. The assigning of grades and criteria will vary widely. This is not to suggest that we language arts teachers don't know what we're doing. "Literacy" is such a complex affair that the range from *good* to *bad* is highly nuanced. Although most specialists can agree in general on the traits of excellent work, we quarrel and debate on the finer points.

Educators, psychologists, and learning theorists can present strong evidence of the ill effects grading has on students. Yet that system is deeply entrenched in the educational system. Students and their parents

Figure 4–1 ○ "Peanuts" (9/9/90), by Charles M. Schulz

claim they need grades, that they "want to know where things stand" even when that knowledge can place students, teachers, and parents at odds with one another. College admissions offices rely on grades as a predictor of success, and businesses and industries look closely at students' grades as one clue to their potential. So the education mill continues to grind out grades.

What is the response of the humanistic teacher who finds grading harmful or arbitrary? What kind of evaluation system can we construct that will be genuinely helpful to student learners and still provide the sort of information demanded by the public and the school system itself?

We will anchor our discussion by noting some important distinctions among the three terms that head this chapter: *assessment, evaluation,* and *grading*. Too often, we find, *grading* is taken as a blanket or cover-all term for the other two, which are, in fact, much broader concepts.

Assessment

Assessment is the most comprehensive of the terms in our lexicon. It involves a wide range of estimates and measures and is *a description of what is happening* or *what has happened*. Assessment generally tries to avoid judgmental statements of *good* or *bad, weak* or *strong, success* or *failure*. Rather, in assessment we try to compile information—as much as we can manage—that provides a snapshot (or holograph) of what our students are accomplishing.

Even though language growth is difficult to measure, there are a number of ways you can assess achievement. For example, you can gain a sense of (assess) what's going on in a language arts class by:

1. Counting the raw number of books read by a student in a term.

2. Observing whether or not your students complete a writing plan, first and second draft, and final copy.

3. Counting lengths of sentences in compositions and computing whether your students' writings are getting longer.

4. Studying how often and how frequently your students contribute to class discussions.

5. Making a list or record of words misspelled early and late in the term.

6. Giving a multiple choice test to determine whether or not your students can match authors' names with the works they have written.

Any of those methods *assesses* language growth in one form or another, and obviously, some yield much more interesting data than others. And it is *interesting*, or better, *informative* data that we seek. We want to collect information that will give us useful insights into what students are achieving in our classes. Among the most fruitful forms of assessment we have used are:

- Logging. Instead of simply jotting down letters and numbers in a grade book, keep a *log* of student accomplishments, an annotated list of what students have done and when they did it. Your computer database program can be helpful here, allowing you to log consider-able amounts of information, then sort through it and print out appropriate excerpts. In fact, much of the actual work of logging can be done by students. Simply ask them to note, daily or weekly, what they have been doing in your class. When parents or principals ask about what's been going on in your class, show them the log.

- Filing. A crude but also an effective technique is to systematically file students' work. You probably can't keep *everything* they produce in your class, but many teachers find it very instructive to select (or have students select) work they see as representing growth and development over a period of time. Coupled with a good teacher log, a filing system is a powerful assessment tool.

- Portfolios. This system of assessment effectively combines logs and files. A portfolio is a carefully prepared collection of student work demonstrating that class goals have been accomplished or showing a representative range of a student's work. Portfolio assessment has become extremely popular in recent years, and there is now even a newsletter, *Portfolio News,* dedicated to exploring new ways of using this technique. Portfolios can help students reflect on their own work, provide information on which to base student placement in classes or courses, and offer detailed information on whether or not a curriculum is succeeding. They can also provide a basis for evaluation and grading. In England, portfolios have been explored as an alternative to the infamous A- and O-level examinations, with student work collected over time providing a richer assessment than a one-shot sit-down exam. In some U.S. colleges, entering students can present a portfolio of their work instead of taking placement exams.

- Classroom observation. Perhaps the most traditional form of assess-ment (yet the one least easily documented) is your day-to-day obser-vation of students. You must be very cautious and self-critical in using your own observations. It doesn't surprise us that most teach-ers can predict quite accurately how most of their kids will do on standardized tests, and this provides some evidence of the reliability of subjective classroom observation. You can watch students in dis-cussion groups, watch them while they're toiling over a composi-tion, interview them in conferences, watch them read silently, study their performance in dramas and role plays, and even see how well-thumbed their textbooks seem to be.

- Teacher as researcher. An important development in recent years has been the recognition that teachers can conduct research to answer their own questions. The teacher/researcher concept simply systematizes classroom observations. You needn't have a degree in statistics or a high-powered computer to collect data on what your students are doing and to acquire valuable knowledge about how learners perform. The general pattern for classroom research is to:

○ Identify a question that you want to answer. (What kinds of writing problems do students solve in peer groups? What books do third graders most like to read? Where do college-bound students experience most difficulties in analyzing literature?)

○ Collect data that will answer your question. Most teacher/researchers will collect several kinds of data. They may look at student portfolios, students' logs, their own journals, standardized test scores. They may also interview the students, offer pre- and postquestionnaires on attitudes, or have a whole-class discussion of what has been happening.

○ Reflect on this information, draw conclusions.

The results are always limited to this particular group of students at this time, and you must be very cautious in not overinterpreting your data, claiming too much for it, or generalizing too grandly on the basis of limited data. In addition, you must guard against tunnel vision, only seeing what you expected or wanted in the first place. In the process of conducting such research, you also guarantee that you have created a solid assessment base for any evaluation and grading that follow.

● Standardized tests. Despite their frequent misuse, standardized tests *do* have a role in assessment. Before employing such measures, however, you probably need to educate people—students, parents, other teachers—about their proper interpretation. At their best, standardized tests merely provide norms and information bases; they are easily misinterpreted and misunderstood, and often interpretations of their results go far beyond the limits of the tests themselves.

Evaluation

The distinction we want to insert here is that assessment *documents*, while evaluation, well, *evaluates.* Evaluation adds judgment and standards to the process.

We sympathize with members of the public who say, "People want to know where they stand. They want to know how well they're doing." Yet often the criticism people receive is decidedly unhelpful. None of us like to be hollered at, to receive scathing criticism, to have our work held up in contempt or ridicule. Although most of us prized our A's and worried about our B's and C's, we probably didn't find our grades especially *informative* in telling us anything about how we were doing in any significant sense. We are increasingly convinced that internal evaluation or self-assessment is at least as powerful as and probably more powerful than external evaluation. Even the kindest and most humane of evaluations isn't much help if it simply holds up a yardstick, rather than explaining the units of measure.

At the heart of any evaluation scheme is a careful and articulate statement of *criteria.* Our students tell us horror stories of trying to figure out what criteria professors are using, usually translated as "trying to guess what he wanted." It's a useful exercise and a service to students for you as a teacher to state exactly what you value, what you see as important: the standards or other measures you intend to apply. (We often give students a copy of the final examination on the first day of class, along with an explanation of how it will be evaluated.)

Among the forms of evaluation that we have found most effective are:

- Self-evaluation at all points in a reading, writing, listening, or speaking project: at the beginning (to see whether or not students are getting the aims and major ideas), in the middle (to see whether they're still with us), as well as at the end. A useful schema we have used for self-evaluation asks the students to:

  - Describe what they have done: what they have written, what they have read, how they went about completing the assignment.
  - Evaluate their work. Did this turn out as they wanted it to? What parts were most successful? Which were least satisfactory?
  - Predict what they feel they will need to do next time to produce even stronger work.

- Peer evaluation, where students gather to assess and evaluate (not grade) one another's work. Peer evaluation is discussed in considerably more detail in Chapter 9 on the composing process.

- "Twenty-six letter grading" (the written evaluation), where we write out assessments of a student's work. Does this seem to reflect the student's full capacity? Does the work meet the basic requirements of the class? What are the strong and weak points of this work as presented? Where are the areas for improvement? What specific things ought the student to work on next time? We find that written evaluation, when separated from the single-letter grade, is perceived not only as nonthreatening, but as directly helpful by students. It is, of course, time-consuming for the teacher.

- Teacher conferencing, where face-to-face evaluation provides a much richer dialogue than written notes.

- Portfolio evaluation, where we assess student's work collected over time and discuss its perceived strengths and weaknesses, areas for improvement, possibilities for additional growth.

- Student evaluation journals and logs, where the students note what they see as the strengths and weaknesses of their work.

- Gut feelings on the part of students and teachers that, yeah, this has it or, thud, something just doesn't seem to be right here.

- Testing, both short answer and essay, especially when there are particular facts and concepts to be measured.

Grading

Tales of bizarre and macabre grading practices abound in our trade. Teachers have allegedly tossed papers down a flight of stairs and awarded grades based on the step on which the paper lands. There are also those who grade religiously "on the curve," statistically distributing grades so that, for every A there must be an F, for every B a D, and the great unwashed wind up with C's. And what about those amazingly precise graders (92.75, A$-$/B$+$)!

Grading is the moment of truth, when assessment and evaluation must be condensed into a symbol. In our experience, grading is far less threatening if a proper foundation has been laid: if criteria of evaluation are clear, if there has been lots of assessment and feedback along the way, if students have been involved in self-evaluation.

Still, if evaluation in language arts is ultimately so subjective, how do we go about grading fairly? We'll confess that we have never discovered a system that we find altogether satisfactory. (If you come up with a perfect grading scheme, we surely hope you'll tell us about it.)

Among some of the better possibilities:

- Self-grading. If students have been given the responsibility of assessing and evaluating themselves throughout the term, it seems sensible and fair that they should have some of or even all the responsibility for the final grade. We have, on occasion, had students recommend grades for themselves and found that, on the whole, kids do a responsible and reasonable job of settling on a grade. Some teachers we know use a system of *matched* grades, in which both student and teacher come up with a grade independently and split the difference.

- Portfolio grading. Portfolio grading generally matches the student's portfolio (including student self-assessment) against aims or goals for a class or unit. The portfolio is then searched for evidence of performance.
- Minimum plus. In this system, the teacher sets minimum standards for a passing grade and additional work to be done for higher levels. For a C a student might complete certain core reading and writing; for a B, she reads additional books; for an A he undertakes some original writing as well.
- Point systems. Here various tasks are assigned point values: reading a book carries, say, ten points; writing an essay carries fifteen. Ranges are set up for A, B, and C work, and students store up points in gradebook heaven as the class progresses.
- Analytic scales. Here the work for a class or course is broken into categories: class reading, writing, oral language, drama, etc. On a scale of one to ten, the teacher ranks student performance; for example:

Drama Work

Low 1 2 3 4 5 6 7 8 9 10 High

The various categories can also be weighted so that, for example, reading is thirty percent of the grade, drama ten percent, writing forty percent.
- Contract grading. In the previous chapter, we suggested that contracts provide an especially effective way to individualize student work. They also offer what seems to us an especially equitable way of grading. Like the point system and minimum plus, contract grades award *productivity*—the more you do, the higher your grade. However, as we note in that chapter, contracts require the student to specify aims and goals, the criteria by which the work will be assessed and evaluated, a timetable for proceeding, and checkpoints along the way.

Toward pass/fail systems of grading

A few schools and colleges have done away with letter or other symbol grades in favor of pass/fail or credit/no-credit systems. In our dream world, such a scheme would be standard practice, rewarding students for meeting class requirements skillfully and well without inducing the competitiveness and anxiety of conventional grading. Pass/fail grading does not result in any lowering of standards, for students can all be held to high levels of achievement. (There need be no "gentlemen's C" in a pass/fail system.) Furthermore, this sort of evaluation allows grading, evaluation, and assessment to be fully and smoothly integrated, maximizing the effectiveness of the whole process. The times are changing—slowly—and one of our hopes is that you will witness the increased use of pass/fail systems in your teaching lifetime.

A note on mass testing

The use of mass or standardized testing instruments by schools, school districts, states, and even national authorities and agencies has increased steadily in the past several decades. A common response to complaints about the quality of education is to institute yet another examination. There is even recurring discussion about national examinations, including high school exit requirements, linked to a set of national curriculum standards. Having had considerable experience with mass assessment, particularly at the state level, we remain dubious of the value of such measures. Indeed, we think that much of the effort that has been put into mass testing in recent years would have been far more profitably directed toward teacher in-service programs, curriculum development, or, perhaps best, book acquisition programs for the schools.

The National Council of Teachers of English has issued frequent warnings and resolutions about the misuse of mass test data, yet misinterpretations of test scores are common, especially among the public and the press. Every major announcement of test scores is almost invariably greeted with a new round of criticism of the schools, the teachers, and sometimes even the American way of life, even though the relationship between test scores, school quality, and performance in life are tenuous at best.

At our most cynical, we view such measures as primarily political in aim and purpose. It's easier to test students than to provide them with adequately funded schools. It's simpler to complain about performance as measured by a set of digits than it is to understand the deep and complex problems of educating diverse youngsters in today's world. Further, strong evidence suggests that mass tests favor white majority students and serve to disqualify and discourage the children of minorities from some educational opportunities.

Yet the tests persist and are quite likely to increase in number during the shelf life of this book. Teachers (in particular new teachers, who may not yet have tenure) need to attend to the tests, and in fairness to kids, we do owe it to them to help them score as high as possible.

Some possible strategies for dealing with mass testing:

- Learn what is on the tests your students will take. We're astonished by the number of teachers who justify the teaching of grammar by claiming, "They need it for the S.A.T." In fact, knowledge of formal grammar was removed from the Scholastic Aptitude Test in 1948. It is important to know what your students will (and will not) need to know.

- Study your curriculum and your teaching plans carefully to see how they already are covering basic test matters. Any decent reading and writing program—in particular one that has students read and write often—will naturally cover a great deal of what appears on virtually any nationally standardized examination. Be prepared to highlight your coverage for the benefit of students, parents, and administrators.

- Cautiously add additional elements to your program to make certain you fully cover required items. We add *cautiously,* because you don't want to let your class be shaped by the test, and you do not want to insert items that are foreign or even contradictory to your own philosophy or to accepted research.

- Help students prepare to take the test. If sample test items are available, run a few practice sessions shortly before the test. This will help your kids feel more comfortable in the testing situation. We also recommend that you look for commercial test preparation books. Our experience shows that such books contain accurate test items and give students a solid indication of what to expect. (A few teachers argue that prepping students for tests is unprofessional or even unethical. We believe that to give students actual *answers* to test questions would, of course, be highly improper. But we also believe it is not only professional but highly desirable to share public knowledge about tests with your students. Indeed, it's a disservice *not* to.)

- Know in your heart that a full, rich language arts program is, in the long run, a better course in literacy than a curriculum based on the demands of tests and testmakers. Have confidence that if you get your students reading and writing, if you encourage them to play with language and feel comfortable with it, if you help them assess their work and understand their own strengths and weaknesses, they will do as well as possible on the tests, probably outstripping peers whose teachers teach *only* to the test or allow their program to be constricted by it.

Summary and Troubleshooting

Dear Abby Fidditch

n concluding this section on curriculum and class planning, we let an old friend do some talking for us. "Abby Fidditch" is an unwillingly unemployed former language arts teacher who lost her job when the voters in her district defeated their fourth straight school bond issue, this shortly after the auto assembly plant closed and put three thousand parents out of work. Abby has taught in one-room schoolhouses and giant urban high schools; she has taught *Hamlet* and *Charlotte's Web,* old grammar and new grammar, smart kids and not-so-smart ones. Many of her former colleagues write to her from time to time for advice, and in her imposed leisure, she replies. We hope you'll find these letters and her answers helpful.

• • •

Dear Abby Fidditch,

What do you do to relieve pressures and tensions within a faculty to make it a more productive unit? If it's not jealousy, it's apathy. I'd like to get my colleagues jazzed up and trying new things, but all my attempts have been frustrated. I am,

A Dangling Modifier

o o o

Dear DM,

I can certainly understand your frustration. I was once a member of a faculty who would only talk to one another when they went bowling. Our curriculum was spare, to say the least.

But there are some ways I found to stir things up and to get people talking. I told the bowler/teachers that we needed a parental relations program to communicate more successfully what we were doing. When we began to talk with one another about that, we began to agree (and disagree) on some key points in the curriculum.

I also found it was very important for me to restrain my criticism of fellow teachers. I have had to stifle my objections on many occasions, but I have learned as well that people like to be asked about what they're doing, if they think you won't be critical of them.

It's also important for teachers (especially new ones) to seek out kindred spirits and to work with them. You'll probably never unify your faculty completely, but you can at least cooperate and support people who see things more or less the same way you do.

Though the unified faculty is a positive goal, in some schools you may just have to dangle.

Abby

• • •

Dear Pedagogical Poetaster,

How do you cope with the problem of imposed goals and objectives? It's all well and good for *The English/Language Arts Handbook* to talk about teacher autonomy and designing your own units and imaginative grading systems and all that, but I teach in a district that has detailed lists of objectives for kids to master, and most of these have to do with things like spelling and vocabulary. There's also a new district competency test administered every year, and teachers whose kids don't do well are called on the carpet. I think the imposed goals and tests are rather trivial, but I have to worry about my students (and my own you-know-what).

Subjected and Objecting

○ ○ ○

Dear SO,

You seem to hit the nail on the head when you say that the goals and tests are "trivial." The people who wrote them were probably sincere, but they have taken a narrow view of the language arts.

Tempting as it is to cover your you-know-what, don't let the skills list dominate your teaching. Integrate the required list with your own objectives. You teach basic skills by the hundreds every time you enter the classroom. In the course of an ordinary composition or reading assignment, you probably cover most of the skills on the list. Develop the habit of noticing how your own teaching covers the minimums. Then jot down some notes to show you have done the work.

Nobody wants to hold the children back or to get booted in the you-know-where. But it's equally important that you not let the demands and objectives prevent you and your students from achieving all that you and they possibly can.

Abby

• • •

Dear Superteach,

I'm really being driven crazy by the idea of individualized learning. I believe in it; I think it's important; I hate the idea of lockstep instruction. But there's a real world out there, and an even more real world inside my classroom, where I have a great mix of abilities, including lots of students who speak nonstandard dialects, some who barely speak English. I feel,

Overwhelmed by Individuals

o o o

Dear Overwhelmed,

Slow and easy does it, I say.

For me the best routes into individualizing were freereading periods and in-class writing. Both are pedagogically sound uses of time, but they also have the advantage of getting everybody to shut up while you figure out what you're doing. I brought lots of reading material into my classroom, everything from comic books to serious literature, and I had students write in their journals daily, at first just a few minutes, eventually up to half the language arts time slot.

Those two strategies allowed me to have conferences with individual students and to get a variety of activities going in the classroom. After my students became accustomed to the routines, I started moving into more complicated work with thematic units, a greater variety of literature, and writing beyond the journals.

I was also inspired by a teacher in my building who said she made a checklist of kids she *wasn't* reaching. In a tough class, that might be twenty-five people in September. She kept on keepin' on: bringing in books, trying writing ideas, casting about for activities to reach each one of those kids. By June she would report that she had the list whittled down to maybe a half dozen. She never claimed or expected to reach every last one of her students. In my book, she was the real Superteach.

Just Plain Abby

● ● ●

Dear Alphabettor,

Tell me more about grading. It drives me crazy. My students are all hungry for grades and are not likely to do anything in the class unless it's for a grade. Then when I give out grades, they all go into a funk (except the A students, who lord it over everybody else). I've tried a lot of the schemes in *The English/Language Arts Handbook,* but still have these sorts of problems. I need some practical help.

Unglued and Ungraded

o o o

Dear Double U,

I haven't an easy solution to offer you. I've struggled with grading all my pedagogical life, and I uneasily admit that I often had to spend as much time working on the grading scheme as I did on my syllabus. But I did find a way to ease my conscience.

First, I realized that the grading system is not of my making, not of my imposition. I don't want it, like it, or need it. My employers do. So I eliminated some of my own agonizing by focusing on the fact that I was not responsible.

Second, I set about to *neutralize* what I saw as the negative effects of grading systems. Toward the end of my teaching days, I did most of my work with contract teaching, where kids would elect a grade and work for it. This was not a perfect scheme. The grades were often pretty high. (But so what! Maybe I was just teaching well.) There was still some "grade grubbing," kids doing stuff just to get it done and earn their A. But mostly, contract grading let me talk with kids as partners rather than enemies.

Third, even when I used other systems of grading, I worked hard to help the students understand and even create the criteria for grading. Then I told them my job was to help them get as high a grade as possible. In this way, too, I found I could operate on their side, rather than appearing as the Angel of Death whenever grading time came about.

Abby with an A
(Well, OK, maybe a B+, but no lower)

• • •

Dear Behavioral Modifier,

Why is it that nobody has much to say about the most pressing of teaching problems: discipline. You can't plan and teach and evaluate creatively unless you can keep the class under control, and everybody knows that's harder and harder these days. So what about it? What about the trouble-makers, rowdies, disruptors, and malcontents we real-world teachers face day after day?

Just Plain Tired

o o o

Dear Elixer of Youth,

Let me tell you what I learned indirectly from a methods class at Grimm University: the rules people give you about discipline almost invariably *don't* apply very well to particular classes. "Don't smile for the first six weeks," they told me in college. I smiled by accident and found a class of kids smiling back. "Start tough and then lighten up," somebody advised. I started tough and when I tried to let up, the kids were so afraid they wouldn't talk. There are guidelines and limits, of course, but I've found that with discipline problems I can only work with kids one at a time, trying to be fair on the one hand and true to my values on the other.

I also am firmly convinced that discipline problems grow in proportion to the irrelevance of the curriculum. If you want discipline problems, try teaching Henry James. If you want to calm a class down, get them reading and writing about their own world. It's not a magic cure, but I find that I'm best off concentrating on curriculum rather than discipline, that the former helps me understand and control the latter.

One Disciplined Cookie,
Abby

t · w · o

Ideas for Teaching Literature and Reading

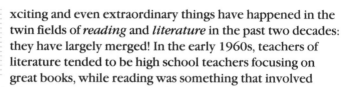

xciting and even extraordinary things have happened in the twin fields of *reading* and *literature* in the past two decades: they have largely merged! In the early 1960s, teachers of literature tended to be high school teachers focusing on great books, while reading was something that involved phonics or look-say instruction in the elementary grades. But contemporary research into both areas has pointed to a resolution by focusing on a common (but by no means ordinary) element: the reader.

For instance, the work of Kenneth and Yetta Goodman (1987, 1988) at the University of Arizona and Frank Smith (1971, 1985, 1988) at the University of Victoria has suggested that we have traditionally placed too much stress on plodding comprehension of text and too little on the reader as an active "meaning making" person. Louise Rosenblatt (1978, 1983) and Alan Purves (Purves, Rogers, and Soter, 1990) have written about the transactional, response-centered approach, which empowers students by having them make sense of texts for themselves. Teachers of reading have moved away from their phonics lessons and pronunciation drills to discuss the concept of "whole language," which is centered on encouraging students to bring prior experience to bear on their reading.

This new research helps cut through a number of traditional questions and dilemmas surrounding the teaching of literature and reading. Are we teachers of literature or of basic skills? Are we teachers of "great" literature only, or can students read popular materials as well? When do we "break" students of the habit of reading books for children and young adults rather than adult fare? What are the differences between literature and nonliterature? What reading skills do students need to have before we turn them loose to read on their own?

Such questions now collapse, for we are teachers of literature *and* reading *and* skills; we teach popular forms *and* classics; we offer (and ourselves enjoy) literature written for little kids *and* big kids.

Our philosophy is integrated around four central aims for reading/literature:

1. *Get them reading.* Nothing happens until students make contact with print. We want to make English/language arts classes havens of print (in an increasingly nonprint world), places where students constantly encounter books, magazines, newspapers, brochures, pamphlets. (We're not opposed to having nonprint literature there as well, but in appropriate proportion to the print materials, which we see as the language arts teacher's primary medium.)

2. *Treat reading as a meaning-making activity.* When a student meets a black-and-white printed page, something *new* is created, a set of meanings based on what the author said, meshed with the understandings and the experiences of the students. We try to concentrate instruction on helping students explore their reactions intelligently.

3. *Let evaluation and criticism grow naturally from students' responses to their reading.* To focus on reader response is not to ignore critical or evaluative reading. However, they must react to the book first, analyze and critique second.

4. *Help students recognize that reading and literature are not remote from life, but are an expression of it.* It dismays us that students often see books as irrelevant to their daily lives, that many seldom read after they have finished their secondary school or college experiences. Most English/language arts teachers know the practical power of reading, yet we have not been particularly successful in helping our students come to see it. One can't *prove* that reading is useful in life, but one certainly can create viable opportunities for students to *discover* that.

A good reading and literature program will thus draw on the natural interest of the printed word, elevating it from an arid classroom study to become part of the lives of young people.

Chapter Five

The First "R"

Of all the basic skills taught in elementary and secondary schools, reading is (arguably) the most vital. Reading is perceived as a key to success and satisfaction in school and college, in business and industry, at home and during leisure hours. Reading is omnipresent. In one of Stephen's college classes, students were amazed to realize they have reading material at their fingertips every waking hour: most found themselves reading something within minutes of rising each day, and many fell asleep with reading material in hand. Out in the workaday world, they encountered stop signs, soup labels, billboards, and the daily mail. One student observed that even as he went through the checkout lane at a minimart he was faced with a stack of leaflets advertising free tutoring for illiterates. ("How is an illiterate going to read the leaflet?" he mused.)

Which brings us to the point that despite the prevalence of print in our society, the teaching of reading is one of our greatest scholastic failures. Statistics on illiteracy are notoriously unreliable, yet one regularly hears that there are in the neighborhood of twenty-five million "functional illiterates" in the United States, people incapable of operating successfully in a print-oriented society. Responding to that concern, various literacy tutorial projects have attracted enormous publicity in this country, which, to bring this discussion full circle, has led to printed illiteracy leaflets at minimart checkout counters.

Everybody from the school board president to the parent of the kid next door has theories about the reading "crisis." The press, for its part, tosses about statistics freely (a single issue of one newspaper cited figures of forty and twenty-five million functional illiterates in two separate articles, neither figure documented by anything more than secondhand evidence—some authority's best guess). Even worse, the media and the public search for scapegoats to blame for the reading problem, as legislators look for some sort of standardized test that will simplistically solve it.

Despite the public uproar, the inflated statistics, and the scapegoating, it must be acknowledged that there is a grave reading problem. By almost any standards, too many children and adults either can't read or don't want to read, and until the day we are all equipped with Dick Tracy–style wrist televisions and videophones, there will be a need for people to learn to read.

The reading problem is best described in the plural—problems—and there isn't just a single scapegoat to string up from the library flagpole. Fortunately, research in the field of psycholinguistics and reading has offered some enlightenment on what has been happening to readers and nonreaders in school.

We know that in the past, reading programs have been based on the assumption that reading is simply a process of *decoding* or *translating* print into oral or silent language. Whether one stressed phonics (breaking words into their component parts) or whole-word (look-say) approaches, the programmatic emphasis was on getting students to sound out or pronounce words on a page. It was assumed that if students knew how to say the words comprehension would follow.

The stress on decoding has produced at least two kinds of troubled readers: the *strugglers* and the *perfectionists*. The strugglers are those who have not fully mastered the complex rules of oral reading; they thrash about trying to pronounce the words placed before them on the page. The perfectionists are performers who have mastered word-recognition skills and can produce flawless oral reproductions but when asked to explain what they have read demonstrate a low level of comprehension. (You may have had the same experience in a foreign language class, where you learned to read the language aloud properly but didn't understand a word, or when you were asked to translate aloud and struggled so hard that by the time you finished a sentence you forgot how it began.) Usually the strugglers end up in a remedial program, where, ironically, they are often taught even more decoding skills and kept away from real reading materials. The perfectionists are allowed to continue their regular classwork, where a teacher may or may not recognize that their comprehension is low.

The public and media periodically voice concern about the decline of phonics instruction, but the fact remains that even today an exhorbitant amount of school time is spent teaching children sound/letter correspondences rather than helping them read for meaning. Elaborate programs have been constructed to teach letters and sounds, including such gambits as letter-shaped puppets and toys and celebrations of a "letter of the week." Spelling and vocabulary instruction continue the decoding emphasis, based on the assumption that if we teach unfamiliar words in isolation, somehow reading and comprehension will result.

Reading is obviously much more than word calling. Any decoding a person does must be in the service of something higher: getting *meaning* from the printed page. In this respect, reading is not so much a mechanical process as a cognitive or *thinking* process. Readers bring a language system and their own life histories to the reading situation. They have control over the syntax of their language; they have a host of experiences in their heads. All of these are brought into play as they read. Programs that focus solely on decoding or memorizing facts can severely hamper the development of broad, flexible reading/thinking abilities.

The alternative to decoding is an approach most commonly known as "whole language." Based on a considerable and growing body of research, it argues that reading is something "learned, rather than taught." People master reading when they need to get meaning from a page, have some clues about how the reading system works, and are put to work in a setting where they can make meaning for themselves with coaching and tutoring as needed. The *whole* in whole language has multiple meanings: it refers to the notion that reading is learned as a *whole* process (as opposed to bits and pieces of language), that one must make *whole* meanings from *whole* or complete texts, that one must treat the language arts as a *whole,* with children reading their own writing as well as texts, with writing being generated in response to reading, with oral language instruction underlying integrated work in reading and writing. Whole language suggests that we:

- Give students freedom to choose what they want to read. If what they're reading interests them, if it's about something they know, if it's related to their purposes for reading, then they are much more likely to gain meaning from their experience.

- Use real books—fiction, nonfiction, poetry, plays for children, young adults, and adults—rather than pedagogically contrived snippets or excerpts.

- Allow students to stop reading works they are not enjoying, skip over material they already know, read selectively and "predictingly" (that is, figure out meanings by any strategies that come naturally to them).

- Emphasize reading as communication rather than a series of skills to be mastered.

- Encourage students to become active and critical thinkers, responding to and evaluating what they read.

- Attend to affective and aesthetic responses, don't just stress comprehension of black-and-white facts on a page.

Initial reading instruction

The topic of newcomers to reading is too complex to be taken up in detail in this book, but we will offer a few general guidelines that have grown from the research in this area. We are advocates of the approach called "language experience," which has nonreaders and nonwriters dictate stories to an adult, who, in turn, helps the children learn to read from their own writing. The ingenious aspect of this approach is that it is *always* meaning centered (since the stuff of reading is the child's own experience), that it grows from oral language competence (which develops in advance of reading and writing), that it teaches children to recognize the words they use most frequently in their day-to-day conversation. The seminal book on this method is Lee and Van Allen's *Learning to Read Through Experience* (1963). Interestingly enough, language experience was first developed as an approach to teaching English as a second language. It is not something that is appropriate only for kids who already have a solid English foundation.

Closely allied in philosophy to language experience is something called "invented spelling," where, from the earliest ages, youngsters are encouraged to think of themselves as *writers,* to make an effort to get their ideas down on paper. (Our youngest son came home from his first day of kindergarten having "written" with invented spelling. What a wonderful way to begin school and literacy instruction!)

At first children may produce mere chicken scratches, but they tell what those scratches mean to a teacher, who, in turn, writes down the story in Standard English spelling. Over time, children come to recognize and control the written language, and their spelling regularizes, coming closer and closer to the conventional.

The manner in which this language is learned seems baffling to the uninitiated. How can a child possibly spell without lists and drill? What sort of magic (or fraud) is involved in saying that kids don't need to be drilled in sound/letter correspondences, that they can pick up words in context (or out of thin air)? It sounds like the emperor's new clothes or Dr. Harold Hill and his seventy-six trombones.

What happens with invented spelling can best be described using the venerable "osmosis" metaphor: people absorb language from the concentrated language experiences that surround them. The great drive people have to understand print—based on their "need to know" about the world around them—helps them detect the regularities in print. It's the same mechanism that allowed us to pluck meaning from the babel that surrounded us when we were infants. When nonreaders and nonwriters encounter print regularly, when they try their hand at spelling, when they read some of their own writing and the writing of others, the systems mutually reinforce one another. Reading (and writing) are learned as wholes in a complex process that deserves the adjective "miraculous."

The miracle can take place in many ways. Some kids learn to read at home on their parent's knee. Some kids learn to read words flashed on the television screen in commercials. And, of course, many learn to read from a teacher. Reading is a miracle, but we know how to predict and support it in the schools:

- Fill the classroom with books (or give students ready access to a user-friendly library).

- Make available "wordless" picture books, which allow the nonreader to make meaning by learning to interpret pictures.

- Encourage children to write—in the air with a finger, on paper with a pencil—and provide support from a teacher who will help dig out the intended meaning of scrawl or scribble.

- Read to students frequently, lovingly.

- Encourage children to state their own reactions to books.

- Instigate plenty of conversation about life and literature.

In short, the whole language method focuses on immersing kids in reading and making reading meaningful and inviting.

Of course, as inviting and noncontroversial as that may sound, the approach has not received global acceptance. Even as we write this chapter, our local newspaper contains letters to the editor protesting a whole language textbook series adopted by the district. The series, which in our judgment is generally sound and inviting, has been attacked for its "overly realistic" (that is, true-to-life) stories, its alleged emphasis on witchcraft and violence (mostly traditional fairy tales), and its failure to teach traditional phonics. One parent wrote that she would rather have her children stay home than be exposed to that "crap." Another likened the stories in the series to a grisly murder that had taken place down in the valley.

As they say in the media, "Stay tuned."

Working with less able readers, nonreaders, and kids who don't like to read

Regardless of the outcome of the whole language wars, which we expect to continue for many years to come, the fact remains that at any level you will encounter many of the students identified in the heading above.

There will be students who don't and won't read the assigned material, students who cannot read well, students who will read but fail to comprehend, students who will read and take every word they read literally. You'll have students who lack confidence in their ability, children who are blocked by a fear of making mistakes, kids who have highly developed skills at masking their reading problems.

There are a number of strategies you can employ at any level to reach these problem students (and most of these are useful with skilled readers as well):

- Develop the classroom environment. Create a classroom reading center as a place that sets the tone for the reading program. Figure 5–1 shows one such center, with bookcases, magazine racks, drugstore "spinner" racks for paperback books, and a comfortable chair.

- Individualize reading assignments. Although there are certain texts you'll want all students to read in common, it's extraordinarily difficult to find texts that are appropriate for and interesting to all readers. With the help of the librarian and the interest inventories we describe in Chapters 2 and 3, make it a point to create possibilities for individual reading.

- Discuss obsolete and inaccurate "rules" students may have been taught about reading. We frequently encounter students who think they must read every word on the page, who believe that you should never glance back at something you might have missed, who are convinced that they don't read fast enough (which may be true, but certainly does nothing for their confidence and competence), who swear that anything in print is true, who believe (but seldom practice) the adage "Always look up the meaning of a word you don't know." The newer psycholinguistic research offers other views: that you can guess intelligently at unfamiliar materials, that glancing back is fine, that you should read at the pace that works for you, that it's probably better to skip many words than to break the reading flow by looking things up in a dictionary.

- Use tapes, films, and records. Use audiovisual materials before, during, or after reading. Filmed versions of novels and stories may often differ somewhat from the original but offer points of discussion as well. Above all, they give students a visual frame for their reading. Tapes and records of authors or actors and actresses reading works can provide an incentive to read and help students develop an ear for the voice, sound, and rhythm of literature.

- Do booktalks. Since you're a reader yourself, you can give a great boost to reading simply by talking about good books you've read and sharing your own response and reaction.

Figure 5–1 ○ A classroom reading center

- Conduct prereading discussions. Talking about the book or story before students begin to read creates context. You may wish to discuss characters students will encounter, or you might discuss students' impressions of the historical or cultural setting of the book. Especially useful is to get kids going on the broad theme or topic of the book, exploring these ideas before introducing the text itself.

- Use picture books. One of the older rules about reading claimed it was "cheating" to look at the pictures for interpretation. Granted, one can go wrong figuring out what a text means *via* an accompanying picture, but looking at graphic materials is a part of the arsenal of any skilled reader. For younger children, picture books abound; we wish there were similar ones written for secondary students. Adult "cocktail table" books are an especially valuable source. Also check your library's media center for visual files, filmstrips, and photographic collections that might enhance a particular text. (And don't forget your own collection of posters, calendars, and photographs from summer vacations.)

More strategies for teaching reading

Collaborative writing and editing

It may seem odd to see writing listed as an approach to reading, but as we have suggested, the two are closely and pedagogically intertwined. As students write and revise, they read, both their own work and that of other students. As is the case with the language experience approach, the content of student writing is likely to be of high interest to other members of the class, and the vocabulary and syntax is generally close to the students' own speech. (Perhaps too close, at times, but we'll take that up in our chapters on writing.)

Some ideas for getting students reading/writing together:

- Create a classroom newspaper or newsletter. As the students work on this document, they will naturally engage one another in fine tuning their reading skills. As an alternative, create a class computer bulletin board or on-screen newspaper, where students can type in ideas and stories, respond to one another, and read the large volume of writing that often results. (A low-cost alternative to the computer bulletin board is the original bulletin board, a chunk of cork that can be covered with students' notes and replies.)

- Write collective stories. Elementary teachers know all about "experience charts," where students dictate a class story based on something they've done together. Small-group story writing works well, too, with groups of three to five children writing either fiction or nonfiction.

- Write serials, in which different members of the class take responsibility for installments in the continuing adventures of a hero or heroine.

- Create editing partnerships and groups. (More on this in our composition chapters.) Suffice it to say that getting students to work successfully in small groups to edit one another's work is a powerful way of teaching reading.

- Collaboratively celebrate students' writing accomplishments. Designate an "author's chair" in your classroom, from which students read their finished work to the whole class. Publish student writing in a class magazine or anthology. Hang writing on the board for parents' night.

Reading with a purpose

Why, after all, do we read? Answers: to learn, to discover information, for aesthetic pleasure. Yet many school texts and assignments leave purpose out of the equation. Or, more accurately, assignments often subvert the kinds of purposes listed above to an overriding aim of teaching reading. We're all for teaching reading, of course, but if that becomes the primary purpose, no matter how well intentioned, much of the drive is taken out of student's will or need to read.

Try some of the following activities to show that reading has purpose and aim:

- Have a treasure hunt. Create lists of clues to send students around the classroom, school, or community. Or have some students prepare the hunt for others.

- Get a blueprint of the school or a map of your town and have students write, then follow, directions for getting from one place to another.

- Bring in hobby or craft books and let students master a new skill.

- Have students read *TV Guide* and plan their television viewing for the week.

- Bring in wonderfully entertaining poetry and give the class a fun day of reading-induced laughter.

- Have students do book talks. These are not old-fashioned oral book reports, but informal conversations in which students chat about what they are reading and gleaning from their reading.
- Invite a senior citizen to class to describe a lifetime of reading.

Reading in the content areas

The concept of reading in every subject area is one that English/language arts teachers should support and encourage. We can't afford to restrict reading to the language arts period in the elementary grades or the English class at the secondary level. The organization of different fields and disciplines—science, math, art—requires different reading strategies. We need to be conscious of those differences whenever we assign textbook reading.

Some possibilities for promoting reading in the content areas:

- Hold a faculty meeting on the problems students have reading various kinds of texts. What are the common elements? How do problems in the disciplines vary? If you're a specialized teacher in a high school, encourage teachers of other disciplines to work on those problems in their own classes (they are in a better position to do that than you are). If you're in a self-contained elementary classroom, you're ideally positioned to focus on reading skills throughout the day.
- Get your school to move beyond textbooks in teaching content areas. Nonfiction books for children, young adults, and adults are often much livelier and accessible to school-aged readers than are the tomes we give them for texts. At the least, encourage other teachers to supplement text chapters with interdisciplinary reading libraries.
- Cross-disciplinize your own teaching (or team teach with another person). Much reading is naturally interdisciplinary. Books on anthropology touch on social issues and problems. Books on science deal with side-effect problems for humanity. Literature talks about life, death, love, hate, warfare, and other interdisciplinary "good stuff." Capitalize on this natural interdisciplinarity to strengthen students' reading skills in many areas.

Reading resources

We have hinted strongly about a major tenet of our philosophy of teaching reading: if you put kids in contact with relevant and interesting reading materials, *reading happens.* There is growing evidence, in fact, that a great many reading skills are picked up by people in the process of reading itself, as they struggle with and solve reading problems. For this to happen, however, you need to have a rich variety of reading material available. Yet as school budgets continue to be restrained and restricted, it becomes difficult for teachers to stockpile the classroom.

Here are some ideas for increasing the range of materials available in your classroom:

- Attend rummage sales, garage sales, and auctions as a source of cheap used paperbacks, old magazines and comics, and other unique and interesting materials. (Yes, we're suggesting that you spend your own money. Take it off your income tax.)

- Write or visit county, state, and federal government offices for free pamphlets and booklets.

- Enlist students and parents in the effort to increase the range of reading materials. Parents are often willing to contribute old books, as well as magazines and newspapers, to the school reading room.

- When making decisions about the departmental or school budget, explore the possibility of buying single copies of good literature rather than sinking large sums into multiple copies and classroom sets.

- Explore the mail-order book clubs as a way of enticing kids to buy their own books. Or establish a paperback bookstore in the school and stock it with fetching titles.

- Build up the recorded literature collection by surveying catalogs and making recommendations to the media-center director.

- Get to know your school and public librarian and find out about book acquisition procedures. In our experience, librarians are discouraged by faculty or public apathy in requesting books. Through your professional reading, identify the books you want available; send the list to the librarian. Even in financial hard times, you're likely to see the collection shaped to your needs and interests.

Multiethnic and multicultural literature

We close this chapter with a special problem: including more ethnic, minority, and international literature in the language arts program. We put ourselves in the camp of the pluralists who want to see the range of cultural materials expanded in the schools, and we are strongly opposed to the "cultural literacy" movement, which argues for focusing instruction on the classic literature of the Western world. In our day and age, we need to expand children's horizons, not restrict them.

Twenty years ago, many teachers responded to the need for multicultural literature by creating special courses and units: Afro American Literature, Hispanic Literature, European Ethnic Minorities. (Many courses in Women's Literature—the "majority minority"—were also developed at this time.) Elementary teachers created international units and held cultural fairs based on reading about how other people live.

These courses and units have served an important purpose, but we think there is a need to move further: schools need to integrate multicultural literature throughout *all* classes and courses. In the long run, we cannot afford to isolate or ghettoize literature of ethnic minorities, reading about other races and cultures. Multicultural reading ought to be happening every day in every class. We know that every culture has powerful literature to offer us and that students can invariably benefit from learning about cultures other than their own.

Unfortunately, few teachers have been trained in this area. The colleges have introduced some multicultural literature, but by no means has the professoriat been able to integrate such literature throughout the curriculum. You're on your own, then, in finding material, but fortunately there are many sources of help:

- Read the professional journals. In particular, *The English Journal* and *Language Arts* regularly publish good columns introducing new multiethnic/cultural materials.

- Check for bibliographies available in school and public libraries where, again, expanding consciousness has led librarians to prepare special collections.

- Consult members of racial or ethnic minorities. Ask them to suggest titles and other materials to be brought into your class.

- Teach thematically. Thematic/topical teaching maximizes the possibility of introducing diverse literatures. Such themes as "Old World/ New World," "Equality," "Conflict," "Generations," and "The Family" are common to virtually all cultures and literatures.

Figure 5–2 provides a checklist for your consideration when you are selecting books for your teaching.

1. Have I included literature that challenges my students' values as well as literature that reinforces them?
2. Have I made available literature that represents the ethnic backgrounds of the students in my class?
3. Have I included literature that shows people and life-styles new for my students?
4. Have I been attentive to the images of male and female presented in the literature I have chosen?
5. Have I been careful to counter stereotypical views of people, values, and life-styles with more precise, detailed, and authentic views?
6. Have I chosen literature that emphasizes similarities and universals as well as differences and unique qualities?
7. Have I focused on the work's literary merits as well as its social and political merits?
8. Have I been sensitive to stereotypes that might be damaging or hurtful to students who are in the minority in the class or school (be they Anglo, black, Oriental, male, or female)?
9. Have I provided a richness of alternatives so that students may have choices in their reading?
10. Have I provided opportunities for discussing images of people, their values, and their life-styles as they are presented in literature?

Figure 5–2 ○ Checklist for selecting multicultural literature

Chapter Six

Reading and Responding

n her classic book *Literature as Exploration,* first written in 1938, Louise Rosenblatt speaks of reading as a "performing art." Not only does literature perform for us, she observes, but we learn to "perform" upon texts, creating our own interpretation. As students mature, as they go from initial readers to child readers to young adult readers, their ability to perform on texts becomes more sophisticated. Her "transactional" approach argues that "literature" exists midway between a text, with its black marks on the white page, and the reader, who "performs" on the text.

Although Rosenblatt's work did not receive as much initial attention as did the New Criticism (launched in the same year, 1938, with the publication of Cleanth Brooks's *Understanding Poetry*), her theory has, in recent years, received enormous support. Those citing her research are as diverse as school reading researchers (emphasizing the effects of prior knowledge on interpretation) and academics who espouse subjective criticism (suggesting there may be as many texts as there are readers).

A response-centered approach makes four assumptions about the relationship between literature and the reader:

1. *Experience with literature is personal.* A student's reaction to a book or story or poem is based on a complex set of past experiences. How students respond depends, to a considerable extent, on who they are, what they have experienced, what they have read previously and recently. If we want students to be moved by literature and to be responsive to it, we must help young people find literature appropriate to their emotional development, their age, their interests, their needs, and their reading levels.

2. *Engagement with literature is a natural process.* We don't have to trick kids into reading and reacting to good books. Experience with literature (as with life) is fundamentally absorbing. In working with students, we must be very careful to support and nurture engagement, not cut it off prematurely.

3. *People read different materials for different purposes.* We read to be well-informed consumers and citizens; we read out of curiosity and a desire to know about mysteries; we read to enter new worlds; and we read to identify with others. Recognizing this, teachers should encourage students to read all kinds of materials, not just standard school texts and anthologies.

4. *Students' reactions to what they read are based on both their purpose for reading and on the nature of their involvement with the text.* The basics of the plot are what excites one student. Another is engaged by a particular character. A third is fascinated by the pictures. We need to allow for a variety of patterns of engagement and response.

Approaches to literature in the classroom

Our own teaching in secondary schools started in standard fashion: we would present a text to the class, tell a little about the author or period, then lead a discussion that largely followed the lines of the New Criticism—teasing out the multiple meanings and structures of the text. Those discussions often found us answering most of our own questions or carrying on a dialogue with one student while the rest of the students hid their heads in books. Later, as we explored response theory, that pattern changed. Although we still spend some time talking with the whole class, a much larger proportion of our time is spent organizing small-group and individual reading programs and discussions. So we have come to see the literature/reading classroom operating with a balance among whole-class discussions, small-group explorations, and individualized reading. We'll look at these in order.

Shared experiences

Traditionally, classroom experience with literature has meant a professor or teacher presenting a view of the meaning of a text through lecture or pseudo-Socratic dialogue. The contemporary word *sharing* is not euphemistic: it *isn't* a cover up for some sort of sentimentalized chitchat about literature. Rather, *sharing* describes a class and teacher exploring books, with all readers invited to contribute to the discussion. A genuine response can sometimes be quite heated; it can lead to anger and tears. We also find the common class experience to be a useful way to help students learn to "perform" for themselves by seeing how other people engage with and respond to literature.

Some alternative ways of approaching common class readings:

- Use short selections (children's books, poems, one-act plays, short stories) that can be read and responded to in a short period of time—a half hour or an hour. We find this preferable to working through long literary works—say a full-length novel—over an extended period of time.

- Screen creative film shorts, videos, and feature films related to topics of interest to the class, then follow those with selected short readings.

- Assign TV shows related to issues and topics of interest to the class as a whole; then do the reading and discussion.

- Treat students' writing as literature to share with the class. Give it the same respect you would professional writing.

- Back up shared readings with recordings of authors reading their own work or actors and actresses doing dramatic readings. Or have your students present and tape dramatic readings for next year's class.

- Have students present alternative oral readings of the common text, then discuss how various presentations shape the meaning.

- Discuss your own reading, not only literature, but newspaper items, magazine articles, pulp thrillers. Invite your students to share their outside reading as well.

- Use bulletin boards to post poems, articles, student writing, and excerpts from plays and novels.

The discussion of literature

As we've noted, the more we teach, the less time we spend in structured discussion of literature. Occasionally we'll be able to get a lively discussion going, but we find it fairly difficult to engage thirty or more students at once in discussing a piece of literature. We hate to recall how many times we've carefully prepared discussion questions only to have students sit like porcupines, quills out, when we ask them to talk. But despite our wounds, we do have a few bits of advice to offer:

- Preface group discussions with oral reading. Read large chunks of the literature aloud to the class to make certain your students have experienced it (even if the students supposedly read the literature for homework).

- Allow plenty of time for gut reactions. Good literature often elicits a strong emotional response from students. They need an opportunity to say what they feel before they move toward formal discussion.

- Preface discussions with writing—five minutes or so for students to jot down their responses and reactions.

- Ask honest questions. Don't ask, Who can tell me the symbolic significance of the porcupine in this book? when you already have an interpretation in mind. The best kinds of questions seem to be those that ask for student engagement: What did you think of this book? How did you like the hero? Have you ever done anything like this yourself? What about that porcupine?

- Let "literary matters" emerge through students' responses. Instead of plunging into the discussion with a question about plot or character, let students discuss their reactions to books; then help them understand their responses in terms of the structure of the book—its character and plot.

- Ask questions that you would like to respond to yourself. Prepare for this by doing your own reading pencil in hand, writing down questions that occur to you, as reader, along the way.

Group experiences

We use small-group work extensively when we teach literature. Sometimes our students will discuss reactions to a story or poem or book that everyone in the class has read; at other times we have groups work on different selections. In both cases, group experiences with literature allow for a wide range of responses from people whose values and opinions may be very different from one another's. Exchanges with people who have different interpretations not only help students grow as readers, they help people grow in self-awareness as well.

Some alternative approaches to group experiences with literature:

- Within a thematic unit, allow groups of students to choose from a broad range of fiction, nonfiction, and poetry.

- Have small groups prepare oral interpretations of poems, plays, and stories to present to the class.

- Let groups specialize in an author, learning all about the work and life and reporting back to the class.

- Type out the questions you would ask if you were conducting a whole-class discussion of a literary work. Then give those questions to small groups for discussion. How much do their answers vary from those you would expect if you had guided the discussion?

- Give small groups the assignment of tracking or mapping a particular element in a work of literature—the development of characters, the twists of plot, even recurring symbols or images or motifs.

- Provide a list of interrelated short stories, poems, or plays for small groups to choose and read from according to their interests (sports, fantasy or science fiction, detective or mystery stories, Dr. Seuss).

- Let small groups develop as reading clubs, focused on favorite authors or genres.

- Set groups to work reading in anthologies or collections, looking for good individual works they can recommend for the whole class to read. (Those conventional anthologies *can* be useful.)

- For your own edification, have the students discuss a poem or story in small groups *without direction* from you. Tape-record the conversation or ask a student to take notes on the directions the conversation takes. You may be surprised by the depth and range of discussion (*provided* the students are reading something they find enjoyable or engaging in the first place).

- With secondary students, to prepare for examinations or college, set up study groups to read and review classic books commonly discussed. Have groups share synopses and interpretations.

Individual reading

Individual reading is at the heart of the teaching process. After all, what we want to accomplish in the literature/reading program is to lead students toward individual competence. We advocate giving kids lots of time in school to pursue their individual reading, particularly given the competition for their out-of-school time and attention. To foster the individualized reading program:

- By hook, crook, or school budget, build up your classroom library. Research shows that much of teaching reading involves getting books into young people's hands (the magnetism of literature will take care of the rest.) The closer the books are to the kids, the more likely you are to make contact.

- Explore and exploit your community and school library. Book repositories may be the stereotypical bibliodungeon, but not to students whose teachers have gotten to know the resources and who can guide the students to what they want.

- Allow a full class week early in the year for students to read silently in class, at the library, or in the reading room. Monitor and assist their choices. If the free reading week works, repeat it at intervals throughout the school year. (For fun and accountability, keep track of how many pages, chapters, and complete books are devoured by your charges during that week.)
- Set aside a reading/conversation corner where students can discuss books they are reading.
- Hold frequent individual conferences with students to discuss their individualized reading.
- Do frequent book talks to publicize books available for individualized reading; have students do book talks as well to sell titles they've recently read and enjoyed.

Extending the range of response

A good English/language arts class will include a combination of reading experiences. It will provide large-group sharing of diverse responses to individual works, small-group explorations on common or group-selected texts, and plenty of time for individual reading and responses. It will also encourage students to perform on texts in a variety of ways. Options for response must allow for different kinds of students and many types of reading materials. The suggestions that follow allow you to vary the ways in which students synthesize their reactions to reading.

Talk and drama

A good book, poem, play, or story often leads naturally to substantial talk. In addition, literature is naturally dramatic, and a powerful piece of literature can be focused through the use of classroom drama. You can have your students:

- Talk informally about characters they liked and disliked, scenes that made them cry or laugh.
- Ask for a conference with you when they have a response to share privately.
- Sit in a circle and give minireviews of books they're reading.
- Talk about their favorite books to younger children.
- Tell the whole class about books they're particularly enjoying, perhaps reading aloud passages that have high impact.

- Do improvisations based on key scenes from a story, perhaps exploring alternative endings or different possibilities for characters' actions.
- Extend or create scenes that are presented sketchily or are alluded to but not shown "on stage."
- Prepare a readers theater production of a work, acting out scenes with script in hand, and without costumes or sets.
- Videotape dramatizations of short stories, poems, scenes from novels and plays, newspaper articles, etc.

Writing activities

Teachers are increasingly aware of "the reading/writing connection": that reading naturally leads to a host of imaginative and expository writing activities, that student writing is, itself, part of the literature of a classroom. To integrate the field from the reading end, let students:

- Rewrite the ending of a story or novel.
- Write a sequel to a story, novel, or play, describing characters or actions following "The End."
- Write an exchange of letters between characters from different books.
- Maintain a journal, logging their reading achievements and their reactions to what they've read.
- Write a poem based on mood, images, or feelings created by a story or play.
- Adapt a short story into a play.
- Describe how they would film a scene from a novel, play, story, or poem.
- Above all, write before, during, and after readings to explore ideas, anticipations, expectations, disappointments, irritations, joys, and mirthful moments.

Media activities

Students need not always respond to literature in words. Have your students:

- Make a videotape based on a poem or story, being more concerned with capturing mood and emotion than on reenacting the work.

- Make a poster or visual representation of a literary work, capturing the basic emotions or ideas of the text.
- Make book jackets, magazine spreads, or advertising posters that will attract a book buyer.
- Present pantomime or charade book reviews.
- Collect magazine photographs that capture their response to a work.
- Draw maps based on stories, both literal maps of the setting(s) and figurative maps of the relationships among characters and events.
- Illustrate favorite poems and stories (including their own).

Critical and evaluative reading

One of the charges often leveled against a response-centered program is that it fails to develop students' abilities to evaluate what they read, to tell good from bad. "If students simply react," goes this argument, "how will they ever come to know that some books are better than others, and that any old reaction to a book just won't do?"

All of us want our students to appreciate good literature. Without being snobbish, we can say that some books stand the test of time better than others (see the next chapter), that some are fuller and richer examples of the writer's art and craft than others. We don't want our kids to pick dreck over substance, easy and simple reads over those that engage and challenge the mind. The response-centered approach doesn't ignore such matters; rather, it tries to promote growth in critical reading from within the student.

How can we nurture the growth of artistic, aesthetic, and critical awareness? We think the following principles are important to keep in mind:

1. *Both students and teachers have "taste," but their tastes are often very different.* It may seem to you that what students appreciate is stereotypic, even simplistic. It's important to recognize, however, that from kindergarten on, children are establishing their own identities and trying to establish their relationships with the world in which they live. They're looking for answers, and they respond to literature that seems to offer them answers. To undercut their choices and their taste is to underrate the power of literature to enrich their lives.

2. *Tastes change as people change.* This is true for adults as well as young people. How have your values shifted in the past five or ten years? What do you care for today that was undreamt of in your

philosophy a few years back? We find it a truism that as long as people are in an environment that offers them new experiences, they expand and enlarge their interests. We worry that too often kids are challenged prematurely with books designed to improve their taste. The result is that they quit reading and their growth comes to a halt. A response-centered program offers students new opportunities for experience and enlarges their horizons gradually, letting the natural growth in critical reading take place.

3. *Growth in awareness comes as a result of building on previous literary experiences.* It's important to consider the cumulative effects of reading on growth. A good experience with one book helps pave the way for success with the next. Enjoyment of a simple book creates a foundation for something a bit more complex. Thus, we emphasize the importance of exposure to a wide range of literature in a response-centered program, coupled with opportunities to react to a text in one's own terms in a community of readers.

Here are some activities we use to catalyze and promote this natural growth in criticality:

- Read a novel aloud to the class over a period of several weeks, perhaps a chapter a day, perhaps as little as ten minutes a day. As you read, present your observations about the book and invite students to exchange viewpoints. In this way you model adult ways of responding while acknowledging that kid critiques follow different patterns (which, in the long run, may mesh with and enrich adult responses).

- Ask open-ended questions, then probe for explanations. Don't begin with formal evaluation of a work. Let students' unexpurgated likes and dislikes emerge first; then nudge students to back up their responses with illustrations from the text.

- Celebrate tangents. The most fruitful discussions we've had with both young and older students have grown through side trips and excursions we could not have anticipated. These are not digressions, and you're much too savvy to let the kids deliberately derail your train of thought. It therefore follows that tangents *are* a form of critical response, one to be understood rather than condemned.

- For secondary students especially, avoid teaching literary terminology in advance. We know that terms like *plot, theme, character, narration, irony, symbol, setting, imagery, dialogue, metaphor,* and *rhythm* are useful in many ways in discussing literature. However, mastery of terminology is not a substitute for or easy route to literary evaluation. We introduce literary terminology in class discussions as it seems helpful in encouraging students to discuss their own reactions. Ah, you liked the way the characters talked? We call that good *dialogue.* You thought the comparison of love to fire and ice was neat? That's a *metaphor.* We're constantly surprised by how often opportunities to present this enabling terminology come up in class.

- Encourage comparisons of literary works. Help students link their past reading to the present by talking about books previously read by the class or by inviting students to draw their individualized reading into whole-class discussions. We also find it useful to compare text and film versions from time to time.

- Make small groups responsible for interpreting accessible literature. Patrick Dias (1990) taught us to let go of the podium and to have small groups come up with interpretations and evaluations on their own, without teacher intervention. We've been pleasantly surprised by the sophisticated interpretations that emerge.

- Use writing extensively. Have students keep response journals as they read; let them write response and reaction papers once they've finished. In place of the traditional book report, have students present their critical evaluation of a book, magazine, poem, or story. Let them write postcard critiques on an index card or insert short reviews into the book jackets of library books (with the librarian's approval, of course).

- Start a book review newsletter in which your class recommends good titles to other classes or grades in the school. In November, send the newsletter home to parents with the suggestion that it be used as a holiday shopping list.

Finally, you should never underestimate the power of a book, poem, story, or play to teach itself. Literature *does* enculturate students, enlarging their range of experiences, refining their tastes and sensibilities. Good books can often do this without the domination of the teacher. But it's also clear that books need the backing provided by good supportive English/language arts teachers in order to work their best magic.

Chapter Seven

The Classics, Popular Culture, and Cultural Literacy

With his book *Cultural Literacy* (1987), E. D. Hirsch launched an enormous controversy in the teaching of arts and sciences. Drawing on some of the research we cite in the previous two chapters, Hirsch observes that readers bring prior knowledge and past experiences to bear on reading an unfamiliar text. If students have a paucity of knowledge, he argues, they will have difficulty appreciating the standard classic works that form the core of a culture. Hirsch believes that youngsters nowadays are not "culturally literate." He argues for increased teaching of core or common elements of the culture and confidently subtitles his book *What Every American Needs to Know.*

Hirsch realizes that some people call him snobbish and even racist (his book is dominated by allusions to the works of white, male British and American authors). However, he states that his concept of cultural literacy is intended to bring a wider spectrum of children into mainstream culture. The pluralists and populists might not like it, he explains, but all children must learn the core in order to participate fully in the nation's cultural and economic life.

In an era when the schools are widely perceived to be failing, Hirsch's book is receiving strong public response. He supplies support for those who would like to reduce "nonessential" offerings in the schools and get back to a basic, core curriculum, with heavy emphasis on traditional mathematics, science, history, and literature.

For those who have been following new developments in English/language arts, however, Hirsch's message is troubling, first because of its emphasis on a traditional core of learning, and second because of its misunderstanding of the nature of the reading process.

While research has shown that prior knowledge has a great deal to do with success in reading new texts, the research has also discredited the practices of teaching snippets of knowledge in isolation, a finding Hirsch seems to have missed or selectively ignored. If we force children to read "great" books that are beyond their reach, we do little more than discourage and alienate them. Further, Hirsch's list *is* snobbish, dominated by the sorts of books deemed important by mostly white, mostly male university professors in prestige schools like the University of Virginia. Even if Hirsch's list were valid, it's doubtful that forcing children to learn a bit of culture every day would bring any child, majority or minority, into full participation in the culture.

(We also have serious reservations about what Hirsch thinks it means to "be an American." But we will let that pass in order to get on with the discussion of teaching.)

Ironically, the cultural literacy controversy has erupted at a time when more and more language arts teachers have turned to quality children's and young adult literature as a source of material. Further, many teachers are expanding the multicultural content of the curriculum, and a number of teachers and librarians are exploring ways of extending the curriculum to encompass the materials of mass or popular culture, including newspapers, television, magazine, film, and records. Cultural literacy as presented by Hirsch clearly contradicts that impulse.

We've never heard anybody argue against the value of classic books, and most people would agree that at some point in their lives, students probably ought to encounter them. And there hasn't in recent years been any appreciable withering away of interest in the common culture. In secondary schools, especially, despite the wealth of alternatives, students spend extraordinary amounts of time with conventional literature anthologies, plodding through such hoary classics as Jonathan Edwards's "Sinners in the Hands of an Angry God" and William Cullen Bryant's "Thanatopsis."

In this chapter we argue for a middle ground, or, perhaps better, for a comprehensive view of "cultural literacy" that gives the classics their due but recognizes that we are living on the brink of the twenty-first century, not in the late nineteenth, and that the nature of culture has changed. Specifically:

1. *All children are "literate" in a culture already.* By *literate* we mean that they live in a culture and are negotiating it for the most part successfully. It may be a culture dominated by television, family, siblings, and peers. It may be the culture of an all-white Boston suburb or a racially mixed blue-collar neighborhood in Sacramento, but it is a culture, and it is complex and rich.

2. *People become literate in new or different cultures in response to opportunities and exposure.* By *exposure* we do not mean a guided tour through anthologies like *Skipping Through American Literature* or *The Pomp and Circumstance of BritLit.* Rather, people become enculturated as their personal interests, ideas, motivations, and opportunities expand. Memorizing bits of cultural knowledge will neither enculturate minority (or majority) children nor pop

them free from their present culture and into the "mainstream" (which, in the United States at least, we defy Hirsch or anybody else to define and describe accurately).

3. *Cultural literacy is personal and plural.* Although one can compile lists of commonly read works, it's a grievous error to assume that there is a monolithic cultural literacy. People's knowledge of the culture is unique and idiosyncratic. It is *personal,* based on their needs and interests over time and circumstance.

4. *Classic and popular culture are both part of a continuum, not contradictories or opposites.* In fact, even the word *continuum* may be inappropriate, since it implies a one-dimensional scale with the classics at one end and popcult at the other. A better metaphor might be that of the earth's atmosphere: it contains a mix of oxygen, nitrogen, auto exhaust, mouthwash fumes, and other gasses we don't want to think about. It's a jumble of molecules. Most teachers would like to enrich that air with the oxygen of what we see as good or better books for kids. We'd like to cut down on some of the noxious fumes of, say, literature that is exploitive, excessively violent, or written to manipulate kids rather than to inform them. But we can improve that air quality only by getting kids out into the fresh country air of reading, not by locking them in a musty library stocked only with classics.

In this chapter, then, we begin with popular culture, showing that it is more than "pop and pulp," more than assigning TV shows kids would watch anyway. After we explore some ways of using these materials in a variety of elementary and secondary school classrooms, we go on to discuss the classics, here directing our remarks mostly to secondary school teachers (though by no means forgetting that the classics and young people's cultural literacy include elementary school favorites like *Mother Goose, Peter and the Wolf, Through the Looking Glass,* and *The Five Hundred Hats of Bartholomew Cubbins*).

Popular culture in the classroom

Study the names in Figure 7–1, a poem of thanks to the founder of our country for some of our popular culture heroes and heroines. If you're like us, you may find yourself illiterate in some aspects of twentieth-century popular culture; there are a number of names here we didn't recognize on first reading. The list helps demonstrate that popular culture is more than the here-and-now, more than passing fads and fancies. As serious scholars of popular culture tell us, its study provides us important clues into people's beliefs, values, traditions, and life styles.

Thank you *George* for . . .
Soupy Sales and Bloomingdale's
James Moody and Howdy Doody
Frank Buck and Donald Duck
Edith Head and Grateful Dead
Elsie Borden and Flash Gordon
Margaret Mead and Allen Freed
Billy Budd and Elmer Fudd
Double Decker and Chubby Checker
Bar Bells and Orson Wells
Mason Jars and Hershey Bars
R. H. Macy and Dick Tracy
Jane Fonda and Satchidandanda
Gandy Goose and Lenny Bruce
Magic Marker and Charlie Parker
Benjamin Spock and Monte Rock
Betty Boop and Hula Hoop
King Kong and Ping Pong
Pinky Lee and Sandra Dee
Peter Max and Cracker Jacks
Babe Ruth and Spooky Tooth
Lady Day and Sugar Ray
Herbie Mann and Charlie Chan
Frankie Lyman and Neil Simon
Huckleberry Finn and Rin Tin Tin
Henry Miller and Phyllis Diller
Sarah Bernhardt and Werner Erhard
Stanley Kubrick and David Brubeck
Larry Parks and Groucho Marx
Jungle Jim and Tiny Tim
Satchel Paige and John Cage
Buddy Holly and Toonerville Trolley
Buckley's Nazz and Satchmo's Jazz
Gil Hodges and Buck Rogers
Easy Rider and Duke Snider
Fatty Arbuckle and Artie Garfunkel

Liz Taylor and Popeye the Sailor
Willy Mays and Gabby Hayes
Paul Bunyan and Damon Runyon
Submariner and Ike and Tina
William Boyd and Pink Floyd
Lauren Hutton and Willie Sutton
Carmen Miranda and Andy the Panda
Helen Reddy and Ferlinghetti
Admiral Byrd and Mortimer Snerd
Mack Sennet and Tony Bennet
Lucille Ball and Huntz Hall
Bill Haley and Barnum and Bailey
Clarence Darrow and Mia Farrow
Joe Papp and Al Capp
Red Grange and Dr. Strange
Freedom Train and Frieda Payne
Claude Rains and Lionel Trains
Johnny Carson and Greer Garson
James Dean and Mr. Clean
Don Knotts and Alan Watts
Count Basie and Edgar Cayce
George Meany and Harry Houdini
William Cody and Truman Capote
Amos N' Andy n' W. C. Handy
Fred Astaire and Buddy Baer
Pearl Buck and Daisy Duck
John Lindsay and Alfred Kinsey
James Cagney and Jerome Ragney
Al Capone and Vic Damone
Johnny Cash and Ogden Nash
The Human Torch and Larry Storch
Ticker Tape and Moby Grape

—from *Hey Babes*, by Bert Padell, published by Acropolis Books, Ltd. Reprinted with permission.

Figure 7–1 ○ A poetic history of popular culture

Popular culture is more than today's funny papers (that expression itself is a popular culture phrase of an earlier era; nowadays we just call them comics). It's more than the top forty in rock'n'roll or country and western; it's more than the fluff'n'stuff of *Entertainment Tonight*. Figure 7–1 just hints at the variety and richness of the American experience as reflected in its popular arts: the entertainments, diversions, and aesthetic experiences of the masses, which include all of us in some contexts.

Nor is popular culture something exclusively American. As our British readers would be quick to remind us, England's popular culture is much older than ours and includes folks named William Shakespeare, Charles Dickens, the Brontë sisters, and Arthur Conan Doyle. The popular culture tradition in Australia, New Zealand, and Canada is perhaps a bit shorter than ours in the United States, but it is filled with interesting characters and personalities and art, from convict poetry to Footrot Flats, from *The Thorn Birds* to hockey player/artists.

Although the popular arts, by definition, appeal to a large number of people, they are not necessarily inferior or mediocre in quality. We think that the study of the popular arts, both of today and of previous periods in history, can be an enjoyable and rewarding English/language arts experience for several reasons:

1. *The study of popular culture enriches students' understanding of their country and its history.* The fiction and poetry, magazines and newspapers, radio and television programs, movies and plays that we enjoy provide insight into our tastes, values, and beliefs. Through a study of popular culture, students can begin to answer questions: What is peculiar or unique about our culture? How have we changed through history? What traits and beliefs have endured? How have we come to be what we are today?

2. *The study of popular culture helps students understand their own tastes and values better.* Students can examine their own interests and compare them with those of their peers, their parents, and people in other times. Such study also gives them a chance to examine some of the sociological, economic, and commercial roots of their taste.

3. *Popular culture is diverse and rich.* Students of varying interests and abilities will be able to find something they would like to explore in greater depth. In addition, the materials of popular culture are at our fingertips in paperback books, magazines, newspapers, TV and radio programs, and movies, an especially important factor in an age of tight school budgets.

To show the potential of these materials, we want to review two approaches to popular culture, *historical* and *genre.* In choosing such apparently "literary" modes of organization, we show how popular culture can be meshed with traditional study. At the same time, we don't want to scare you off. As you'll see, these approaches are appropriate for heterogeneous kids from kindergarten through graduate school.

The historical approach

- Choose a historical period that interests or intrigues your students or is covered in their text. U.S. students might explore the popular culture fads and fancies of the Civil War era, the Gay Nineties, the Roaring Twenties, Prohibition, the Rock'n'Roll Fifties. Your library probably has a number of illustrated "cocktail table" books on any of these periods, and for any era in the twentieth century, films or videos are likely to be available. Examine the art, music, science and technology, and fashion of the time, and have your students write about what they see and understand.

- Choose a single important day in twentieth-century history and have students study its cultural milieu. (The beginnings and/or endings of the World Wars are particularly good ones, inviting study of popular culture worldwide.) Have students examine newspapers and magazines (available at most reasonably large community libraries) and discuss the news of the day, trends in fashion, popular songs and other music, theatrical entertainment, and radio (and possibly television) offerings.

- Have students reproduce or imitate a popular art form from an earlier era. They can write dime novels, create minstrel or vaudeville shows, write cartoons and comics. Or, invite your students to write period fiction or drama, a short story or play set in a period that interests them, reflecting what they've learned about the mass culture of the era.

- Recreate literature from a period that interests you, with students taking on the roles of historical characters or simply trying to read a poem or story from what they take to be the perspective of the writer.

- Have students interview parents and grandparents about how they entertained themselves. What did they read? What did they listen to on the radio? What songs did they hum? What were their favorite films, television programs, cartoon characters? From this, have your students create a chronology or time line. Some parents and grandparents might even enjoy coming to class to talk, perhaps bringing along some memorabilia (a 45 rpm record of Bill Haley and the Comets singing "Rock Around the Clock," for example).

- Have a treasure hunt in which students search attics, basements, and bookshelves in their houses for books, magazines, and newspapers saved by their family over the years. What has survived? Why? What does it tell about values?

- Visit garage sales and rummage sales to pick up old children's and young adult books. You can create a popular culture library for pennies. Let your students read, analyze, and discuss these "survivors."

- In the same manner, look for school books from earlier eras (hell's bells, your school book room probably has a bunch of these). Have students discuss these in terms of educational practices of earlier days. How have things changed? How would they feel if they had to study, say, a 1950s-style spelling book?

- Have students bring in family collections of school yearbooks and picture albums. What can they learn about the values, interests, and fads of those times by studying photographs and inscriptions?

The genre approach

Popular culture clearly follows trends and formulas. One successful television show spawns a dozen like it; a best-selling novel will be followed by myriad imitations; one detective or spy or cowboy or sci-fi movie creates the pattern for others. As students look for these common elements, they are sharpening their skills for literature study as well, where one sonnet leads to another, one heroic couplet is followed (alas) by two thousand more, and a surprise ending to a short story sets a pattern followed for generations to come.

- Teach a "best seller" unit (to older students). You'll have to do a bit of research yourself, looking back through, say, *Time* or *The New York Times Book Review,* to get a list of best-selling books over the years. Many of these will still be available in your community library. Have your students examine them, perhaps read them cover to cover, and create a description of how the genre of the best seller has evolved.

- Teach a Newbery/Caldecott unit (to younger *or* older students), examining the winners of these children's literature awards over the decades. Again, your school or community library is likely to have copies of most of these.

- Have students look into the ever-popular genre of "the Western" with authors as diverse as James Fenimore Cooper, Zane Grey, Henry Wilson Allen, Jack Schaefer, and Louis L'Amour. How is the West depicted? What are the formula plots? How are women and minorities depicted?

- Analyze one of the series books for upper elementary/junior high students: the Hardy Boys books, the Nancy Drews. What patterns do students see here? Kids might also like to look at older series, say, the Tom Swift series (both senior and junior), or even the Bobbsey Twins.

- Plunge into the mystery/detective genre, with writers such as Arthur Conan Doyle, Mary Roberts Rinehart, Willard Huntington Wright, Manfred Lee, Agatha Christie, or Erle Stanley Gardner. What are the qualities of some of the main characters? What do villains have in common? How does the writer create suspense?

- And, of course, there's science fiction, which invites both historical and contemporary analysis. Some students will enjoy going back to the works of H. G. Wells and Jules Verne to see how it all began, while others will enjoy plunging into current sci-fi materials to study patterns in the creation of heroines, aliens, hostile planets, modes of transport, and even language and communications systems.

Of course, genre study is not limited to the printed word. Television and films demonstrate patterns as well. Have your students:

- Watch a soap opera for a week (either a prime-time soap or one taped during school for replay later). What are the typical problems that soap opera characters encounter? What is the status or profession of these characters? What life-styles do they represent? What are the clichés and customs of soap opera?

- Write a soap opera for children or for teenage boys or girls. How would they adapt the conventions to reach their own kind?

- Discover the patterns of situation comedies. What kinds of characters, experiences, and life-styles are represented? To what extent do the sitcoms accurately portray life today?

- Describe the image of women and minorities as presented in television dramas, sitcoms, or soaps.

- Characterize the heroines and heroes of television dramatic action series.

- Analyze the role of violence in television and film.

- Study and discuss the content of Saturday morning cartoons.
- Examine lists of Academy Award–winning movies, read about the films, perhaps see some that are available on video.
- Hold a Walt Disney Film Festival and figure out the formulas for the classic cartoons and/or the family escapade genres produced so successfully by Disney.

Nor should we forget music, art, and drama. Invite your students to:

- Study a musical genre: rock'n'roll, jazz, the blues, "highbrow" or symphony music. How have these changed over the years?
- Study a single musician or rock group. How has, say, Michael Jackson or Madonna carved out a niche for himself or herself? What are the characteristics of the model?
- Go to a play, preferably several, and write down all they can about "how to put on a play." In doing so, they'll discover many of the formulas of this genre.
- Go to an art museum (or browse through contemporary and classic art books brought in by the teacher). What's going on in the world of oils, acrylics, water color, collage, and whatever they do to make that modern stuff?
- Study trends in photography over time, from still photos of the Civil War to contemporary photography. This is a particularly good unit for science buffs, who can discover how technological developments in films, printing papers, lenses, and camera mechanics and electronics have allowed artists new possibilities for graphic exploration.

A warning concerning monoculturalism and popular culture

Throughout this book we argue for a curriculum that is pluralistic and multicultural. In a sense, the study of popular culture attempts to do just that: to bring a wider range of materials into the curriculum. But popular culture can also be narrowly interpreted as the culture of majorities; after all, filmmakers, TV producers, journalists, and writers generally play for the largest possible market. In the United States, television has made some efforts to center shows on minority concerns, yet, as your students will discover (if they pursue one of the genre activities suggested in the previous section), the life of a minority person on television is far removed from that of many people. We must be extremely cautious, then, that "popular culture" not be interpreted simply as the culture of the majority.

As we state earlier, *every child is part of a culture,* and that culture is a *popular,* that is *living,* culture. Some of the following activities help ensure that popular culture studies become and remain genuinely pluralistic:

- Through reading reviews and summaries in *Language Arts* and *The English Journal,* learn about best-selling writers from other countries. Bring these to the classroom and/or put these on individualized reading lists. Do the same for children's literature published in other lands.

- Study the popular culture of a country far removed from our own. What is happening with art, music, literature, and television in countries in Asia, Africa, and South America?

- Remember that folkways are a part of popular culture. Have your students read folktales of majorities and minorities; have them listen to folk music from many different cultures.

- Subscribe to a newspaper with good international coverage and keep your bulletin board filled with clippings that help reveal the cultures of other lands (and not just the latest McDonald's to open in China).

- Have students study how international and interracial problems are handled and discussed in science fiction. How does this differ from what they see in today's world?

- Regularly assign watching of documentary programs on public television or the other educational channels that show popular culture in lands other than our own.

Defining the classics

For openers, it follows that among the classics we include literature (and arts) from many different lands and cultures. In Chapter 5 we review some basic resources and starting points for the teacher who doesn't feel familiar with a wide range of literatures. To encapsulate: read the professional journals, look through catalogs and book lists published by the various teacher organizations, and talk with your school and local librarians. It may take some digging, but you'll find international classics available.

But what is a classic, anyway?

Our colleague and friend Bill Palmer, of Alma College in Michigan, told us about a useful exercise he conducts in which he asks his students to define "classic" in a number of categories. What is a classic car? A classic (as opposed to classical) piece of music? A classic play in football or basketball? A classic recipe? A classic style in fashion? Finally, Bill asks, "What's a classic in literature?" In the activity, students talk about the points or features that give long-lasting credibility or substance to ideas, artistic creations, and material objects.

Stephen tried a variation of this activity with some English-as-a-second-language students at the American School in Taipei, Taiwan. When asked about classic movies, two informants declared that the newly released *Back to the Future, Part II* was a classic. When Steve questioned how a brand-new film could earn this label, one answered, "Because this movie is going to be around a long long time." "Besides," added the other, "they're already making Part III." Although we might not share their tastes in popular culture, we think they had the idea of "classic" quite right.

The classics of literature for children, young adults, and adults need no apologists or defenders; they don't need to be artificially propped up by being forced or obligatory reading in school curricula by people like E. D. Hirsch.

Yet many of the standard classics of world literature seem to leave young people cold. In particular, there seems to be a conflict at the secondary level between the great books many *hope* students will read and the books they *will* read. Hirsch and his followers regard this as representing some sort of decay in education and the minds of young people. We think there's a far easier explanation.

The simple fact is that the language, values, morals, and manners of *Hamlet, The House of Seven Gables, Uncle Tom's Cabin, Things Fall Apart, Tales of the Lao, Dr. Zhivago*, the *Odyssey*, or *The Rubáiyát* are often confusing and inexplicable to youngsters who live in contemporary cities and suburbs, who work at McDonald's for spending money, who watch and enjoy a great deal of contemporary television. Understanding classic literature comes relatively late to most young people and even to twentysomethings and thirtysomethings and beyond. (Susan didn't have the great "aha!" and come to appreciate *Great Expectations* until her fortysomethings.) Though teachers and parents want their children to be exposed to the best that culture and literature has to offer, early pressure to read books that are too difficult often destroys students' interest in reading and the possibility they will *ever* read the classics. The authors of the classics don't need to be artificially supported by English/language arts teachers, and they don't need to have us killing off their potential readers in our zeal to enculturate.

Teaching by ideas

The heart of teaching the classics is, we think, getting kids to wrestle with ideas, to discover that the ideas in classic literature remain important today, that the great books speak to us now. We've all seen teacher-centered, idea-centered classes in which the instructor presents mostly his or her opinions about a classic. This won't do, of course. What we must do is help students perform on texts, discovering ideas planted in the text, linking them with present-day experiences, forging interpretations and responses to the literature.

This can be done with single texts, although we prefer to link works thematically or topically. A unit for high schoolers on "Love and Romance," for example, can include both contemporary adolescent fiction and such novels as Charlotte Brontë's *Jane Eyre,* Emily Brontë's *Wuthering Heights,* Thomas Hardy's *The Return of the Native,* and Leo Tolstoy's, *Anna Karenina.* Classic plays for the same unit could include Shakespeare's *Romeo and Juliet* and Edmond Rostand's *Cyrano de Bergerac.* Sir Walter Scott's *Lady of the Lake* might be woven in, along with Greek myths of Cupid and Eros, Chinese tales of courtship, and even Biblical stories, including the tale of the Garden of Eden (if your school censors will allow *that* bit of suggestive literature).

A thematic unit on "Values and the Individual" might include works as diverse as Bunyan's *Pilgrim's Progress,* Conrad's *Lord Jim,* Dostoevsky's *Crime and Punishment,* Hugo's *Les Miserables,* Thoreau's *Walden,* Twain's *Huckleberry Finn,* and Whitman's *Leaves of Grass.* That's a pretty heavy reading list, of course, and we present it simply to show that works from the common core of Western culture *can* easily be treated thematically. From that list, you can easily go on to add materials from popular culture, international literature, and contemporary books written for young adults.

Whatever the pattern you choose and whatever the literature, it's important to recall that reading (like writing) is more than a collection of decoding skills and involves far more than digging out meanings intended by the author. The reading of a classic, like the reading of any book, needs to be prepared for, supported when underway, and followed up to ensure that classic engagement has taken place.

Prereading activities

- Pose for discussion some of the ideas and issues you anticipate the students will want to discuss in the text. (Don't make this your own pet list; consider your student/readers.) Before even having students open the text, explore some of the ideas. Then suggest how students will find new permutations of these issues inside the book covers.

- Talk with students about the actions and beliefs they want to see in their heroines and heroes.

- Use film versions—cautiously—to preview a story. Rather than showing the whole movie, we suggest that you get the video and fast-forward to a few key scenes that will prepare the way for better reading.

- Spend some time providing necessary historical background if the book is far removed from the students' lives in time or place. However, be cautious about overkill here. A light overview is often sufficient to set the stage; the book itself will often supply the necessary details of history or geography for comprehension.

- If the history is complex, create a time line of the period, showing major events and allowing students to write in key events from the book as they occur.

- Bring in picture books that show the country where the story takes place, if possible then and now.

- Read some sections of representative language aloud so students can begin to hear the sound of the book and its words. If vocabulary is likely to be difficult, prepare "cheat sheets" of key terms. (Here again, we caution against overdoing the vocabulary work or turning a potentially rewarding encounter with a classic into a mere vocabulary lesson.)

- Create an improvisational drama in which students role-play issues and problems that come up in the book: conflicts over love, values, religion, politics.

Activities during reading

- Have students keep a reading log, a running record of reactions, projections, imaginings, and reflections.

- Let students select from a list of major characters in the book and keep an imaginary diary for him or her, recording responses to major events.

- Pause regularly and have students free write their reactions to the book, including frustrations and lack of comprehension. Use these to gauge the success of the unit and to modify your strategies as needed.

- Have the students keep lists of questions as they proceed: questions about the author and his/her approach, questions about character and motivation, questions about the time and place of the novel. Then when you ask, Are there any questions? kids may actually have some.
- Invite students to sketch, draw, or diagram key scenes.
- Bring in a speaker: a librarian, art historian, history buff, local college professor. Use these people to enrich the students' understanding of the book.
- Have students do dramatic readings or readers theater presentations of key scenes. We recommend that you let students prepare these; don't just read around the class, having students take turns.

Follow-up activities

- Discuss the ending in detail, including the possibility that the students would like to have had it end some other way.
- As a whole class, discuss how the classic has shaped the students' thinking and affected their ideas: What characters and situations had the most impact, and why? How have students' concepts and feelings changed and grown as a result of the novel? How do they imagine it was received in its own time? (Back this up with reviews of the period, if possible.)
- Extend the study beyond the book itself, moving the students into the culture of the time and place. Possibilities include:
  - A period "fair"—Victorian, Romantic, Wild West, Colonial, or international.
  - A facsimile newspaper reporting events from the novel and including editorial commentary and book reviews.
  - An investigation of music from the period or region.
  - A photographic display of technological inventions from the era.
  - Biographies of authors, politicians, and artists from the period or country.
- Spend a class period having students play the role of their (least or most) favorite character from the book.
- Have students choose a contemporary problem, issue, or setting and discuss how characters in the novel would respond to it.
- Let the students write to the spirits of the author and major characters.

Summary and Troubleshooting

Four Problems in Teaching Literature

ere are some problems that were posed for us by a group of undergraduates, savvy in the ways of school, who had just completed student teaching and who had also just finished a course in the teaching of reading and literature. We asked them to brainstorm about their concerns, then to group their questions into major issues or problems. They came up with four gems.

Problem one: The nonreader

No matter how clever and skillful our teaching strategies, there are always kids who struggle with texts, who cannot process print successfully. In particular, there are the growing numbers of students who are not native English speakers/readers. If you've read the chapter on popular culture and the classics, you know that we're committed to literature instruction that begins with the student's own culture. For ESL speakers/readers, that means acknowledging their competence in their native language. We are advocates of bilingual instruction, which offers instruction in both English and the native language, and are strongly opposed to the English Only movement that would limit bilingual education and reduce acceptance of multilingualism in society. In many cases, then, nonnative speakers may be encouraged to do free or guided reading in their native language, while focusing on English in their common class readings. As we have suggested, too, *all* readers need plenty of support, and oral and dramatic reading (in English) is an especially valuable tool to use with both ESL and English-using students who have difficulty processing text.

We also think the policy of "the right book in the hands of the right kid at the right time" helps to solve these problems. Stephen once caught the dickens on a radio call-in show for saying that it was OK for kids to read comic books. (He was also chastised for calling young people "kids." "Kids are goats," said the caller, who didn't like the sound of comic books in school, either.) "Comic books" are only a metaphor for "the right book," suggesting that people must read at a level where they can make contact. If comics do it, that's an excellent *first step.* A daily newspaper will work for some students. So will a job application blank. Or a wordless picture book or a nursery tale accompanied by a cassette tape or a book read to a child who sits in a teacher's or parent's lap. The point remains that reading means making sense of material for your own purposes, and no amount of agonizing over the alleged quality of that literature will make a nonreader read it.

Problem two: The basal reader or adopted anthology

We don't envy the position of textbook publishers, who are open to criticism on many fronts. Publishers have been attacked for the inanity of stories like the old *Dick and Jane* readers. There have been resolutions passed against basals at national English meetings because of their overemphasis on snippets of literature and a phonics approach. Yet publishers also receive complaints that they have forgotten phonics in favor of look-say and whole language approaches. When basals have employed literature from outstanding children's writers, parent groups have hauled the books to school board meetings to object to everything from perceived satanism to alleged fodder for bad dreams.

High school literature anthologies have been attacked both for their deadly dull chronological-historical approach and for their just plain fatness (or avoirdupoisity—they're a drag to carry around). Yet when publishers have offered thematic, multivolume, slim texts focusing on accessible literature for a wide range of readers, those series have not sold well. The upshot is that publishers tend to stay with their bread-and-butter programs, and these, in turn, tend to be conservative, well in arrears of the best current thinking about reading and literature.

So most of you teach or will teach in systems with adopted textbook programs. Teachers—new teachers in particular—are expected to teach the text. It's well and good to talk of individualized, multicultural, multigenre reading, but the textbook must, of necessity, remain at the core.

There are several ways you can work with or around the adopted textbook:

1. It's important to emphasize that *if a text is stressing an obsolete or wrongheaded approach, it's probably not going to produce results anyway.* If a text overworks phonics or reduces literature to mere history (with the most difficult and obscure works first, the fun stuff at the end), it will not advance the literacy of students. You need not feel that you are shortchanging students by not dwelling at length on the text.

2. *Textbooks can be restructured and refocused by their users.* In the end, *you* determine how the material is to be taught. Even the worst of the elementary school basals and high school anthologies that we've encountered contain a number of good stories, poems, plays, essays, and even study questions. If you pick and choose, you can use the textbook flexibly and even as a *convenient* collection of materials.

3. *You can always supplement the textbook.* We learned as first-year teachers that *nobody* objects to "enrichment." There's very little to prevent you from going well beyond the text to use school and community libraries and resources. Frankly, we find that the biggest obstacle to moving beyond the text is *teachers'* conviction that they must cover the text, a set curriculum, or a list of common readings. If you were raised in a system that taught mostly common books, or if, like many of us, you were taught literature in a conventional fashion but came to love it nevertheless, you may find it difficult to let go of your own traditions. We have struggled with this ourselves, having written our share of college papers involving abstract analysis of the critical content of books and not having had such a bad time doing so. But our own teaching of diverse students persuaded us that what worked for us and for a lot of other English majors just wasn't the ticket for a majority of students. As we suggest in the previous chapter, this doesn't mean abandoning our literary heritage (even as that heritage is translated into basals and anthologies), but putting it in a fuller, and, we think, richer context.

Problem three: The critical self/ the critical colleague

Many teachers suffer from a self-censor who constantly critiques and carps, who can never let anything go, who can never say, "That's good enough." This critic is one's own past training and experience speaking. For example, we use a great deal of small-group work in our reading/literature classes, yet there's a part of us that continually asks, "Shouldn't you deliver a lecture on this? Shouldn't you be leading a scintillating whole-class discussion?" If that self-analysis stays within reasonable limits, it can offer some interesting challenges to your philosophy, forcing you to say, for instance, "No, I don't think a lecture is what these students need at all. They talk more and learn more in small groups than they do in class discussions anyway." Keeping a teacher journal and conducting good teacher research is one way to channel your dialogue with this alter-ego teacher.

Of perhaps greater concern are other teachers, often those at the next grade level, whose teaching philosophy differs from yours and who peer at you over half glasses in the hallway.

These teachers, whose reality and life-and-death power sometimes grow in the imagination, look at the students you send each year and find them wanting. The students' grammar skills are weak, and they obviously haven't studied enough spelling (issues we take up in subsequent sections). In literature/reading, the complaint seems to be that the previous year's teacher (you) did a poor job of covering the syllabus, including that basal text or anthology discussed as Problem 2.

These teachers speak louder as students move through the grades and into the secondary schools, and the most vocal of all is the college professor who indicts the entire K–12 school system: "Why, I can't even make an allusion to *Huckleberry Finn* or 'Paradise Lost' without explaining it" or "My students can't seem to write a single coherent paragraph analyzing and critiquing a literary work articulately." As college professors, we frequently receive letters from secondary school curriculum committees asking us to identify a dozen or so works that the students entering the university should have read. Presumably the same letter goes to other professors, leading to the compilation of a book list or syllabus for juniors and seniors. We respect the intention of the letter writers, but we decline to send our choices. Instead, we mail a letter like the following:

> We strongly urge you not to compile a book list of "must reads" for your students or to focus this year's instruction on getting students ready for next year.
>
> Far more important is that your students be *readers,* that they know how to find and choose books they want to read, that they read actively and inquiringly, that they feel confident in speaking up or writing out their reactions and analyses.
>
> Instead of a set curriculum or list, we encourage teachers K–12 to make their classrooms into reading centers with as many different kinds of texts as their students can read profitably. That will include some classics of children's, young adult, and adult literature, but it may include a lot of reading material that won't "stand the test of time," yet will be enjoyed by the students anyway.
>
> The student who will be most successful in college (or the next grade level) is not necessarily one who has read traditional masterpieces cover to cover, but the one who has just plain read *widely:* fiction, nonfiction, drama and poetry; science fiction and fantasy; good children's and young adult literature; some best sellers; some entertaining romance novels, detective fiction, some scare-the-socks-off-you thrillers. The good reader will also be one who has thought about the content of films and television, who can see beyond their surface content, who can react to and critique the popular media as well.

There's no crash course in "college reading" that will prepare your students. What's needed is a K–12 reading/writing curriculum that helps your students grow from their present level to one just a little bit more sophisticated. If everyone focuses on that goal, college will take care of itself.

Problem four: Censorship

Censorship is an absolute killer of intellectual inquiry, teacher morale, and a progressive reading/literature program. It's also something akin to guerrilla warfare and terrorism, for there simply isn't much of a defense one can offer when it occurs. Yet, lest we sound too self-righteous about the whole thing, we can understand the position of the censors: that they are deeply concerned about their children's welfare, that they believe books can harm people (just as English teachers believe books can help people), that as taxpayers they feel they have a right to say what goes on in the schools.

Probably the single best defense against censorship is an articulate school book adoption policy. How are the books for English/language arts classes selected? What is the policy on individualized reading of books from the school library? From the public library? If there are books that, for one reason or another, have been identified as inappropriate for use in the schools, they should be identified clearly. In formulating policies of this sort, parents should be integrally involved, though in an advisory capacity, with the paid professionals—the teachers and administrators—forming the policy that is finally approved by the board of education.

Nevertheless, numerous censorship cases have arisen even after procedures have been established and followed. All it takes is one parent's writing one letter to the editor saying, "I don't care what they did in committee, I object to this book." In addition, school-book censors are well-organized nationwide, so that often, despite policies followed, a vocal and often articulate minority can turn a community into a battleground.

To our way of thinking, however, the simplest inoculation against censorship is also pedagogically sound: individualize your reading program. Although censors are occasionally successful in getting titles removed from library shelves, they have never been able to censor what somebody else's child chooses to read on an individual basis. If your program is individualized, and if, perchance, a parent objects to a book his/her child is reading, common sense suggests that you let the child drop that book and choose another. The case ends there. As a way of heading off problems, you might even send home book lists from time to time, showing parents the range of choices open to their youngsters.

Nevertheless, if you find yourself or your school to be the target of censorship, ask for help. Such organizations as the American Civil Liberties Union, the National Coalition Against Censorship, the Coalition for Academic Freedom, the National Education Association, and the American Federation of Teachers all have an interest in the rights of the teacher to teach. The National Council of Teachers of English can also supply support, as can its political action group, Support for the Learning and Teaching of English (SLATE).

t·h·r·e·e

Ideas for Teaching Oral and Written Composition

n English/language arts studies, composition was the growth industry of the 1980s and continues to thrive as we approach the end of the century. Composition still struggles for equal time with reading and literature, but it is not the clichéd stepchild that it was as recently as two decades ago. In the elementary and secondary schools, thousands of teachers have learned about new approaches to composition that emphasize ways of engaging students in *using* language rather than concentrating on language form. At the college level, a generation of composition specialists—people who actually like to teach writing as well as literature—have deepened the body of formal research into composition. And at both levels, a growing body of writers/teachers/researchers is exploring new approaches to improving writing instruction.

The approach we explore in this section of *The English/Language Arts Handbook* is what we call *experiential*. The label is deliberately ambiguous, for it applies to both students' *experiences* generally—what they "do for a living"—and *experiences* using language: their everyday, year-in-year-out uses of written and spoken language. Our philosophy can be summed up in two basic premises:

1. *Children learn to use language through the experience of using it for purposes they see as valuable and interesting.* We didn't invent that idea: John Dewey articulated it both earlier and more eloquently. Another way of phrasing this notion is simply that people learn what they do. If we want students to learn to write, they need to write; if we want them to use oral language better, we need to find them tasks and occasions that allow those skills to develop. However, as we suggest earlier in this book, we don't mean to imply that all language learning takes place by magic. Obviously having a teacher around to structure and support language learning helps a great deal. At the same time, we ignore students' street experiences with language only on peril of disenfranchising our classes in the eyes (and mouths) of those students.

2. *Students' experiences provide the fundamental energy that drives their language. To compose* means much more than *to send a message.* Before a message can be sent, it must be ordered in the mind. (Or, if it is ordered at the point of utterance, it must at the very least be based on prior experiences.) Those experiences can be gleaned firsthand just by living, through the school of juvenile hard knocks, but they can also be gained vicariously, through media and literature. (It would be nice to think that significant experiences can be had through schools as well, given the portion of their lives students spend there.) The important point is that our composition program must pay as much attention to the qualities of students' experiences as it does to language and the processes of composing.

Chapter Eight

The Process of Composing

T he title of this chapter has become something of a buzzword and a shibboleth in our profession. Under the leadership of Wallace Douglas (1963), Donald Murray (1968, 1982), Donald Graves (1983), and others, we have experienced a "writing process" revolution that some have compared to one of Thomas Kuhn's (1962) "paradigm shifts," in which a profession makes a fundamental change of philosophy, when, finding the old order wanting, it settles (with considerable excitement) on something new.

Process writing, the new order, overthrew an earlier focus on *product* or language form in the teaching of composition. In brief, the process philosophy argues that instead of giving students forms and structures to master, we need to guide them in the skills, activities, and *processes* of composing, showing them how to engage in the acts of composition successfully. If process is attended to, the products will follow naturally.

We've been convinced of the validity of the process approach for a long time, but at the same time, we're concerned that the "paradigm shift" may turn out to be simply a new pedagogical formula replacing an old one. We've witnessed "process" teaching in which grammar and form were still stressed through all stages of writing; we have witnessed a mixing of pedagogies in which teachers supply vocabulary words and have students go through the "process" of making up artificial sentences illustrating the "proper" uses of those words. Jeff McNelly's "Shoe" cartoon (Figure 8–1) hints at this problem.

We also understand the arguments of so-called traditionalists who point out that formalists, too, have been concerned with helping children find something to say before they compose (the classical area of *invention,* which has become *prewriting* in the process pedagogy). We agree with those who argue that discussion of form must necessarily be a part of instruction in process, lest students get the impression that the free-flowing, underpunctuated, eccentrically spelled stuff they write in their journals is good enough for business letters or college applications.

Figure 8–1 ○ "Shoe" (10/12/90), by Jeff McNelly

There must be—there are—middle grounds in all this, positions that allow a teacher to place appropriate emphasis on skills and processes to help kids compose successfully in recognizable and conventional discourse forms.

Our own middle ground is an experiential approach, which takes neither a rigid *product* nor a *process* stance, but rather focuses on the *experience* of composing about the *experiences* one has in life. Real life shows us plainly enough that students need to put their writing into "grammatically correct" (or simply "appropriate") language. It also teaches us that real writers sometimes agonize over what they write, often do multiple drafts and revisions, but sometimes bat out a polished piece and get it right the first time.

Our approach to the process of composing, then, is not a formula or pattern for implementation, but a philosophy or attitude that asks:

1. *What is it that children really know* or care about learning?
2. *How can we provide opportunities* for them to do that?
3. *How can we help them discover language and form in language* to express the outcomes of their learning, thinking, and feeling?

In particular, it's important to emphasize that we don't see any need to isolate skill instruction from the actual process of composing. Traditionally, that instruction has been offered at two points: before the fact of composition (through lessons in grammar, rhetoric, style, vocabulary, spelling, etc.) and after the fact (mostly through error correction). Current research points to a flow or continuum between getting ideas into language and figuring out just how to do that. Skills mastered in the context of composing are more likely to stay with the learner than those learned in isolation.

An oral language base

You may have noticed we've shied away from using the term *writing*, using instead *composing* or *composition*. Actually, we don't *like* the term *composition*, which has very much a schoolroom sound and, for some reason, always reminds us of a big wad of fresh, wet bubblegum stuck to the bottom of a shoe. *Composing* is more to our taste, especially because of its musical overtones. The point we wish to emphasize, however, is that we're talking (note the metaphor—we're obviously writing, not talking) about creating things in language. We can compose our ideas in song, speech, art, dance, or mime. When we compose in writing, we can do so in exposition and argumentation, or in poetry, drama, and fiction.

Sheila Fitzgerald of Michigan State University regularly reminds us not only that composing is more than writing, but that most people do far more oral composing in their lives than any other form. She argues with her Irish rhetorical skill that we need more talk in the classroom.

Some ideas we've found useful in building up that oral language base for composing include:

- Be a little less eager to quell the tumult at the beginning of the class hour or when gibblegabble erupts. Before gaveling the place to order, spend a few moments reflecting:
  - What are students talking about?
  - Why is their language so animated?
  - How skillful is their oral language: does it make sense or are they talking nonsense? (If it makes sense to them, which it usually does, you have some clues to the students' existing oral competence.)

- Create time in the class for discussion of ideas and topics proposed by the students: discussion Fridays, for example. Some teachers put a "suggestion box" on their desk as a way for students to propose topics.

- Be willing to drop what you're doing when students obviously have 🗙 something powerful and important to talk about.

- Use partnership and small-group work frequently. (An Australian teacher once told us that her methods instructor thought small-group work was so important that he made it a *fiat*: "*Never* talk to the whole class at once." That may be extreme, but it helps underscore the value of talk in small groups.)

- Let students choose oral projects along with or instead of written work. This is not to diminish writing, but to appeal to the common-sense observation that many people would rather talk than write. In addition, if students are regularly allowed and encouraged to make oral reports and talks, the traditional stigma/phobia attached to The Public Speech will diminish. (Many people would rather die or even be forced to *write* something than give a speech; yet those people have quite good oral language skills and can speak articulately in less formal settings.)

- Use oral language as a starting point for writing. Give students time to talk through their writing ideas, to prewrite a paper orally.

- Encourage talk in response to reading and literature, beginning with students' own deeply felt reactions, then moving on to discuss how the literature provoked their reaction.

- Explore the differences between speech and writing. Have students talk about an idea, write about it informally in their journals, then write it as a more formal paper or composition. What differences do they see? Do this, as well, by comparing radio news with newspaper coverage of the same event, or a televised speech (by the president, let's say) with written reports or transcripts in the paper.

- Help students understand the range, beauty, and flexibility of vari- eties of spoken English. Find locals who use Indian, British, Jamaican, Asian, Hispanic, Black, southwestern, southeastern, Brooklynese, Bostonian, or down east dialects. Have them come to class to talk about themselves and their language; help your students see how the varieties of language function.

- Perhaps most important, turn your class into The House of Story-telling. Stories are the stuff of life (or, in academic terms, "narrative is a primary act of mind"). Bring performing storytellers to your class (your state arts council or humanities committee will often provide funds). Encourage your students to be storytellers, swapping anec-dotes, experiences, tall tales, jokes, might-have-beens, wishes for the future.

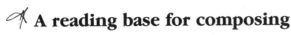 A reading base for composing

We discuss reading and response in detail earlier in this book. Suffice it to remind you that, in general, good readers tend to be good writers and speakers. The nature of the link is not altogether clear, and it would be naive to suppose that by "making" a child a reader you will "make" him or her an articulate speaker or writer. Nevertheless, virtually all research points to the fact that the composition classroom should be a reading classroom. Stock yours with books, magazines, newspapers, literature on audio- or videotape, and student writing itself.

Knowing yourself as a writer

The *Paris Review* interviews with writers, begun in the 1960s, helped to develop interest in the process of writing by exploring how the professionals did it. We were fascinated to learn that Robert Frost composed only on a lapboard, that Mary McCarthy fictionalized parts of her autobiography because she felt her fictions were closer to the truth, that Henry Miller felt a dynamism when composing on the typewriter (and had a hard time writing after his eyesight failed) (Plimpton 1962).

Aside from the general interest of such *factoids* (as Cable News Network calls them), we came to see that professional writers varied widely in their habits and began to question the wisdom of having students all write at the same time on the same topic. Now, we can't arrange for all students to exercise all their idiosyncrasies in the classroom. (We heard of a kid who said he wanted to do his writing in his locker, by flashlight.) And we need to follow Wallace Douglas's (1963) advice to distinguish between writing *behaviors* (pen versus typewriter, lapboard versus desk, morning versus night) and the more fundamental *processes of composing* (finding ideas, getting started, editing our work). But we find it very helpful to learn about our students' writing behaviors and processes with questions like these:

- What's the best piece of writing you think you ever have done? Describe how you did it.
- When do you like to write best? What's the worst time for you to write?
- What weird and strange things do you do when you write?
- Do you ever put off starting a writing assignment? Why is that?
- What kind of tools and equipment do you like? Do you use a word processor? Paper and pencil? Colored pens or felt-tips?

Figure 8–2 ○ A classroom writing corner

- Can you write when there's music playing? When the TV is on?
- Do you prefer to write in class or at home?
- What can we do to make this class a more comfortable place for you to write in?

Along these lines, we very much like the idea of setting up a "write place" (see Figure 8–2) in the classroom where students can go to work on their writing projects.

Idea gathering

One of the purposes of the "write place" is to provide starting points for writing, ideas for the student who is fresh out. You can stock a corner in your room with:

- Photographs clipped from magazines and newspapers, providing inspiration for writing.
- Writing ideas culled from professional magazines and educational journals.
- Story or drama starters: ideas for interesting tales, like "something involving a Martian, a schoolteacher, and a police officer."
- Jokes and riddles with "now you do one" instructions.

However, in the long run, student writers need to move beyond such stimuli or writing "prompts." The experiential approach recognizes that the cry, "I don't have anything to say," really means, "I'm not certain that what I have to say will be accepted here" or "I'm worried that if I say this, people will think it's silly."

We try to build confidence in our students by:

- Helping them become oral storytellers. (See previous comments on oral language.)
- Administering interest inventories: What do you like to think about? To read? To do on your own time? What's the most magical moment you've ever experienced? Did you ever almost die? Have you had a friend move away or die or drop out of your life in some other way? If you weren't here, where would you like to be?
- Having them set aside a portion of their notebook for writing ideas. When students write regularly and know their ideas are valued, they start coming up with more and more ideas for papers.
- Bringing in newspapers and having them clip out articles and headlines that interest them. We find that virtually any newspaper can be mined for a good fifty to one hundred topics, day after day after day. Try it with students of all ages.

- Jotting down writing possibilities on the board following a class discussion, reading, viewing of film or video, or common experience (a trip to the zoo, museum, library).

- Asking them to maintain a journal or logbook. Teachers we know have students write for ten minutes at the beginning of class, write whenever they have a chance, write at home several times per week, write every day, write about themselves, write about world events, write about television, write about brothers and sisters and parents, write about other school subjects. The journal—not graded, not corrected for spelling or punctuation—becomes a repository of ideas for exploration through writing.

Writing to somebody with a face

Our experience suggests that writing is best motivated when students try to reach real audiences, whether large or small, close or distant. Working on this premise, some graduate students of ours at the University of British Columbia developed a plan for a course called "Writing to Somebody with a Face," aimed at having *all* writing read by someone other than the teacher. Their course involved students in writing all manner of letters, memos, notes, and essays.

Some places/people to write:

- Other students, of any age or geographical location. Set up a letter exchange within the class or between classes or between schools. Check your school or local library for the addresses of pen pal associations. A new wrinkle on the pen pal theme is to link students via computer networks so that communication/correspondence is instantaneous.

- Political figures. Most politicians will write back, even if only a form letter. Have students write to congressional leaders, town council members, the mayor, the U.S. president, world leaders.

- Business leaders. Write with questions about careers, the economy, the writing demands in the world of business.

- Television networks (to critique programming).

- Celebrities (though warn kids not to expect a personal response).

- Newspaper editors.

- Family, friends, and relatives.

The writing workshop

The background work—what some teachers call *prewriting*—helps students come to writing confident they have *something to say* and an audience that is *prepared to hear it.* (Note that we have again unconsciously applied an oral language metaphor to writing; obviously advance preparation is as useful to speakers as it is to writers.) Some suggestions:

- Develop strategies to break down the common writing period in which everybody writes the same thing at the same time. The writing workshop model encourages students to pursue their work at their own pace. In its simplest form, the workshop consists of set days of the week when students know they will be working on their writing. In a more complex formulation, students are in reading *and* writing workshop five days a week, following their own pace in all their literacy work.

- Establish a "works in progress file." Students can keep one or several papers in a file for future revision. Most writers find that letting papers cool in the file for a period of time allows them to approach their work with fresh insights. As time passes (and as you offer various avenues for publication) your students polish up works for presentation to an audience.

- Promote critical/editorial talk. Not nasty, red penciling talk, but productive engagement among peers who help one another solve problems at all phases of the writing process.

- Discuss ways to organize. Show students how to "cluster" or "web" ideas (see Figure 8–3) as a method of discovering different ways to approach material. Offer brainstorming as another technique, and perhaps the traditional formal outline as another. Get an organizer or hypertext program for your computer and show students how to use these tools. (Some students/teachers even like to plan using a "paint" program, which lets them add embellishments. Figure 8–3 was prepared on such a program.) On a word processor, show students how to begin organizing with words and phrases that, through the wonders of electronics, can be expanded, deleted, and rearranged so that what starts as a bare bones list grows into a completed work. Or show the pencil-and-paper gang how their journal entries can grow in the same ways.

- Use contract grading. We praise this method earlier in this book and find it especially advantageous in a writing workshop. Here students are basically told that the more (quality material) they write, the

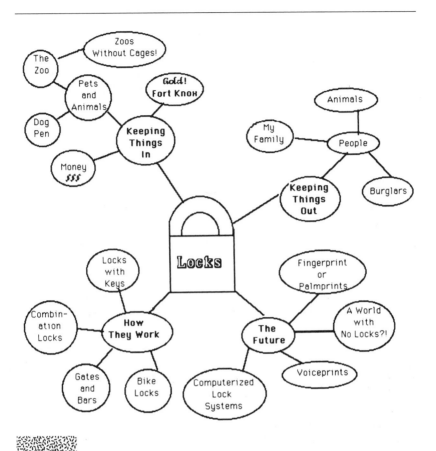

Figure 8–3 ○ **One way to cluster ideas**

higher their grade will be. Because you don't grade individual works, you are freed to become a collaborator in the writing workshop.

- Have works in progress readings, where your young writers select the best, most engaging, most *tantalizing* paragraph or sentence or page in their draft writing and read it to the group, thus generating interest in the final product.

- Distinguish among some of the following terms and concepts in writing:

    ○ A *freewriting* draft.

- A *first* or *rough* or *hack* draft, the one in which you just get it down, just say what you have to say, knowing you can go back to it later.
- *Cut-and-paste* (something we used to do literally with scissors and tape, now adopted by some computer programs as a metaphor for moving text around on the page).
- *Revising,* making changes in the *substance* of your work—adding things, moving them around, finding the right word.
- We like to make a distinction between revising and *editing,* which (in our writing workshops) refers to fine-tuning of style, vocabulary, effectiveness.
- We make a strong contrast between this and *copyediting* or *proofreading,* which (again in our parlance) focuses exclusively on matters of surface correctness: usage (or "grammar"), spelling, punctuation, capitalization.

● Develop an organizer chart or file so that you can keep track of where students are on given writing projects. Some teachers we know have students create a file card for each piece they begin writing, then update and refile it in a box on the teacher's desk as the piece progresses. Others have figured out ways to do this on a wall chart or poster, with the students again taking responsibility for the record keeping. One elementary school teacher has students write their names on snap-on clothespins, to which titles of works in progress are attached; the pins are then clipped to and moved along the edge of a "writing process" chart.

● Put concerns about correctness in context. We discuss this vital issue in Chapter 10, "The Red Pencil Blues."

Publish, publish, publish

Make the writing public. Don't let kids toss finished papers into their backpacks; don't let those compositions sink to the bottom of the gum-wrapper-etcetera compost heap in student desks. Some possibilities include:

● Organize a writing fair where students present their best work, nicely copied and bound, illustrated or "graphicked" as much as possible.

● Designate an author's chair, where kids who have finished work sit and read to the class.

- Write for national contests and publication. (Check your library for books for young writers that list places of publication. Also check *Writer's Market Place* or *Literary Market Place* for possibilities.)

- Establish author's day. Formats for these events vary from kids coming together informally to read their own work to visits from professional authors who talk with the students about their work. One cautionary note: young authors need to be celebrated *daily*, in the individual classroom, not just once a year in a flashy (but fraudulent?) public extravaganza.

- Instigate arts and crafts projects. Our book *Gifts of Writing* (1980) suggests a number of ways in which kids can create attractive books of their own, including cloth-bound books, minibooks (postage-stamp-sized), big books (done on poster board), bigger books (done on the painted sides of refrigerator cartons), scrolls, accordion books (that fan out and stand on their edges), folding books (a single sheet of folded paper, in Shakespearian quarto fashion), and others. Our motto in that book is "Make your writing look as good as it reads." The title of that book suggests another element of our philosophy: that students should come to think of their writing as something to give, with pleasure and pride, to other people.

- Give performances. Turn short stories into readers theater presentations; present and videotape one-act plays; get older kids in a drama class to present the poetry of your young writers.

- Put short chunks of writing on the chalkboard—a bit like building a sand castle, but a good way to give short-term publication to a bit of writing.

- Use an overhead projector, *not* to model errors or show how to fix something up, but to celebrate a completed piece.

- Put things on the bulletin board. (A British teacher once told us her supervisor would chastise her if she didn't change her bulletin board daily; the only way she could do that, of course, was by putting up lots and lots of student writing. Jolly good show, we say.)

- Make posters: collect poems on a theme, short essays, minifiction stories and post them in rooms and hallways.

- Publish literary magazines: create a constant flow of leaflets and fliers in the school—kid written, edited, and produced.

- Keep an annual scrapbook in your classroom featuring what students regard as their best or most typical writing, accompanied by an autobiographical note and a photograph. Treasure these, and we're not just being sentimental.

We discuss the role of computers in editing and revising papers in Chapter 10, reviewing how they can help students get their papers into the best possible shape. Computers are also enormously helpful at the publishing end, too. Students can:

- Use desktop publishing programs to lay out final copy for magazines, books, newspapers.
- Insert clip art, original paint-program drawings, or artwork that has been scanned and digitized.
- Print multiple copies of their work.
- Print "on screen," that is, rather than printing hard copy, use the screen for final display.
- Display their writing on computer bulletin boards (and receive electronic responses).

Finally, we suggest a way of publishing that was told to us by John Dixon (1976) in a summer institute in London. He got the idea from a British secondary school headmaster. The headmaster had a blank bound book with a green cover. Whenever he encountered some good or interesting writing, he would cry out, "I must save that forever! Copy it into the green book, please!" We rushed right out of the institute and found a green book and have been using it quite happily in writing classes ever since. We've added one twist: at the end of a class or course, we give our students a mock final examination, an author identification quiz based on readings from the green book. Our students invariably, and perhaps not surprisingly, score 100 percent on the exam. The writing that has gone into the green book has become *memorable*—what a great boost to the ego and competence of the people who have written in it!

Chapter Nine

Extending the Dimensions of Literacy

We are daily confronted by a broad band of language forms: radio, television, advertisements, plays and drama, street mime, signs and placards, musical lyrics, soap operas, newspaper editorials, found poetry, sports stories, offers we can't refuse, memorandums, letters, literature. In the schools, however, we tend to zero in on a single composition form or discourse mode: exposition. Although elementary school children are free to write stories, poems, and plays, such "frivolity" decreases by the middle school/junior high years as teachers concentrate more on preparing their charges for the expected rigors of college or the "real world." It all ends with the *magnum opus* of many people's high school writing years: *The Research Paper.*

Without denying the usefulness of clear, coherent, expository writing, we want to point out that the function of the *word* in society is changing dramatically in this electronic age. Much exposition comes to us by way of television, film, computer terminal, even fax. Although we don't rely on print the way we used to, print is anything but dead. We may not read extended expository essays very frequently, but we see print employed in new and imaginative ways on everything from faxed restaurant orders to a PBS series on the history of language. *To compose* is an act whose boundaries are expanding as rapidly as new media extend their limits.

We cannot possibly teach all students every discourse form they will encounter in the remaining sixty (or will it be one hundred?) years of their lives. But we can prepare students for this expanding world of discourse if, instead of restricting literacy to exposition, we see that our aim as composition teachers is to aim for diversity. A good comp program, we think, will allow students to compose in as many forms as possible, in imaginative as well as expository forms, in public as well as private forums. Students will write to inform as well as to entertain; they will write plays and dramas as well as tightly organized essays; they will compose in popular and media forms as well as traditional school genres. A list of just a few of the possibilities is provided in Figure 9–1.

PERSONAL WRITING
Journals
Diaries
Sensory writing
Writer's notebook
Feelings
Sketches
Observations
Reminiscences
Autobiography
Monologue
Free response
Calendars

IMAGINATIVE WRITING
Fiction
Fantasy
Adventure
Science Fiction
Riddles
Jokes
Poetry
Collaborative novel
Stories
Dialogues
Epitaphs
Songs

INFORMATIVE/PERSUASIVE WRITING
Essays
Editorials
Reports
Letters
Telegrams
Bulletin boards
Labels and captions
Reviews
Newspaper artcles
Magazine essays
Booklets
Directions

POPULAR FORMS
Ads
Commercials
Propaganda
Posters
Flyers
Popular journalism
Satire
Imitations
Song lyrics
Concert reviews

DRAMA/ORAL ENGLISH
Mime
Charades
Improvisation
Creative drama
Writer's showcase
Debate
Discussion
Show and Tell
Interviews
Puppetry
Game shows
Choral reading
Readers theatre
Conversations

MEDIA COMPOSITION
TV scripts
Radio programs
Slide-tape
Soundtape
Montage
Collage
Animated film
Commercials
Videotape
Bulletin boards
Magazine layout
Storyboard

Figure 9–1 ○ Extending the range of composition

To explore the possibilities for composing, try an experiment using this list. Simply pick a topic or idea—politics, preserving the planet, our town, dinosaurs, love—and brainstorm for possibilities: how can you (or your students) "compose" about this subject in, say, media forms or drama or imaginative writing? (Figure 9–2 shows some of our noodling on the topic "Our Town.") For any one of those topics, students can follow the rubric or checklist in Figure 9–3, which shows how they can develop it further.

Sometimes teachers question their own competence to teach beyond the familiar domains of expository writing: I'm not a poet, advertising whiz, or script writer. I've never made a video. How am I supposed to do this? Figure 9–3 provides one answer: engage the students in figuring out how a medium or mode of discourse works. (If you'd like, you can call this "rhetorical analysis.")

Have kids collect and study samples of the form—reading some short stories, watching some television, analyzing a collection of poems. From this, have them offer some generalizations: What makes a good story? A good television show? An enjoyable poem? The purpose is *not* to come up with hard-and-fast rules for the genre, but to help the students grow toward an intuitive understanding of its general guidelines. In such analysis they may discover that successful stories have many elements (not just plot, character, climax, or a surprise ending). In studying TV they may discover a formula for situation comedies, but they may also see that their favorites break the formula in certain ways. As they read poems, they may discover (thank goodness) that not all poems rhyme, that not all poems describe birds or flowers, that poems, too, succeed by breaking some of their own rules, by challenging and surprising a reader. This rhetorical analysis is not strictly a secondary school or college-level activity, by the way; the very youngest children can see systematic elements in the stories they read and like.

We also find it useful with students of all ages to imagine the process of composing the writer (or filmmaker) must have gone through. Literary critics and some composition specialists argue against such an approach on the grounds that the final "product" does not reliably display the stages of composing. Taking that argument as an advisory, we nonetheless think you can raise some interesting questions, cautioning that you're not trying to create a strict record of what happened, merely imagining some of the ways the author might have proceeded:

- What's your image of the writer as a person based on this work?
- Where do you suppose the writer got the idea?

List Composition
Topics for: Exploring "Our Town"

PERSONAL WRITING

Visit your old elementary school and write about your memories.
Write about some of your favorite "haunts."
Tell about what makes your neighborhood unique.

IMAGINATIVE WRITING

Write a poem about your street.
Imagine Our Town in 2001. What will it be like?
Write an imaginary story about a crime or mystery set in Our Town.

INFORMATIVE/PERSUASIVE WRITING

Write a letter to the editor of the paper about a change that is needed.
Describe the resources of Our Town to a person who has just moved here.
Investigate the entertainment sources available in Our Town to a person your age.

POPULAR WRITING

Write an ad or commercial for Our Town.
Interview a public official about his or her role in Our Town.
Debate a needed improvement in Our Town.

DRAMA/ORAL ENGLISH

Dramatize the founding of the city in 18--.
Prepare a reader's-theater reading of writing about Our Town.
Bring in historical artifacts from the "early days" and discuss.

MEDIA COMPOSITION

Borrow the videotape unit to prepare a short program about the community.
Prepare a feature story - with photographs- of the downtown area.
Create a slide-tape introducing a stranger to Our Town.

Figure 9-2 ○ Identifying composition topics

WRITE YOUR TOPIC HERE: _Our Town_

WHAT FORM (DISCOURSE MODE) WILL YOUR COMPOSITION TAKE?

Video of old houses and buildings.

WHAT ARE YOUR AIMS AND GOALS? WHAT DO YOU WANT TO

ACCOMPLISH OR COMMUNICATE WITH THIS COMPOSITION?

I want to show that there are still many historical buildings in Our Town.

WHO IS YOUR AUDIENCE? _The Cable TV channel audience._

WHERE CAN YOU FIND SAMPLES OF THE FORM YOUR COMPOSITION WILL

TAKE? _Discovery channel, Public broadcasting._

WHERE WILL YOU FIND INFORMATION ON YOUR TOPIC? _Library._

Interviews with owners of older buildings. Visit with local architect. Visit to Our Town Historical Society.

WHAT PROBLEMS DO YOU THINK YOU MAY HAVE IN DOING YOUR

PROJECT? HOW CAN WE SOLVE THEM? _Mostly using the equipment. I will take the beginning video class at TV Channel 11 before I start the project._

Figure 9–3 ○ Developing a composition topic

- Where might he or she have gotten "models" for the characters? Ideas for the plot? Background information for a story or article?
- What clues are there inside the piece about how the writer proceeded (e.g., references to interviews or books).
- How did the TV scriptwriter create a set of characters that would be entertaining for the audience? What other characters do you suppose

the writer considered including? (If you were the writer, what additional characters might you have included? Whose personality would you change for the better?)

● Can you think of alternative ways this writing might have been organized or presented? Can you think of alternative beginnings or endings?

A magazine like *Writer's Digest* is good to have around for such discussions, since it often includes a number of quotations from writers on their writing along with some good tips for writers that give insights into how to go about writing a short story, a script, a poem.

It's useful, too, to look around your community for people who might come in to talk about their writing experiences. Chances are that your town has at least one writer for children (published or unpublished); somebody who has scripted and produced a play (perhaps a pageant for church or temple); someone who writes about sports, business, world news, community events for a living; a person who writes locally produced television specials; somebody who is willing to talk about autobiography or family history.

You can also depend on students' knowledge of real-world discourse to provide them what they need. Most kids can tell you the formula for their favorite TV show without even pausing to think about it. They have picked up the conventions of science fiction or adventure stories from TV as well. (There's some danger, of course, about their doing copycat writing, but for the novice, even imitation can be productive.) Having students write in a variety of media is not as difficult as it might at first seem.

However, if you still have doubts, there's yet another alternative: *compose with your students.* Abandon your assigned or self-appointed role as expert and plunge in with the kids. "Well, how *do* we go about producing our own cable TV show? Whom can we ask? What can we read? Let's start working with a script and some equipment and see how it goes."

A potpourri of ideas for expanding the dimensions of literacy

● The TV networks make much over their new fall program offerings. Organize your class to review the new shows and/or to produce satires or imitations of some especially bad or good ones. (We find kids' impulse to satirize quite intriguing from a rhetorical standpoint. To do successful satire, you must have understood the conventions of the mode or genre. That kids do satire so naturally shows that they're soaking up more than content from public discourse; they're learning its rules, too.)

- Try a paired biography early in the school year, where students team up to write each other's most engaging stories.

- Have students write their name and a personal slogan on a lapel button.

- As an alternative to "My Summer Vacation," have students write tall tales about their summer away from school.

- Let students choose pen names for their writing early in the year. This gives them a feeling of being a "writer."

- Start an open-ended story as a class project. Someone in the class leads off by writing (or tape-recording) the opening. In succeeding days, weeks, and months, students add to the skein of this yarn.

- Have students bring an object they value to class and create stories, poems, or skits about it.

- Get a video camera and do an "Introduction to Our Class" as your first video. Give each student thirty seconds to tell name, interests, and a quick anecdote or joke.

- Explore nonverbal communication by banning talk for one class period, yet conducting business as usual. Use a second period to discuss orally what happened.

- Bring in a cardboard box, two dowel rods, and a roll of shelf paper. Have students create a scroll television, putting together drawings, clipped art, and text.

- Explore the language of advertising by having students do a sales pitch for something generally unsellable (e.g., a year-old boiled egg).

- Borrow a set of art slides from the art department or library and have students put together a slide show using well-known paintings and taped readings of their favorite poems.

- Borrow from the world of Dr. Seuss and have your students write about imaginary animals or imaginary extraterrestrials who come to visit your school.

- Create a "checkbook" character. Acquire some blank checkbook registers and have students compose a mystery spender through his or her checkbook entries.

- Invite proposals for a new comic book or television series based on a superhero/ine.

- Send students out with tape recorders to collect sounds. In class, rerecord these to create a story in sound.
- Get letter writing started early in your class, both imaginary letters and those that will be mailed. Letters can go to:

  - Yourself!
  - A close friend.
  - An archrival or enemy.
  - Family.
  - Relatives.
  - Teachers.
  - Your boss (if appropriate).
  - A minister or social leader.
  - A scientist or inventor.
  - Ricky-the-Martian.
  - Thumbelina.
  - A movie, television, or rock star.
  - A person who lived in the past.

  Topics for letters can include:

  - Current problems.
  - World issues.
  - Popular culture and tastes.
  - Tall tales (and true).
  - What the writer wants to do in the future.
  - Speculations on 2001 or 3001.
  - An ideal world.

- Send the students out with video camera or tape recorder to interview friends, parents, teachers, or strangers on topics of current concern. Edit these into a radio or video program.
- Use video or tape recorders to save students' readings and dramatizations.
- Keep abreast of new computer programs that invite fresh modes of composition:

  - Interactive programs that allow students to select a variety of visual materials and compose their own art/writing projects.
  - Networking, which allows students to talk/write to one another through electronically linked computers.

- ○ "Draw," "paint," and "draft" programs that permit students to illustrate their work or to compose in words and pictures.

- ○ Desktop publishing programs that offer new degrees of freedom to student writers/editors/publishers.

Imagination, creativity, and writing

Like many writing teachers, we've long been uncomfortable with the traditional division into *creative* writing and the *other stuff,* usually meaning nonfiction prose, which parses out as "exposition." Obviously, creativity is not limited to poetry, drama, and fiction; nor is it limited to people who prefer to compose in those forms. We like David Holbrook's view of creativity offered in *The Exploring Word* (1963) and *Children's Writing* (1967), where he suggests that all students are capable of "creativity," that is, of dealing successfully with their own experience and getting that into words.

Some of our colleagues prefer the term *imaginative* for the writing of poetry, drama, fiction, and what they call *imaginative nonfiction,* the latter including a wide range of contemporary prose by writers such as Annie Dillard, Tom Wolfe, John McPhee, Rachel Carson, Stephen Jay Gould, Isaac Asimov, and Joan Didion.

In any case, we want to be on record as favoring the synthesis of imagination and writing in *any* form (including schoolroom exposition and the research paper), even though, in the next three subsections of this chapter, we discuss the teaching of *drama, poetry,* and *fiction* as modes of composition.

Composing through drama

We have emphasized the importance of an oral language base in composition. It's important to stress that it has a *dramatic* base as well. In *Teaching the Universe of Discourse* (1983), James Moffett shows that all communication involves a kind of dramatic tension between *I* (the speaker, writer, actor) and *you* (the listener, reader, acted upon). In drama, people play all of those roles, alternating between the *I* and the *you.* Whether one is talking about the relatively easy task of having students read aloud or the complex one of launching a full-fledged stage production, drama deserves a fuller, richer role in the play of English/language arts.

Elementary teachers are often more comfortable with *creative dramatics* than are secondary teachers. Imaginative play is an important addition to the language arts program at any level. For secondary students, scripting and theatrical presentations seem to come more easily. At both levels, the *writing* of drama is a powerful exercise in the imagination and in composition skills. A play draws on our natural sense of oral language and dialogue; it requires us to tap our own emotions and put them into characters on stage; it even forces us to *organize:* to figure out where to put the furniture, how to get the body off stage, how to include off-stage information so our audience will know what is going on.

Some ideas for drama in the classroom

- Try some drama warmups, activities traditionally used by drama coaches to loosen imaginations and muscles:

  - Students lie on the floor, and as you name parts of the body, ask them to become aware of each part, investigating how it moves, what they can do with it. (An activity best done with preadolescents, 'nuff said.)

  - Bring in a bag of objects (hairbrush, sponge, cup, book, egg beater). Ask individual students or pairs of students to choose an object at random and create a dramatic skit that centers on it.

  - Pair students off and have them take turns doing mirror images of each other, imitating gesture, movement, and facial expressions.

  - Ask your student to imagine they are blocks of ice, melting in warm air; an ice cream cone at a 4th of July ball game; a hotdog in a microwave.

  - Have your students pretend to be swimmers underwater as you describe what they see on a South Pacific dive.

- Have your students pantomime:

  - A great machine in which they are interconnecting parts.

  - A bank robbery, with students playing robbers, tellers, security guards, customers, and even the video camera that is catching the whole thing on tape.

  - Assembling some object from imaginary parts.

  - Fishing, with one of the boat partners doing all the catching.

- Explore radio plays with your students. Tapes of old radio dramas and comedies are widely available. After listening to some samples, your students can write scripts and then tape-record (or present live) a drama of their own, complete with sound effects.

- Use puppets for improvised plays and skits; puppets offer self-conscious students, in particular, the kind of anonymity they may need to participate fully in drama.

- Do shadow plays with younger students, again supplying just the bit of protection from audience scrutiny that some kids need to take off.
- Create a variety of television-style talk shows as a bridge between drama and oral language. Students improvise their conversation, but must remain within appointed roles.
- Make connections with literature, finding its dramatic elements and bringing them on stage. Have your students:
  - Read, read, read aloud so they become comfortable with interpreting literature in their own voice.
  - Turn works of literature into readers theater, where various members of the class read dialogue parts while one person, perhaps you, reads the "he/she saids" and the "stage directions."
  - Dramatize a poem, song, or story, translating it into their own words.
  - Conduct imaginary interviews with characters from a story, poem, play, or novel.
  - Role-play a favorite poet.
  - Place characters from a historical novel in a contemporary scene.

(Keep the video camera around for many of these events.)

Composing through poetry

Poetry is the most difficult of the imaginative forms to teach, we feel, because students often develop early misconceptions about it. As children, they delight in the sing-song qualities of verse, and before long, they think that all poems must rhyme, a notion reinforced in many language arts classes where rhyme and meter are presented as the most important characteristics of a poem. As students get older, they often encounter modern poetry that seems obscure and difficult or ancient poetry that also seems obscure and difficult. If they write poetry, it's often in a fixed form, which subordinates ideas to structure. And for some reason our profession has developed a tradition of teaching poetry *units*, which walls off poesie and ignores its natural connections with human thought and other discourse.

Some ideas for "teaching" poetry (or better, simply *using* poetry as a natural form of expression). First some don'ts:

- Don't isolate poetry in separate literature or writing units. Offer poems as reading along with other literature; present poetry as a writing option alongside fiction, drama, and nonfiction.

- Don't overstress poetic traits and the characteristics of meter, rhythm, and metaphor. To do so is akin to saying that the most important thing about the essay is its paragraph structure.
- Don't describe poetry and poets as different from the rest of the literary universe. Don't claim that poetry is "more powerful" than prose or that poets have "deeper sensibilities" than other people.

Some positive suggestions:

- Help kids *find* poetry in the world around them: clever, powerful language in advertising, political statements (it's occasionally there), literature.
- Help kids *find* the poetry in their own writing (it's frequently there). When you discover them using language in creative, powerful ways, tell them, "*This* is poetry."
- Immerse students in good poetry. The best way for them to learn the characteristics of the genre is to read a lot of poems. From that, students will learn how poems work.
- Teach poetic form and devices as ancillary to meaning, secondary to interpretation.
- Encourage students to think of poems as a way of expressing ideas, even complex ones, *especially* complex ones, about their views of the world.
- Have students who like to write poetry collect and bind their work in the fashionable "thin volume."
- Create a Poetry Kaleidoscope, a bulletin board that is a constantly changing display of poems, both by the kids and by writers you and they admire.
- Get a poet to come to your school, probably with the aid of a grant from the state arts council. Help students see that poets are ordinary but not-so-ordinary people who write about the same sorts of things that the students cover in their writing journals.
- Flood the school magazine or newspaper with *your* kids' poems, which will be much more attractive and readable than the sing-songy pseudopoetry that's probably being published there now.
- Invite older students to explore fixed modes of poetry—like the sonnet—carefully and cautiously. Although we question the wisdom of having all students write in obligatory forms, we also recognize that there are kids in any class who can quite successfully compose in set verse forms, from haiku to heroic couplet (with the limerick happily in between).

Composing through fiction

Of the so-called creative forms, getting students to write fiction is probably the easiest. We all have storytelling impulses within us, and youngsters come to the elementary grades ready to create wonderful fictions (and ready to have those same impulses channeled into drama as well). John Rouse (1978) has reminded us, too, that so-called nonfiction is "fiction" of sorts, that any "true" story is something we abstract from experience and interpret for a reader.

To sustain and develop your students' powers as fiction makers:

- Let them write stories just about any time. (The best writing teacher Stephen experienced was a fourth-grade teacher who simply set aside every Wednesday as story day. The kids would come to that class with the story already half written in their minds.)

- Explore stories as a way of presenting information (an exciting alternative to the research paper). To do this, students develop a story that is centered on the topic they researched.

- Help students make connections between "nonfiction" and "fiction" stories by having them create fictions "about somebody your age, with your interests and concerns."

- Get a fiction writer to come to your class to talk about his or her ideas, work habits, and views of what good stories are all about.

- Bring in videos of classic short stories you've had your students read. Ask them to compare the filmed and written versions.

- Treat the characteristics and traits of good fiction within a context of meaning. That is, as students write stories and read stories, occasionally ask them to describe the nature of the stories they think are most successful. What are the characters like? What plots work best?

- Have students create a collection of *What if*'s as story beginnings. What if a student actually told a teacher what was on his or her mind? What if an alien came to our school? What if national television came to our school? (That possibility is explored in Steve's *The Burg-O-Rama Man.*)

Brass tacks writing ✍

"Sure, it's important to extend the imagination, to let students write creative forms as well as exposition. But what of the need for students to write for the job, for college, for the real world?" Enter "brass tacks writing."

We debated that phrase for some time before selecting it for use in this book. Some would call what we're discussing here *practical discourse,* the writing of business, academia, and society at large. However, that ignores the reality that fiction, poetry, and drama are also practical modes. Others prefer the term *exposition,* but as we will show, writing in this domain involves much more than essay writing or exam writing or research papers. Brass tacks writing includes memorandums, letters, editorials, application blanks, proposals, and a host of other forms.

Brass tacks (or "nuts-and-bolts") writing is the sort the public generally regards as basic, the kind that will help kids succeed in school and society, the stuff that Johnny and Jane allegedly can't produce.

We think composition programs can meet the demands for brass tacks writing in new and interesting ways. Kids need not shut off their imaginations when they write essays or business letters. What they have learned writing drama and stories can serve them well when they write examinations and term papers. Organizing a poem can also help students learn to organize a persuasive essay.

Workaday writing

One of the easiest ways to help students focus on the use of writing for practical purposes is to have them empty a wastebasket. That's right: dump it out on the floor and sift through the trash, looking for writing that has been *used* by virtue of its having been thrown away. Our own wastebasket—dumped at this writing on the study floor—is representative; it contains:

> Brochures from a bank, credit card company, and public utility informing us of bargains and proper procedures (all came tucked in with the monthly bill).
>
> Canceled checks and a scratch sheet for an unbalanced checkbook.
>
> A Three Musketeers bar wrapper listing caloric contents, fat levels, and other undesirables.
>
> Three drafts of Figure 9–3 for this chapter.
>
> A used grocery shopping list.
>
> A set of instructions on how to assemble a desktop bookshelf.
>
> Notes on a series of poems by Marianne Moore.
>
> A letter from a friend.

Workaday writing is more than writing that gets tossed in the wastebasket. We also have notebooks full of workaday writing (including several filled in preparing this book) and files and folders in varying states of disarray where we keep materials. Generally, workaday writing is *that which gets a practical job done,* and the point of the wastebasket exercise is to show just how much of such writing there is in the world.

Another interesting trait of workaday writing in schools is that *the teacher seldom grades it.* This is writing that students do for their own purposes: to remember things, to organize ideas, to collect information. As a teacher, you can increase the amount of writing students do while showing them the value of brass tacks writing and not burdening yourself with themes to grade. Just raise their practice levels and consciousness of functional writing. Have students write:

- Class notes of all sorts: notes on their reading, notes on lectures or presentations, notes on projects or experiments. Teach kids how to take reliable and dependable notes, and from time to time project a student's notes on a transparency to help the others see how it is done.

- Learning logs. These are a step beyond garden variety notes. Here students not only write down facts and concepts, but reflect on the ideas as well. "How do we *know* Christopher Columbus discovered America?" "How can we be certain that it's oxygen that helps things burn?" Learning logs can also be collections of students' *mis*understandings (with instructions for them to contact the teacher whenever they write, "I just don't understand [*insert puzzlement of your choice*])."

- Freewrites responding to class material. Ask the students to anticipate concepts or to write about prior knowledge before you teach; have them write midstream or summary commentaries as and after you teach.

- Questions that are submitted to the teacher or to fellow students on ideas covered in class. You can write replies, have students write replies, or use these for discussion topics.

- Microthemes: postcard essays written in response to a poem or story or textbook chapter.

- Abstracts, summaries, précis: to condense some reading into note-card-sized form.

- Progress reports on reading, writing, and dramatic projects.

- Evaluations of their learning, of their own performance, of a class unit or semester course.

Brass tacks writing projects

To make brass tacks writing seem real to your students, let them actually do real brass tacks writing. There are numerous opportunities for students to write in many different forms and genres around school and community. They can write:

- Letters to editors, public officials, teachers, the principal, or their parents arguing for ideas or privileges they see as important.
- Proposals to the audiences above outlining specific plans of action: how to save recess, how to save a community wetland.
- Feature or information articles for the school (or possibly local) paper.
- Critical reviews of new television programs and films, possibly published in the school paper, perhaps posted on a hallway bulletin board.
- User's manuals for complicated computer programs used in the class. (Kids often write simpler instructions than those created by the program developers.)
- Software. (A kid-developed program in Basic or Logo or Toolbook or Hypercard would certainly qualify as an organized piece of logical language use.)
- Investigations of problems: recycling, bicycle paths and bicycle safety, environmental impact. (Forward these to appropriate public agencies for review and response.)
- Press releases for school events.
- Posters dealing with important issues or advertising school events.
- Directions on how to write a good essay, poem, story, or play; how to play a sport; how to do well in school.
- Dramatic scripts for video plays, cable TV presentations, live plays presented to dramatize an important issue (recycling, for example).
- And imaginative forms that persuade—poems, plays, stories that awaken readers to important issues, problems, and concerns of young people.

Such writing projects carry students beyond the classroom, prepare them well for real world writing. We can't, of course, get kids ready for every last business letter they may have to write ten years after they've graduated; we can't anticipate what sorts of writing skills they'll have to demonstrate to keep a job in industry. However, we can provide them with numerous writing activities throughout their school years so they're positioned to use their literacy in the real world when it matters.

The academic writing scene

The projects and activities we have suggested on the past several pages prepare students for college as well as real life. Brass tacks writing usually emphasizes the traditional academic skills of marshalling evidence and presenting it effectively to an audience. Our own experience teaching college freshmen suggests that rather than mastering a limited range of forms like "the five-paragraph theme" or "the research paper," students need to develop fluency in a wide range of brass tacks writing forms. If they achieve that broad competence, they can quickly and successfully adapt to the specific demands of Professor Smith's history term paper or Dr. Jones's logbooks in computer science.

However, there are some specific strategies that senior high teachers can undertake to ready their students for academic writing:

- Survey the kinds of writing demands placed on college students. Actually, let your students do this as a good brass tacks writing project: have them write to last year's seniors who have gone on to college, asking those older, wiser folks to send back copies of their college papers, complete with professors' comments; then ask them to analyze these papers to learn the range of demands and responses.

- Teach students to use a concise handbook of usage, spelling, and writing form. Help them get to know their chosen handbook backward and forward so they can solve their own manuscript problems some distant 2:00 A.M. in the dorm.

- Help students learn to analyze assignments. Here again, real samples will help. What does Professor Smith mean when she says, "Analyze the poem any way you wish, but use supporting evidence"?

- Have your students get to know their own writing process and study habits. Self-knowledge of strengths and weaknesses, of successful and unsuccessful strategies, can go a long way toward helping students get themselves organized during the early, chaotic, bewildering days of college.

- Encourage students to think of audiences for academic writing. Usually this is the professor or graduate student. We wish that most academic writing was done "for real," but in fact it is often designed to reach a limited audience indeed: the person who will grade the paper. Knowing that helps students understand what to put into their writing.

- Above all, help students K–12 become inquiring, researching, thinking, *composing* human beings. More than knowing the mechanics of the research paper and the five-paragraph theme, college-bound students need to be spirited thinkers and writers. If teachers will help them *compose* in the fullest sense of that word, exploring the extraordinary dimensions of imagination and discourse, academic writing will be handled with competence.

Chapter Ten

The Red Pencil Blues

The scene: A language arts classroom, could be upper elementary, could be secondary. *The cast:* Typical students and teacher.

Teacher [*entering from the hallway door, brandishing a sheaf of papers*]: Class, I have completed grading your papers.

Class [*sotto voce*]: Mutter, mutter, mutter.

Teacher [*distributing papers to the class*]: On the whole, these were much better than the last ones. In fact, I'm encouraged that you're really working hard to improve your writing.

[*As the students receive their papers, they flip to the back page, searching for the grade.*]

Student 1 [*aside*]: Whadid she give you, Stan?

Stan: C-plus. [*He stuffs the paper into his bookbag.*]

Student 1: Wadid she say about it?

Stan [*shrugs*]: Who cares? I never understand what she wants. Last time I thought I did great, and she gave me a D. Time before that I turned in a thing I did in fifteen minutes and she gave me an A.

Teacher [*continuing to distribute papers*]: I think we're making real progress in here, don't you?

Students [*in chorus*]: Yes, Teacher.

The details of time, place, and situation may vary, but almost every teacher has played the lead in a scene like this. Having spent the better part of an evening or weekend writing thoughtful comments on papers, we return them to students and watch as the kids flip to the back, see what damage has been inflicted by the grade, and ignore the instructive comments.

We wind up singing the red pencil blues.

Of course, no trendy English/language arts teacher uses a *red* pencil anymore. Research and teacher lore have taught us that "bleeding" on kids' papers, accentuating errors in crimson, has negative effects on their writing.

We have also rejected what might be called the red pencil mentality, which saw the teacher's principal role as that of error corrector, super-grammarian. These days, English/language arts teachers try to make their comments supportive and generally positive, and they try to focus the negative comments, perhaps choosing one particular item for discussion each paper.

Yet theme marking/grading/editing still causes more than its share of problems for teachers and remains what we still refer to from time to time as the theme-correcting *burden.* (In our experience, the number one reason teachers give for not assigning more writing is the fact that they have to comment on it, and they're just not certain it's worth all the time and energy.)

Fortunately, current practices in teaching composition offer some fresh, even inviting alternatives. In particular, the interest in composing as *process* has encouraged teachers to move away from their traditional role of arbiter of finished products toward that of writing guide or coach. We're now more interested in helping students learn how to revise and edit their own papers than in showing them what they did right or wrong after the fact. Even concern for correctness, usage, and mechanics can be incorporated at appropriate stages of instruction.

The newer approach is based on the following scheme:

1. *Treat students' writing as a process in meaning making rather than an exercise in learning to write.* That is, the primary purpose of composing is to create something that other people will read suc-cessfully. Although as teachers we want students to learn to write better, we must carefully avoid turning student papers into a proving ground or testing facility for writing skills.

2. *Engage students constructively in taking responsibility for their own papers.* In the long run, the students themselves will be the ones who must make changes in their papers and accept the praise and criticism that goes with their writing.

3. *Use peers as readers and audiences.* Although fellow students may not be the ideal readers or the most informed responders, they can provide helpful feedback and a genuine sense of readership in the classroom.

4. *Teach from a workshop perspective, offering help when it's needed in the process of composition.* Having students revise, edit, and correct in class is a perfectly valid use of "company time," and a better use of your time than taking home stacks of papers to grade.

5. *Skeptically assess the effects of your comments on student papers; grant students the right to ignore your comments or to act on their*

own best instincts. We English teachers may well have overrated the value of our comments on papers. How will students learn if we do not correct their errors? we often ask. But classroom observation and the experience of writers suggest that even the best-intended, psychopedagogically framed remarks often miss the mark or fail to be helpful. The bottom line is that writers gradually figure things out for themselves.

These five principles do not, by any means, lead to a quick cure for the red pencil blues. Putting them into action is difficult. What do we do with kids who "just don't care" about their writing? Or the student whose chronic spelling problems make his papers absolutely unreadable? Or student editors who give one another bad advice? Or the student who consistently ignores our advice and consistently writes drivel or nonsense?

Too, we know a number of teachers who have tried to organize their classes into workshops where students take responsibility for their own editing and who abandoned the idea, saying that it just didn't work. Students didn't feel comfortable in groups or didn't work on the task at hand or didn't have anything worthwhile to say to one another.

All we're saying, then, is that employing the new pedagogy is no easy task and will not lead to quick successes. But it seems to us superior to singin' those old-time red pencil blues.

How can you go about setting up a writing workshop that will be helpful to students? How can you teach the processes of revision? How can students be helpful to one another as editors? How can correctness and copyediting become natural parts of the workshop? Where does *grading* factor into all of this? We offer some answers to those questions in the remainder of this chapter.

The individual writer

Right out of the chute it may be necessary for you to change some habits. Often students come to you with stereotyped images of the teacher as theme grader, with no inkling that there are other ways to go about writing than to submit a paper and wait to find out what was done wrong. (However, we should also state, from our perspective in the university, that increasingly the students who come into our classes seem to have been in a writing workshop and have had at least some previous experience in this mode of instruction. Praise be to their elementary and secondary teachers of "writing as process.")

Still, at any level, launching a writing workshop (or "wordshop" as we like to call it) requires preparation and explanation. Here are some strategies we've found helpful:

- Distinguish between the phases of revising, editing, and correcting papers. We generally discuss revision as a matter of working with content, editing as focusing on matters of language and style, and correctness as dealing with matters of mechanics and usage. It's most important that students not blur these distinctions. In particular, many of your students will come in thinking that "revising" simply means "proofreading" or even "copy it over, in ink."

- Early in the year, explain the idea of a writer's *responsibility* to the reader. This is not the nagging sort of *responsibility* we invoke to get children to clean up their rooms, but recognition that composing is a personal act with personal rewards and consequences. *You* are the one whose name goes on the paper; thus you are the one who needs to be the bottom line, the "buck-stops-here" writer/editor.

- Provide lots of time in class for students to work alone: to write, revise, self-edit, and copyedit their papers. There are several good reasons for using class time in this way. First, given today's busy schedules, kids will often not have done it at home. Second, and more fundamental, this sort of quiet time allows you opportunities to hold conferences with students (more about this later). Most important, perhaps, is that it helps students see that before you go to the peer group or writing response group, you must take responsibility for making your paper as good as it can be.

- Help students individually and collectively develop criteria for assessing papers they're writing. What will make a good personal narrative or letter to the editor or personal research paper? It's often helpful to develop or have students develop rubrics or checklists of things to look for in their writing: detail, focus, aim, appropriate beginnings and endings.

- Have students develop notebooks or portfolios of their best work and/or work in which they have worked through particular problems of editing, mechanics, and usage, a collection of writing they can use as touchstones for their present assignments.

Peer response groups

The heart of the newer pedagogy is a small group of students who, with teacher guidance and support, offer one another reactions to their papers and editorial advice. Peer groups can meet often during the writing process: we typically use groups shortly after making an assignment (so students can share basic ideas), during idea gathering (so students can discuss raw materials for their composition), during and after rough drafting (to collect audience responses and reactions), at the polishing stage (to work on fine points of mechanics and usage), and when the papers come in (to celebrate).

Some ideas for peer response groups:

- Let students form their own peer groups. Some teachers we know argue against this, preferring to structure groups so that they contain a mix of better and poorer writers, so that friends don't always work with friends. Despite the problems that self-selected groups sometimes present, we think they form a much tighter writing community than structured groups.

- Suggest that students *name* their writing group: The Magic Pens, The Awesome Editors, Will Shakespeare Light and Power Company.

- Assure students that they know how to help one another in class. (They *will* be skeptical.) Two useful exercises:

  o Have students describe the best and worst stories or poems they have ever read. These might be fairy stories for the younger children, British or American literature for the secondary students. Use the discussion to help students see that they already have valid critical standards.

  o Invite the students to write or improvise a parody of a current television show. In doing so, they will automatically employ critical and evaluative standards and (if you want to use some terminology) knowledge of *rhetoric.*

- Encourage students to be *helpful* editors. Each student in your class has certain skills and talents as a language user that he or she can employ. Make it clear that although not everybody (including you) knows everything about writing, in your classroom community you know quite enough to help one another out in important ways.

Strategies for writing groups

- Don't let students apologize in advance for their papers. The natural instinct is to say, "Well, this didn't turn out the way I wanted;" or, "I don't like this very much." Outlaw such self-defeating conversation.

- Give students a variety of ways to present papers. Some kids would like to read a draft aloud to their classmates. Others would prefer a "paper pass," where everybody's draft is read and commented on in silence.

- Model peer-group sessions for your students:

  ○ Project a paper on the overhead (a paper written by one of last year's students) and hold a discussion on how the class could make helpful remarks.

  ○ Pass out some of your *own* draft writing, take a deep breath, and ask the students to help you out. (In so doing, you'll also model how to respond to reactions.)

  ○ Put some students in a "fishbowl"—a small group in the center of the room—to conduct a discussion. Afterward you and other students can discuss how this went.

- Structure some peer-group sessions so that students know precisely what to look for in papers. Have different focus sessions on such matters as:

  ○ Beginnings. What makes a good beginning? How well does this one work?

  ○ Word pictures. Describe for the writer the visual images this creates in your mind.

  ○ Socko, boffo language. Tell the writer about all the knockout phrases in his or her writing.

  ○ Structure. Does this piece flow well from beginning to end? Could we follow it clearly?

  (The best source of ideas for such peer-group activities is Peter Elbow's *Writing with Power* (1981). It contains literally hundreds of ideas for peer-group responses.)

- More ideas for focus in peer groups:

  ○ Have students listen for rhythm and flow. If they don't hear it, what is causing the problem?

  ○ Have the writer give the history of this paper: why he or she chose to write it, the kinds of problems that have been encountered in process.

  ○ Encourage the groups to begin with praise—not hollow praise but focused reactions that say "I liked X because of Y."

  ○ Ask students to read one another's papers aloud. Having somebody else read your paper not only relieves anxiety but helps a writer hear his or her work in perspective.

- Do writing about writing in peer groups. If group members are not talking, if they're not doing substantial discussions of the work at hand, have them write out comments to give back to the writer.

- Have students keep a running commentary as another student reads a draft paper aloud. The idea is for respondents to jot down their instantaneous reactions to the piece, useful information for any writer to have.

- If your students are very reluctant to share comments orally, allow them to write letters to the author about the work. Such letters should *not* be anonymous, but they should be prepared carefully and thoughtfully. Putting criticism in a letter often makes it easier for student editors to comment.

- Have peer groups present one another's writing at the conclusion of an assignment. Student A can read student B's work aloud. Student C can introduce them both, explaining what the group liked about his paper. Or students A, B, C, and D can combine forces and do a dramatic presentation of E's work. (Roll the video camera.)

The teacher's role in response groups

For the most part you want to keep yourself out of the assessment, or at least operate behind the scenes. It's possible for the teacher to sit in on groups, even to make comments from time to time, but you must be cautious that you don't take over the group or disrupt its natural flow. We "float" during response groups, watching for unproductive groups. We have no reservations about intervening if a group isn't getting the job done, and we occasionally offer comments as we tune in to the work of a group. If we've done our job right, however, the groups pretty much run on their own.

Conferences

Holding conferences with students about their writing operates in a middle ground between peer response groups and teacher-written comments. The conference is a particularly efficient use of teacher time, because you can spiel out more words per second than you can writing. More important, you can get feedback from students and zero in directly on their problems. In a few colleges and universities, conference teaching has seemed to work so well that professors have actually abandoned common class meetings and spend all their time working face-to-face with students in their offices. We have strong reservations about that approach, however, because in it we feel both the loss of the classroom community and an increased student dependence on the professor. Some elementary and secondary school teachers, dissatisfied with peer groups, nonetheless run workshop classes where students work alone on papers while the teacher circulates conducting brief conferences. Many combinations are possible.

Our rules of thumb for conferences:

- Keep them brief. It's tempting to develop *your* ideas at great length. Learn how to make your conferences directed, usually to one point that either you or the students have raised.

- Let the students talk. Let them describe the problems they're having, even though their perception may differ from your own.

- Respect students' privacy. The downside of classroom conferences is that other kids can hear what you're saying. Be cautious.

- Let students suggest solutions to their own problems. Don't always be the answer person.

- When you do suggest solutions, present them as alternatives, allowing students to see several possible ways of proceeding.

- Don't let conferences become centered on proofreading. This is not an effective use of your time. Focus your energies on matters of content, style, language.

- Don't be so businesslike in your conferences that you forget to ask kids, "Howz it going, generally?" Take a few seconds to discuss the weather, the ball game, the upcoming dance.

The teacher as editor

We think it's important for teachers to supply as much help as possible *during,* rather than *after,* the fact of composition. We find that the more time we put in on classroom discussions and conferences, the less time we need to spend writing comments on papers. However, there comes a time for just about any teacher when written comments become important. Some principles and strategies to keep in mind:

- Make your first response to the paper that of a *reader,* not a grammarian. React to the content. Make laugh marks in the margin if it's funny. Explain the parts that moved you.

- Think of your response as a *letter* to the student rather than as a set of instructions for rectifying a problem composition.

- Give reasons for your positive responses. It's difficult to avoid the generic "good" or "swell," but at least try to explain what in the paper led to the qualities of goodness and swellness.

- Work hard to understand what students have written. We see that as a major responsibility of the teacher/theme reader. We absolutely disagree with teachers who refuse to read "sloppy" papers or who red line a paper if it contains too many errors or is difficult to decipher.

- Don't feign ignorance or confusion when students have simply written clumsily or outside the boundaries of standard English. Do explain the ways in which writers can make it easier for readers to grasp what they have in mind.

- Make suggestions in terms of the paper's content rather than stressing grammatical or rhetorical terms. That is, avoid abstractions; tell students concretely what seems to be the problem or what needs to be done. *Not:* "You've made an incomplete comparison." *But:* "You never finished telling me why Ford trucks are better than Chevies."

- Make suggestions that help students solve their own problems. Encourage them to go back to revisit their data or experience, thereby adding more depth and detail.

- Encourage students to develop their own standards. Provide support through your comments so that students can develop their own concept of "good writing" and confidence in their own decisions as writers.

- Don't cover too much. Resist the temptation to make this the one composition that will solve the student's writing problems forever.

- Explore alternative ways of writing back to students:
  - Put your comments on "sticky" notes so that you don't have to write on the paper itself, or
  - Reserve your comments for the end of the paper, leaving the pages clean.
  - Test out the interactive network at the computer lab to see if it makes sense to put comments *into* papers via a word processing program.
  - Have students turn in a blank cassette with their papers so you can amplify your written comments on tape.

- Don't read too many themes at once. That's obvious, of course, and sometimes reading the stack is unavoidable. Try staggering due dates, both among and within classes. Orchestrate your oral conferences and your written responses so that you are not compelled to read every last composition in the barrel tonight or this weekend.

- Above all, see your role as that of helper, not enemy. Your job (as we see it) is to help students succeed with the papers they've written. If these compositions are successful with its chosen audience, no doubt the learning we all want to see will take place.

The question of correctness

When the teacher takes editor's pen or pencil in hand, the issue of what to do about surface correctness emerges instantly. What do you do? Should the teacher correct every spelling error? Every error in mechanics? Every nonstandard usage item? Should you put proofreading symbols in the margin—*sp., punc.*—and have the students find the problems and solutions themselves? The dilemma is complicated by the fact that parents seem to be very critical of teachers who *don't* identify every error, and if parents had their way, red pencils might be standard issue for every teacher.

We take up the issue of correctness in more detail in the next chapter. For the present, however, it's important to remark that we think surface correctness *must* be subordinated to matters of content and style when a teacher responds to writing. The growing body of evidence suggests that correctness *does* make a difference to students when they're publishing their writing, so keeping audience at the forefront helps. In particular, having students write in a workshop or lab setting where they can get help regularly makes it easier for the teacher to teach correctness with a fighting chance that the concepts will take hold in students' minds.

The strategy that has worked best for us in elementary school, high school, and college classes is to stress the distinction between content and surface correctness, that the one precedes the other. We also give the students responsibility for handling correctness. Students *can* successfully use handbooks and dictionaries to find solutions to many of their problems. A simple oral reading by the student will also turn up many errors that are simply ones of omission or accident. Peer groups can also do much of the polishing work on any paper that students write.

In some cases, however, we find it necessary to include work on correctness in our written comments. This is particularly true of students who are not native speakers and writers of the language, and it's sometimes the case with students who simply have chronic usage/mechanics problems or even—though we dislike the word—disabilities. Then we will often focus on a particular problem and, for one paper or several, show the student how to manage it successfully for his or her own purposes. We also make it a point to tell the student precisely why we're working this way, and we regularly find ways in our written comments and/or conferences to praise the student for the content of the piece.

And, believe it or not, we have also had students ask us for more help with correctness matters. Sometimes this comes from an inappropriate fear that "my grammar is bad; my English teacher said so." At others, it comes from a realization on the part of the student that he or she has a problem and, quite simply, wants to solve it. In such cases we're quite willing to work with students. (Often we have told classes, "If you want specific help with usage or spelling or punctuation, say so at the top of the paper.") In these instances, our first job is to figure out whether or not the student truly has a problem. If it's real, then constructive teaching is possible through written comments or conferences, and, what's more, is likely to be successful.

Grading compositions

Having remarked above that the theme reader/teacher ought to be on the side of the student, rather than being the enemy, we now turn to the inimical process of grading. If you're not careful, your best-intentioned work with student writers, your carefully and humanely written comments, will be wasted in the eyeblink it takes to see the grade.

In our ideal world, student writing and other composing would always be "graded" pass/fail, successful/unsuccessful, or credit/no credit. And we comment in several of these chapters that *contract grading* is about as close as we've been able to come to that ideal. Another good alternative is *portfolio grading,* where students receive a mark for showing growth over time or for having completed particular kinds of assigned writings. If you find it necessary to put individual letter grades on student papers, we recommend the following ideas:

- State your grading criteria at the beginning of the assignment. In fact, type them up and run off copies for the students to study.
- Engage students in setting standards for grades. What makes a "good" story or an "excellent" piece of research writing? As students develop those criteria, they will also come to understand how they apply to their own work.
- Break your grade into components: clarity, organization, structure, style, correctness. Weight these factors to show students precisely what you value (presumably matters of content over those of correctness).
- Include the writing process as part of the grade. Give credit for preliminary proposals, first drafts, second drafts, polished copy, thus rewarding students who undertake the process seriously and productively.

- Have your students write self-assessments as they turn in their writing. (We don't recommend having students *grade* their own papers.) As students reflect on what they've written, they're more likely to understand the grade that you've assigned to their work.

- Explain your grades. (No easy task.) Never slap a B or C on a paper without explanation or with short phrases like "Too short" or "Not enough detail." Make certain students understand what your grade means and how they can do better next time.

Summary and Troubleshooting

The PTO Discusses Writing

The scene: The assembly room of most any school. *The occasion:* The English/language arts teachers have developed a new composition program and have spent the evening describing it for interested parents at a Parent Teacher Organization meeting. The teachers have discussed writing-as-process, oral language foundations for writing, editorial groups, and the development of editing skills through publishing. The time has come for questions from those parents.

The Principal: . . . and so we thank the language arts teachers for this informative presentation. I know they stand ready to answer your questions.

Parent 1: Well, this all sounds very interesting, but I really am puzzled as to why our children write so badly in the first place. I mean, when *we* went to school, it was pretty much expected that we would write and write well. What happened to destroy that?

Teacher 1: You raise an important set of issues there. With all due respect, I'd have to urge us to be careful about reminiscing about our own past education. Granted, we in this room may have grown up writing, but the "writing problem" has been around for a long, long time. Even in "our" day, in meetings just like this one, parents worried about the bad writing of their children.

Teacher 2: But certainly the role of language in people's lives has changed, hasn't it? We use the telephone more than ever; we get much more of our news and entertainment through television and the electronic media. The students I see don't have the same motivation to write that we may have had in the preelectronic dark ages.

Parent 2: Then why so much focus on *writing?* Didn't somebody once say, "Print is dead?" Or at least dying?

Parent 3: Not in college it isn't. My older kids have had a terrible time writing in college, so I want to know why the school hasn't done its job in the past, why it has waited until now to do something.

Teacher 3: It's an interesting contrast, isn't it? On the one hand, the demands for writing (at least in college) are as great or greater than ever. On the other hand, we have the feeling that electronic media have altered the need for us to write at all.

Teacher 4: And we've tried to account for that in our writing program—or, perhaps, I should more accurately call it a *composition* program. As you've seen, we plan to have students write—or compose—in many different forms and genres, to write poems as well as essays, scripts as well as essays.

Parent 4: That's precisely what bothers me. All this emphasis on *creativity* and *expression*. I mean, come on, now. We're not raising kids to be poets or playwrights; we're raising them to go to school, to get good jobs. I think the program is focusing too much on frills.

Teacher 4: But if I could jump back to the previous point. The one about preparation for college. The new research in writing has helped us see that just concentrating narrowly on practical writing like the essay or the business memorandum doesn't really produce highly literate students. They may know the forms, but that doesn't mean that they'll be able to conquer new writing tasks successfully.

Teacher 3: Ironically, the very fact that we concentrated so much on essay writing in the past may be, in part, why students have so much trouble in college.

Parent 5: But *poetry?*

Teacher 5: We're not trying to make poets out of your children. But we do recognize that writing a poem or a script or a short story or any of the so-called creative forms involves students in organizing ideas and using language in ways that are fundamentally helpful even in practical writing. We don't want kids to write rhyming memos filled with metaphors and similes, but it's true that writing poetry with force and imagery does encourage one to write compactly, precisely, without wasted words. Aren't those also the traits of a good memo?

Parent 6: But it still sounds loose and progressive to me. Like, the other day, my daughter came home with a composition from language arts and there were four misspellings and some grammatical errors. Nobody had bothered to correct these. Don't teachers know the difference anymore? Don't they care?

Teacher 6: Of course we care, and, believe it or not, most of us can still spell and use good grammar. In your daughter's case, what she brought home was a draft of her work. The errors hadn't been corrected because she hadn't reached the proofreading stage. We get to that when students are preparing final copy.

Parent 6: It makes no sense to me. An error is an error. In my day, when we made a mistake, there was no coddling; we were told when we were wrong.

Teacher 6: So how do you feel about writing today? Do you like to write?

Parent 6: Me? Oh good grief, no. I'm not a good writer. Never was. I could never get it right for my teachers, so I certainly don't do much of it now.

Teacher 6: Well, that's part of the point then, isn't it? Your experience is actually quite common. People who have been taught by the red pencil are often so fearful of making mistakes that they don't write. In our program, we put errors into an appropriate context, and we do, honestly, correct them when students are finishing up their work. But to dwell on errors too soon, too much, doesn't correct those errors. All it does is make people self-conscious about their writing.

Parent 7: So where's the proof? I mean, you've given us a lot of talk about this program—a lot of claims that if you don't correct errors and don't just teach essays that students will learn to write. But where's the proof? I mean, do you have some test results we can see?

Teacher 1: Well, there will be test scores coming out. The students have just taken their state assessment, and believe me, we teachers are just as concerned as you parents about how well your children do. If students do poorly in the tests, then our program is very much in jeopardy.

Teacher 2: But where's the proof, you say? We just happen to have copies of a small magazine our students have produced, and the kids, your children, have done *all* of it, from writing and editing and proofreading down to setting the type and doing the page layout on our desktop publishing program. Please study these and see what you think.

Teacher 3: And as you enjoy the refreshments later, please stop along the back wall and study the individual bound books our students have made. How many of us published books of this high quality when we were their age? And remember, please, that these were created by all our students, not just the "gifted" or the "college bound."

Teacher 4: We also want to remind you of our Young Authors' Conference next month, where youngsters of different backgrounds from all over the district will get together to read and share their writing with each other and with adults. We could use some parent volunteers for that program, too, parents to meet with small groups of authors and to help them share.

Teacher 5: In fact, we can use parental support in so many ways. We could use some parents to help in our individual classrooms as well . . .

Teacher 6: . . . assisting students in proofreading their own works, so you could see how this system works. Oh, we have much for you to do.

The Principal: Enough. Let's not scare them off, eh? But clearly, parents, these teachers respect your questions and value your ideas. We hope you'll stick around for more talk and that you'll remain interested in our program far into the future.

f·o·u·r

Ideas for Teaching Language

Language. (lan'-gwij) [Middle English, Old French, from *la langue,* tongue, language] An arbitrary system of signs and symbols by which people communicate and interact.

The dictionary definition just begins to hint at the problems and possibilities of "langwij." It shows, rightly, that our language is deeply rooted in speech and that we use an "arbitrary" or conventionalized set of symbols to get our communication done. The dictionary ignores the magic of language: its miraculous and mind-boggling properties and capabilities, its poetry and its science.

And it says nothing of teaching. The dictionary might have added:

Language. That which drives English/language arts teachers crazy because of their students' misuse of same.

Or, more positively:

Language. The unifying element of the *language* arts.

Or, more positively still:

Language. Source of endless possibilities for exploration and inquiry, from how language systems work, to how they shape and are shaped by people, to how they serve as a medium for expression of learning, emotions, facts and concepts, truths and lies, curses, incantations, and literatures in every land and culture.

Guess which definitions we'll pursue.

Our aim in this section of *The English/Language Arts Handbook* is to demystify language study and explore its fullest dimensions. We'll begin by examining what is traditionally the most limited aspect of language in the schools: grammar, dialects, and correctness. Without ignoring these standard curriculum components (the components many parents and administrators misperceive as the heart of our discipline), we'll go on to show the kinds of language explorations teachers can conduct to help kids feel at home in the linguistic sea on which they are afloat. We'll even show how language study is not only a way of unifying English/language arts studies, but of bringing coherence to the whole school curriculum. Here are some citations which hint at the range of possibilities:

"In the beginning was the word." (Genesis)

"Perhaps of all the creations of man, language is the most astonishing." (Lytton Strachey)

"Language is the Muzak of the mind." (Joseph Morgenstern)

"Lexicographer: A harmless drudge." (Samuel Johnson)

"People's speech is the skin of its culture." (Max Lerner)

"If you will scoff at language study how, save in terms of language, will you scoff?" (Mario Pei)

Chapter Eleven

Grammar, Dialects, and Correctness

O
ver the years, *grammar* has probably generated more discussion, debate, acrimony, and maybe even fistfights than any other component of the English/language arts curriculum. There are teachers who say they are "for" grammar, and those who are "against" (never mind that both *use* grammar every time they open their mouths to speak). There are traditionalists who call for a return to sentence diagramming, cultural pluralists who want a broadening of definitions of correctness, and eclectics who say, "I'll do whatever seems to work (and nothing does)."

The brouhaha over grammar has had a debilitating effect on English studies. Instead of discussing how to get kids to read more, write more, think more, and talk more articulately, we've spent entirely too much time debating whether or not students ought to be studying *transitive* and *intransitive verbs, gerunds* and *gerundives,* and the reality of a *dative case* in English. (Grammatical query: Do language arts teachers *lay* or *lie* better?)

Seldom have combatants in the great grammar debate bothered to begin by following a simple rule from general semantics and common sense: *define your terms.* As lexicographers know, words used in diverse situations take on multiple meanings. What angry parents mean when they ask "Why don't you teach our child *grammar?*" is not what teachers mean when they say "I don't teach formal *grammar,*" which is not what linguists mean when they say "Our *grammar* is better than their *grammar.*"

In case you've never looked it up, here's what Webster's tells us about the origins of "grammar." First the derivation:

> Old French, *gramaire,* from Latin *grammatica,* from Greek, *grammatikē,* from feminine of *grammatikos,* skilled in grammar, from *gramma,* letter, from the root of *graphein,* to write.

It's interesting to note the very close connection between grammar and the written word. Linguists nowadays recognize that there are important differences between the grammars of spoken and written English. However, schoolteachers will be quick to tell you that errors in written English cause particularly violent responses from the public.

Now the definitions of *grammar*:

1. The science of treating of classes of words, their inflections, and their syntactical relations and functions.
2. A treatise on grammar.
3. Manner of speaking or writing, with reference to grammatical rules.

(G. C. Merriam Co., *Webster's New Collegiate Dictionary,* 1985)

A key distinction must be noted between the first and third meanings. The first is that of a linguist or an informed language arts teacher: grammar is a study of the system of English, how words fit together in our language. (From here on, we'll call that grammar[1].) The third meaning, grammar[3], has to do with language in actual use in society. In the eye of the public, grammar[3] is extraordinarily broad in scope, ranging from whether to say "may I" or "can I" to good penmanship to double negatives. In fact, grammar[3] probably ought to be called "language in use," because it has many elements (like penmanship and politeness) that have little to do with grammar.

Grammar[2] is a textbook, technically a "treatise" on grammar. But as often as not, you'll find that a grammar[2] book contains a wide range of information about the language. Some of the material in a typical school or college grammar will have to do with the way sentences are put together, but you'll find many other topics, including how to address a letter and how to look up topics in the library.

For generations, teachers have presented grammar[1] (the system of English) through grammar[2] (handbooks of usage and style) in the hopes of changing what students do with grammar[3] (speaking, writing papers, using good English). Has it worked? Generations of school children know intuitively that the answer is no. Further, nearly a century of research in this topic has failed to show a connection. In study after study, researchers have presented grammar[1] and later measured students' use of language, looking for improvements. And in study after study, they've come up with no significant differences. (For a particularly useful summary of those studies, see Haynes, 1978.)

We must be cautious in interpreting such studies, however. Clearly *some* people (children and adults) are capable of translating the abstractions of grammar[1] into operations they can execute in their speaking and writing. For example, we know people who can distinguish between feeling *bad* and *badly* by observing that one is an adjective that can be applied to objects while the other, as an adverb, describes or modifies an action. Thus *bad* describes one's physical state, while *badly,* used to describe feeling, would describe tactile skill. Others of us either have to look it up every time or memorize a rule or slogan: "To feel badly means you've got no sense of touch."

The research into applications of grammar[1] necessarily has to be conducted with large numbers of students. It's not surprising that the results are a wash. For every kid who can understand the abstractions and apply them, there's at least one other kid who feels bad about the whole thing and cannot make the connections. We've long believed that if you could separate those students who have a propensity for learning through abstract principles and teach them grammar[1], you probably could show some effects on their language use. But we teach heterogenous learners (even in homogeneous classes), so a pure grammar[1] approach is doomed to fail.

We don't want to argue that grammar[1] should never be taught or should be taught only to those who have a propensity for learning from it. But we do want to make clear our research-supported conviction that the wholesale teaching of grammar[1] to all kids with the expectation that they will all become model speakers/writers of Standard English was an inappropriate language-teaching goal from the outset.

If the research evidence does not justify teaching large amounts of grammar[1] in an effort to make children write and speak better, what should we do, especially given the clamor of parents, administrators, and school leaders for more grammar?

Grammars[1], [2], and [3] all have a place in the school program. Teachers would be wrong (not to mention naive) to say that they don't care about correctness or that "grammar doesn't matter." The problem, again, is in blurring distinctions and teaching one form of grammar thinking that it will produce changes in language use. We'll take up each of the grammars in this chapter.

Teaching grammar[1]: The systems of language

Both linguists and teachers have discovered that exploring the way English (or any language) operates can be engaging and rewarding for students if it is separated from the felt need to change people's language behavior. That is, grammar is inherently interesting to examine in its own right. Try some of the following with your students:

- Say "Good morning" to them, and no matter what they say back, ask them how they knew what you meant. How did they know you meant "Hello" or "Let's get started" rather than "Mornings are inherently good" or "This particular morning is good"? Use the discussion that follows to help students see that they are masters of a very sophisticated language system. (Also teach them that wonderful Australian greeting and farewell, "G'day.")

- Bring in copies of Lewis Carroll's "Jabberwocky," with its nonsense words:

> 'Twas *brillig,* and the *slithy toves*
> Did *gyre* and *gimbal* in the *wabe.*
> All *mimsey* were the *bororgroves*
> And the *mome* wrath *outgrabe.*

The italicized words were coined by Carroll to create images, and students enjoy talking about words like *slithy, toves,* and *brillig* to see why and how those words carry meaning, even when they aren't in the dictionary. Further, in an elementary parts-of-speech lesson, students can understand that *outgrabe* is some sort of action, while *toves* are things and *slithy* is an attribute or characteristic of a *tove.* In the process of discussing this knowledge *that the students already possess,* you can refer to terms like *noun, verb,* and *adjective,* which they've probably met before if they're in fifth grade or above.

- Teach parts of speech independently of rules of usage. That is, don't muddy the waters of teaching nouns and verbs by immediately introducing rules for the agreement of subject and predicate. We've found that one can teach recognition of basic parts of speech quite rapidly from the middle elementary years on up.

- Instead of using textbook lessons, teach parts of speech using readily available materials: newspapers, the textbook chapter, school memorandums. Start with the stuff of life: the *nouns* and the *verbs,* the objects and the actions. Introduce *is* as an equal sign, the *verb of being. Adjectives* and *adverbs* follow, along with the concept of modification. Don't fuss overmuch with connectors: *determiners, prepositions,* and *interjections.* Over time, work these gap-bridgers into the discussion. Ideas to try:

  ○ Have a debate over which is more important, *nouns* or *verbs* (a debate that will likely end in a draw).

  ○ Analyze parts of speech in newspaper headlines, noting how the lack of connectors sometimes leads to ambiguities.

  ○ Teach *simple* sentence diagrams. (This may seem like heresy to some antigrammar teachers, but *if* separated from usage rules,

sentence diagramming is easy to master and does give students a
visual sense of grammar[1].)

○ Teach parts of speech through the structural grammarian's device
of *substitution frames*. That is, instead of (or along with) traditional definitions, show students that particular *slots* in sentences
are filled with similar words:

> The (noun) walked.
> The cowpoke (verbed).
> She came (preposition) the party.
> "(Interjection)!" he shouted.

You and your students can experiment to develop a series of
substitution frames that reliably identify parts of speech in (adjective) situations. Along the way you can reinforce students' realization that they have already gotten a great deal of grammar under
control just by mastering the language.

● Try some of the following linguistic experiments as proposed by
Ruth Taylor (1976):

○ *Excluded combinations.* Have students create a series of nonsense
words: *wonkalooney, brigabobble, marmulate.* Then help them
see that many possible letter combinations—zl, cm, pd—were not
selected. Thus students can see that English words are formed
according to system, not just chance.

○ *Pluralization.* Let students write plurals of nonsense words. "One
wonkalooney; two _____." How is it that students can automatically supply the correct plural on a nonexistent word?

○ *Changing parts of speech.* Students can also intuitively change
nonsense words into other parts of speech. Thus, if a person *out-
grabes* regularly, he or she is an *outgrab*—. Taylor proposes,
"What would you call a man whose job is to *zib?*"

○ *The QV language.* The "grammar" of this language is based on two
rules: 1) Each sentence begins with Q, and 2) each sentence alter-
nates Q and V. Thus QVQVQVQ is grammatical, while QVVQQV
contains several grammatical errors. What are they?

○ *Kalaba X.* This game involves some grammatical terminology but
makes teaching the distinction between subject and predicate
clear. Kalaba X sentences always follow this order:
Predicate   Object + Modifier   Subject + Modifier
In Kalaba X, "Mary had a little lamb" is translated:

> Owns lamb little, Mary
> Loves lamb, Mary little

> Loves Mary pretty, lamb
> Owns lamb, Mary pretty.

- If Kalaba X seems too complicated, back up a bit and teach subject, predicate, and object this way. Create some simple sentences, each word written on a separate card. Try:

    > I threw the ball.
    > The dog bit the man.
    > John loves Mary.

    Have the students stand up, holding these cards, to create possible sentences. Which sentences can be rearranged (e.g., "Mary loves John") while still being "English"? Which sentence must be done exactly in the order given? En route, you can help students see how nouns can become subjects or objects and how verbs function as predicates.

- Study Esperanto. This artificial language, created by a Polish physician, L. L. Zamenhof, has been studied and learned for over a century and has an estimated seven million speakers worldwide. The grammar of Esperanto is simple and regular and, taught to students, helps them understand English grammar as well. For the first of a free series of postcard lessons, write the Esperanto League of North America, P. O. Box 1129, El Cerrito, California, 94530.

- Compare foreign languages. If your students are studying some Spanish or French or German, or praise be, if they come to you as speakers of Chinese or Japanese or Yiddish or Italian, have them describe the grammar (or system) of that language.

- Teach your grammar textbook, selectively. If your school has an adopted grammar series or if the curriculum requires coverage, you can do so without destroying students' love of language. Separate the grammar information from correctness. Don't assign all forty-seven fill-in-the-blank usage exercises for each lesson. Supplement sterile textbook examples with newspaper clippings. Help the students keep straight on the distinctions between the three grammars, even if the book doesn't.

How much grammar[1]?

When should grammar[1] be taught? How often? To whom? With what expectations?

We'll start with a negative: we wish diligently to avoid the traditional school pattern of teaching grammar (parts of speech, sentence functions, usage rules) over and over and over. If you look at many adopted text series, you'll see that this is precisely what happens; it's the same material year after year, a text writer's acknowledgment that "grammar" didn't "take" the first or second or third time.

More positively, we find that in every language arts class there are opportunities to discuss language-as-system every day!:

- A kid tells a joke. Did we get it? Nine times out of ten jokes depend on a linguistic trick or turn of phrase, and, we admit it, we'll stoop to analyzing jokes to see how they work.

- Somebody uses a metaphor. We pause for a moment to note how this language works by substituting a surprising word for one we would ordinarily expect because of our understanding of grammar.

- Students are puzzling over a poem—a sonnet by Shakespeare, a limerick by Lear, a goofy verse by Shel Silverstein. Opportunities arise for us to help kids see how *syntax* works, how we go about unlocking language puzzles in literature.

- The daily cartoon strips contain puns, gags, and clever syntax, so we discuss these with students.

Grammar[2]: Books about language

A major publisher reissued its basic high school handbook with the claim, "It's passed the test of time with millions and millions of students." That's the sort of sentence we'd like to turn over to a group of students for linguistic analysis. Like many advertising claims, it implies much and explains very little. Which "millions" of students spoke up in favor of their dear old schoolhouse grammar book? How much time has passed (and how slowly did it creep)? What tests were passed (and who gave them)? The fact is that school grammars (grammars[2]) have largely failed the test of time for millions of students by such simple criteria as a) whether or not the students learned to use language with a reasonable degree of correctness, b) whether they came to understand the nature of language itself, and c) whether they are at ease with themselves as speakers/writers.

As we've suggested, the typical school grammar[2] is an odd mix of description and prescription about language, a mismatch of instruction and drill, a curious combination of half-truths about contemporary usage and the writing process. It's a puzzle why such books, which have remained largely unchanged throughout this century, still dominate so many elementary and secondary school classrooms.

Nevertheless, there are some good books describing language that can be helpful to teachers and students, especially if we keep in mind *why* we are presenting material to students and what we hope to accomplish. We don't recommend adoption of any grammar textbook, and we wish school districts would save their money and spend it on good literature. Instead of spending (literally) tens of thousands of dollars buying (literally) tons of grammar books, school districts should invest in smaller numbers of some of the following:

- Adult books on grammar. No, these are not X-rated. They're accessible "linguistic treatises" that help teachers (and perhaps a few advanced senior high students) learn more about the language. In particular, if you feel a little shaky about your knowledge of grammar (and, in our experience, just about everybody does), you might look at a book that describes grammar from a linguistic, rather than prescriptive, point of view.

  Richard Veit's *Discovering English Grammar* (New York: Houghton Mifflin, 1986), Patricia Osborne's *How Grammar Works* (New York: John Wiley, 1989), and Dorothy Sedley's *Anatomy of English* (New York: St. Martin's, 1989) all help one learn about modern views of English syntax. (If you want a classic linguistic treatise, explore Otto Jespersen's *Analytic Syntax,* published in various editions.)

  Broadening the scope somewhat, William O'Grady et al. have a useful introduction to *Contemporary Linguistics* (New York: St. Martin's, 1990). Gary Goshgarian's *Exploring Language* (Glenview, IL: Scott, Foresman, 1990) and Paul Eschholz, Virginia Clark, and Alfred Rosa's *Language Awareness* (New York: St. Martin's, 1990) are both good collections of essays that explore the full dimensions of language as it functions in society. Many of the articles in those anthologies are quite readable by secondary school students.

  S. I. Hayakawa's *Language and Thought in Action* (New York: Harcourt Brace Jovanovich, 1990) is a many-editioned classic in this area as well.

  We also highly recommend two books that help put questions of "grammar" into a multicultural perspective, Harvey Daniels's *Not Only English* (Urbana, IL: National Council of Teachers of English, 1990) and Robert McCrum et al.'s *The Story of English* (New York: Penguin, 1986). The latter is the book version of a superb PBS television series every school media center ought to acquire for use by students and teachers.

Also important are two contemporary classics describing the grammatical nature of African American English, J. L. Dillard's *Black
English* (New York: Random House, 1972) and Geneva Smitherman's *Talkin' and Testifyin'* (Boston: Houghton Mifflin, 1978).

- Usage handbooks. A good usage handbook is technically not a grammar; in fact, many highly reputable usage handbooks make minimal
use of grammatical terminology, focusing instead on helping readers
with "troublesome" word pairs: effect/affect, lay/lie, have to/must/got
to, and even pailsful/pailfuls. Webster's puts out a good desk reference usage handbook, and you'll also find many smaller paperback
versions at your local bookstore. Usage handbooks have high payoff
value because they tell you what to *do* with your language. Our
particular favorite is a little book by Rudolf Flesch, *Look It Up: A
Deskbook of American Spelling and Style* (New York: Harper &
Row, 1977). It's simple to use, plain in its explanations, up-to-date in
its view of usage (that is, willing to accept popular usage as a guide to
what's "acceptable" in speech and writing).

- Dictionaries. Here again we stray a bit from the definition of grammar[2] as a treatise on syntax. But obviously dictionaries are an important source of linguistic information for students, and most
dictionaries carry enough information on grammar and usage that
they qualify under this category. We think it's important that dictionaries be seen as helpful tools, not as punishment. Thus we don't
have much faith in dictionary drills ("Look up these ten odd words"),
and we don't believe in forcing dictionary use ("Don't ask me what it
means; look it up!"). We do think kids should have dictionaries
handy and feel comfortable using them. One of our favorite activities
is to have students "adopt a word"—a curious one like *skulk* or
winnow—look it up in the dictionary to become an expert in its
origins and meanings. We then hold a get-acquainted session where
people wear their words as name tags.

- Spelling guides. A big problem with dictionaries is that you sort of
have to know how to spell a word to be able to find out how to spell
it. A handy alternative is a list of commonly misspelled words, sometimes available on a single laminated sheet that fits in a notebook.
Such lists are helpful because they can be scanned quickly and you
can find the word you need without flipping through many pages. A
longer version of a spelling demons list is *Webster's Word Guide,*
available at most bookstores.

- The thesaurus. The utilization of thesauri thrusts numerous scholars
into portly misfortune because they utilize phraseology possessive of
inappropriate implications. (We wrote that last sentence by substituting thesaurus synonyms in the sentence, "The use of the thesaurus

gets a lot of students into big trouble because they use words with wrong connotations.") Occasionally the thesaurus is useful for finding just the right word or locating a word that is on the tip of your tongue. (You look up its synonym.) Show students a thesaurus; explain how it works; caution against misuse; keep it on the reference shelf.

- Secretary's manuals. These little volumes, available inexpensively in paperback, are a gold mine of information. A good secretary's manual contains all the usage advice of a schoolroom grammar but places it in a less pedantic, more useful form. A typical secretary's manual contains spelling lists, some basic rules of usage, disputed usage items, letter format, information on library use, and tips on manuscript preparation. Dollar for dollar, they are the most practical grammar[2] around.

- Computer programs. Our profession is debating the use of computer programs that offer help with usage, spelling, and mechanical items. We think these programs can be helpful and will not necessarily become a crutch for an imagined future generation of nonspellers and nongrammarians. (That's the sort of issue mathematicians debated before allowing students to use calculators on tests. Now, having researched the issue, most mathematics teachers see calculators as actually increasing students' ease and ability with numbers.) We're interested in computer grammar[2] programs for their immediate use in helping with proofreading but also for their indirect or spinoff effect of teaching a little grammar, spelling, mechanics, and usage on the side. For example, our word processor includes a "word alert" program (for usage items), "phrase alert" (for clichés and some grammatical constructions like passive voice), and a "punctuation check." When it "beeps" something in our writing, it offers a brief, practical lesson: Don't put a comma after "than." Do you mean "to," "too," or "two"? Students who receive such on line help with their writing can pick up a great deal of grammatical information on their own. The problem with such systems, we find, is that the knowledge they offer is more sophisticated than many novice writers can assimilate. That is, you have to know grammar and usage to use the information. (In turn, if you know grammar, you probably don't need the computerized help system.) On the whole, however, we think most of these programs will be helpful and a quicker source of information than a book version of a grammar[2].

Grammar[3]: Dialects and correctness

As just about everybody knows, English usage is not constant. It varies from one part of the country to another and within regions. The hill country accents of Tennessee are not those of West Virginia; Texans don't talk quite like Oklahomans; you can easily separate a true down-easter from a Bostonian, even though they both speak a New England dialect. Usage varies in vocabulary, syntax, intonation, and pronunciation, and it differs according to ethnic origins, social settings, educational contexts, and content. Moreover, the conventions of usage change over time.

The point is that usage—grammar[3]—is not always determined by hard-and-fast rules or even by written-down rules; it is, as Robert Pooley (1946) noted years ago, a product of custom and tradition. It's also a byproduct of face-to-face contact, for whenever dialect communities encounter one another, they tend to exchange language along with information, commodities, or punches. The basic structure and vocabulary of English grew from such encounters between Celts, Anglo Saxons, Danes, Romans, Normans, and the church. Today it continues to change with new cultural forces and encounters.

For many years, English/language arts teachers taught a status dialect, Standard English (SE). SE is, essentially, the form of the language presented in usage handbooks, the language spoken by six o'clock national newscasters on television. It is a "prestige" or standard dialect more as a result of the power of its speakers (the white majority in England, New Zealand, Australia, Canada, and the United States) than of any innate superiority or linguistic elegance. As linguists point out, all dialects work; each form of speaking/writing is essentially as successful as any other. We're no longer in a position to say that the best or proper form of the language is Standard English. (Actually we should say Standard Englishes, for despite some national or international common characteristics, SE in London is clearly different from that in New York or Auckland or Sydney or Toronto.)

Yet we know that SE (in its various forms) *matters.* Kids who don't use standard spellings will have their job applications rejected; those who employ nonstandard usage in placement tests will wind up in remedial writing courses (even though they may be quite articulate). Folks who write in Standard English have a better chance of having their letters to the editor published; those who speak SE will be listened to more carefully in public settings than those who don't (if the latter can even work up the needed courage and moxie to speak publicly in the first place).

There are several alternative approaches to SE available to the teacher. Among them are:

1. *Enforcer.* The enforcer is the traditional school teacher who will accept only Standard English in the classroom, who feels it is the duty of the school to get all students talking and writing this real-yet-imaginary dialect. Among the enforcers we also list the members of the English Only movement, who are, with considerable success, having

English declared an official language, and trying to force people who do not have English as a first language to convert to our mother tongue.

2. *Legitimizer.* We get this term from Geneva Smitherman who argues in *Talkin' and Testifyin'* (1977) that teachers must accept a broader range of dialects in society as a linguistic fact. It's not accurate, she points out, to claim that kids who don't speak Standard English will fail in life. There are plenty of people speaking an astonishing range of dialects who are doing quite well. Smitherman calls for understanding rather than eradicating dialects. Proponents for bilingual education also fit into the legitimizer camp, suggesting that students ought to receive some instruction in their native tongue so they can acquire quality education, even as they are in the process of learning a new language.

3. *Expansionist.* This third kind of teacher argues against enforcing a rigid standard and says that we owe it to all kids to increase their understanding of language as well. An expansionist argues that the way to change the way people talk and write is not to *make* them change, but to expand their opportunities to use language in real situations. In this camp, too, are the proponents of English Plus (offered as an alternative to English Only), who say that all kids ought to become acquainted with more languages than just their native tongue.

Our program for grammar[3] is *legitimizer/expansionist,* including the recognition that Standard English "matters." We include attention to dialects and correctness. We think it's very important for students to have a *context* for correctness, to come to understand what dialects are, in general, what their own dialects are, the implications of owning and using various dialects, and a sense of the social and political impact of dialects on dialect speakers (of whom everybody is one).

Some activities for the classroom:

- Have students analyze their own language. Encourage them to keep a journal noting how they adjust their language for various settings: when they talk to the principal, when they call a friend on the phone, when they call an information source on the phone, when they speak to their parents or minister or teacher.

- Have them note how their oral language differs from written standard. *Everybody* says (or "sez") *gonna* and *gotta.* What other oral forms do they use, forms like *wanna, doncha, cm'on, comin',* and *goin'?* Help them see that these forms, though nonstandard in writing, are a normal part of speaking.

- Cautiously conduct a study of swear words. When and where do kids swear? How do they know when to turn it on and off?

- Have students role-play language use in various settings: a college professor lecturing a class; a business executive discussing quality control; three ten-year-olds setting up a club; a public address announcer at a football or basketball game; a disk jockey on any of the following stations: oldies, mellowies, country and western, fifties rock'n'roll, hard rock. Have the students discuss the language range and usage employed.

- Do imitations. First caution students that these will be done in the spirit of inquiry, not to make fun of anybody. Then ask them to present imitations of dialects, along with impressions of famous people. Although the imitations may not be linguistically flawless, they provide excellent data for discussion of dialects. How does a person imitate Texan, Appalachian, or New England dialects? What are the speech characteristics of John Wayne, the President, and Kermit the Frog?

- Let a boy and a girl do improvisations of the same role: a business executive worried about the stock market, an angry parent, a person applying for a job, a person trying to find directions in an unfamiliar setting. How do they approach the task differently? How much of this could be attributed to the individual's personal style (John is generally quiet; Mary is socially energetic), how much to male/female role and language differences?

- Create slang dictionaries. The more diverse your class, the better this project will turn out. Have students collect slang or colloquial expressions that separate kids from adults.

- Explore written, or "eye," dialects whenever they come up in literature. How do authors represent various speech patterns? Do these mesh with the kids' understandings (and imitations) of the same dialects? Roger Shuy (1974) has provided an excellent list of possibilities:

Norwegian/English: John Van Druten's *I Remember Mama;* Ole Rölvaag's *Giants in the Earth.*

Yiddish: Arthur Kober's "That Man Is Here Again" and "Bella, Bella, Kissed a Fella"; Leo Rosten's *The Education of Hyman Kaplan,* Bernard Malamud's *The Natural,* and Saul Bellow's *Herzog.*

Chicago Irish: Finley P. Dunne's *Mr. Dooley Says* and James T. Farrell's *Studs Lonigan.*

Tennessee: Mary Murfree's *In the Tennessee Mountains* and Mildred Haun's *That Hawk's Done Gone.*

Quaker: Jessamyn West's "The Battle of Finney's Ford" and Mable Hunt's "Little Girl with Seven Names."

The novels of Chester Himes, Richard Wright, and Ralph Ellison provide avenues for the exploration of Black dialects.

- Explore dialects through recorded literature. Check your school or local library for writers reading their own works. Frequently this will not only give you a sample of the author's dialect, but of the author portraying his/her conception of somebody else's dialect as well.

- Explore dialects through television. In particular, have students watch the news for a week, tape recorder nearby, to catch interviews with speakers of noticeable dialects. Use this raw material for further discussion of how dialects work.

- Conduct a unit in which students explore their own language roots. Although they may not be able to track their own family all the way back to non-English-speaking members, they certainly can learn of the linguistic trails left by their cultural/ethnic group. What languages did your American ancestors speak? What countries did they come from? What part of the country did they settle first? What English words come to us from the language of your ancestry? How did those words become part of American English?

- Discuss linguistic prejudice. Very likely your students will have some, overtly or covertly. What impressions do they have of speakers of a Southern dialect, a Boston or Yankee dialect, Brooklynese, English, Irish, German, Indian, or Jamaican? Help them see ways of separating people from their dialect.

- Study the origins of punctuation rules. Do students know why a period was once called a "full stop"? Why the comma was a "half stop"? Given the origins of these marks as signals for pauses, help students think about their own recurring punctuation problems.

- Spend some time reviewing the history of English spellings. Help students understand how English spelling became regularized and why, because of its diverse linguistic origins, English spelling is so maddeningly inconsistent in the first place. Some students might like to read up on the various efforts that have been made over time to simplify English spelling and purge it of its oddities. Why have such efforts failed despite their logic? From this unit, have students create a personal list of spelling demons and try to figure out why particular words give them problems.

- Have students explore community attitudes toward language varieties. Let them develop a list of common variations or perceived errors in language and ask people to describe their reactions.

- Much has been written and said about the employability of speakers of nonstandard dialects. Have students in your class survey employers to discover what expectations and demands employers have for workers with various jobs.

- Learn about the English Only movement and its efforts to establish English as a national language. Also contact the National Council of Teachers of English for information on English Plus and its view of the use of varieties of English.

- Above all, from this study of grammar[3], help each student in your class develop an understanding of his or her language. In a journal or notebook students might write about:

  o Their own dialect. Everybody has one. What's yours?

  o Where their dialect(s) stand on the social/political scale. Do they have a prestige dialect? one that is regarded as nonstandard for business or college?

  o How their dialect represents themselves, their heritage, their culture.

  o What (if anything) they feel they need to do to change their dialect. (Tread carefully here: Do not force students with nonstandard dialects to pledge erasure. To the contrary, we'd be most happy if, at the end of this unit, students said, "I am pleased with the way I talk.")

  o Recurring problems they have with written English, not just dialects, mechanics, or spelling, but problems getting ideas down on the page.

  o Their own opinion on movements like English Only or efforts to enforce the use of Standard English on all students.

Chapter Twelve

A Curriculum for George Orwell

A half-century ago George Orwell argued that "the English language is in a bad way" in his now-classic essay, "Politics and the English Language" (1946). He was especially concerned about language abuses, which he felt were leading to a blurring of thought, particularly in politics. Muddled language, he said, reflected muddled and outright deceptive thinking, and citizens needed to be on the alert for it. In *1984*, Orwell continued his exploration of language and thinking through the genre of fiction, showing a society whose language was controlled by Big Brother to make antigovernment thinking impossible, whose citizens were trained in "doublethink": the ability to hold and discuss two contradictory ideas simultaneously.

Although Orwell's gloomy prophesies for 1984 did not come true, most observers of the language agree that the abuses he described are still rampant, accentuated by our global communications network. Even today a committee of the National Council of Teachers of English presents a Doublespeak Award to a politician or bureaucrat who utters the worst bafflegab during a year (and there are plenty of candidates). The committee also bestows a more prized Orwell Award for clear and precise use of the language.

George Orwell accurately described a vicious cycle. The English language "becomes ugly and inaccurate because our thoughts are foolish, but the slovenliness of our language makes it easier for us to have foolish thoughts." He was not ready to give up hope, however: "The point is, the process is reversible."

In the previous chapter we discuss the nuts and bolts of grammar, dialects, and usage, but we also need a chapter dedicated to George Orwell to place those concerns in a broader context, that of language in society. As important as matters of correctness may be, it seems to us far more important that children (and adults) come to have a sensitivity to language, a knowledge and awareness of how it functions.

When we see students struggling with writing, unable to write the fabled "cogent, coherent essay," when we see them reluctantly stand up to mumble a vaguely formed opinion, then we see a problem far greater than grammar and correctness.

To some extent, inarticulateness and euphemistic language are a negative byproduct of content and experience: that is, language users sometimes waffle about because they aren't experienced in the world and haven't had much of an opportunity to put ideas in language. That problem is the topic of the first two sections of this book and can be partially cured through a good composition and literature program, where kids have lots of opportunities to read, talk, and write about ideas that range from personal experience to world issues.

But there's an element of language awareness and experience that's important as well. As S. I. Hayakawa pointed out in his language classic, *Language and Thought in Action* (1990), a great many adults don't have the foggiest notion what language is all about. They confuse words— mere symbols—with the objects they stand for. They use name calling as a substitute for rational discourse. They can't follow the semantic implications of discussions. They are vulnerable to the simplest linguistic tricks of propagandists or advertising agencies.

Our "curriculum for George" is, in effect, a program to increase language consciousness and awareness. We think it's important for young people to develop a sophisticated understanding of the complexities of language. There are hundreds of exciting activities one can use in the English/language arts classroom to help students understand the nature and functions of language. Not only are these activities engaging in their own right, they have both indirect and direct payoff in helping students read, write, speak, and even think more clearly, articulately, and powerfully.

Language fun and games

Mrs. Jaypher

A poem to be read "sententiously
and with grave importance":
Mrs. Jaypher found a wafer
Which she stuck upon a note;
This she gave the cook.
Then she went and bought a boat
Which she paddled down the stream
Shouting: "Ice produces cream,
Beer when churned produces butter!
Henceforth all the words I utter
Distant ages thus shall note. . . . "
Edward Lear (1812-1888)

To Make an Amblongus Pie

Take 4 pounds (say 4½ pounds) of fresh Amblongusses, and put them in a small pipkin.

Cover them with water and boil them for 8 hours incessantly, after which add 2 pints of new milk, and proceed to boil for 4 hours more.

When you have ascertained that the Amblongusses are quite soft, take them out and place them in a wide pan, taking care to shake them well previously.

Grate some nutmeg over the surface, and cover them carefully with powdered gingerbread, curry-powder, and a sufficient quantity of Cayenne pepper.

Remove the pan into the next room, and place it on the floor. Bring it back again, and let it simmer for three quarters of an hour. Shake the pan violently till all the Amblongusses have become of a pale purple colour. . . .

Edward Lear

Edward Lear knew just about as well as anybody that language is fun and games. It's important for teachers not to forget the important role that language *play* has in our mastery of English. Both adults and children enjoy the humorous use of language—puns, riddles, jokes, rhymes, puzzles, and satire. Children naturally create humor through language, and they respond to it with ease, without the intervention of teachers or instructors.

Language play goes well beyond humor, for most successful users have a sense of "the play of language," a feeling for words and language that allows them to explore and exploit the richness of English to make their meaning clear. The following sampler of games will give you some of the possibilities.

Word games

- Jumbles. Many newspapers carry anagrammatic jumble or word-search puzzles, challenging the reader to unscramble words or to find words in a maze of letters. These games are challenging for students but also deepen their understanding of the language, including the mysterious patterns of English spelling which make *lyknoplamatic* a possible English word while *lzqorywamatic* is not. After students have played some of these games, invite them to create their own (thus revealing that they have intuited and generalized from the rules).

- Hink-Pink. In this game, students create a rhyming adjective-noun combination and provide its definition, with other students trying to guess the rhyme. For example, a *chief of police* is a "top cop", a *foolish hitchhiker* is a "dumb thumb." A Hinky-Pinky expands the number of syllables so that a *tax on pulchritude* becomes a "beauty duty." Try the Hinkety-Pinkety for *tree surgeon* ("organic mechanic"), or the Hinketetie-Pinketetie for *middle-European farmer* ("Bavarian agrarian"). For sophisticated teachers only, a *New Yorker's whiskey cabinet* (we knew you'd come up with "Knickerbocker liquor locker" for that Hinkety-something).

- My Gramma's Game. My gramma likes apples, not oranges; books, not magazines; floors, not ceilings; pillows, not beds. When the clues are written out, you can see that gramma's preference is for words with double letters. Let your students create their own "gramma likes" games with words that begin with vowels, have three syllables, contain a silent letter.

- Odd Person Out. Who doesn't belong in the following list? (1) J. Randolph Adams, (2) P. Nelson Kennedy, (3) C. Quacken Bush, (4) D. Edward Blake, (5) L. Clark Grant. (Number 4 does *not* contain the name of a president.) Or (1) Grace H. Iverson, (2) Rachel S. Turner, (3) Diana A. Nelson, (4) Alice B. Croft, (5) Janice K. Long. (All except number 3 have names in alphabetical order.)

- Panagrams. A panagram contains every letter of the alphabet: "The quick brown fox jumped over the lazy dog." That panagram requires thirty-five characters to get in twenty-six letters, and language gamesters have delighted in trying to write shorter ones, such as:

  "Pack my box with five dozen liquor jugs" (thirty-two).

  "Blowzy frights vex and jump quick" (twenty-eight, but hardly recognizable as English).

  "Waltz, nymph, for quick jigs vex Bud" (twenty-eight, but requiring a proper name to squeeze in all the letters).

- Single-Letter Words. Try this quiz with your students: What letter of the alphabet is a bug? (B); a beverage? (T); a vegetable? (P); something to look with? (I); a cry of surprise? (O); to be in debt? (O); the person one speaks to? (U). These do not exhaust the possibilities; your students can find more.

- Teakettle. Have your students develop lists of homonyms: sea/see, bark/barque. Then have them make up sentences in which the homonym is replaced by the word *teakettle:* "I will row my *teakettle* (*barque*) and pick up the *teakettling (barking)* dog."

- Spelling and Vocabulary Games. While the purpose of language games is expressly *not* to overwhelm the students with instructions about language, we must point out that a great many language games also *teach.* Scrabble reinforces vocabulary and spelling and pushes students into exploring new words. The old parlour game GHOST does the same: Participants sit in a circle and add letters to a one-letter base; the person who cannot think of a letter that would lead to but not actually complete a word is the loser and receives a penalty letter from the word G-H-O-S-T.

● Punctuation Games. In *Fun with Words* (1972), Maxwell Nurberg poses some of the following punctuation puzzlers:

  ○ Punctuate the following, once as a request for information, once as an insult: *Whats the latest dope*

Answers: "What's the latest dope?" "What's the latest, dope?"

  ○ Punctuate the following so that it invites one to take a plunge:

Answer:

Exploring the alphabet

Our colleague Diana Mitchell brought a number of children's alphabet books to her junior high school class and asked the students to discuss how writers go about presenting the alphabet. Sometimes, for example, the writer will give an object for each letter (*A* is for Apple; *B* is for Ball). Another strategy is to combine words beginning with particular letters in what's known as an Alphabettor: "Avery's animals attacked altogether, biting bees, bears, and birds, caught and captured by Cooley's cautious company . . . " Diana's students then developed and illustrated their own alphabets to share with younger children.

Other alphabet activities include:

- Study the origins of the English (Roman) alphabet. How did it emerge from drawings and hieroglyphics?

- Study weirdnesses in English spelling. Create your own list of spelling demons, the words people *always* seem to get wrong, and figure out why these particular character combinations cause problems. We nominate *necessary* and *traveler* to get you started. Students might also discuss spelling rules such as "*i* before *e*, except after *c*" and determine why that rule works.

- Have the class propose some simplified spellings. Tell them that for years, the *Chicago Tribune* tried to get "through" spelled as "thru," but called it quits when the idea didn't catch on. Why do we cling to our odd spelling system?

- Bring in a guest speaker of Chinese or Japanese and have that person explain how these are word/symbol languages rather than alphabetic. Ask them to explain how a Chinese typewriter works or to discuss the debate in Japan over the use of the Roman alphabet to represent traditional Japanese words.

Language and pictures

Many teachers have their students write *concrete poetry* (or *pattern poetry*), in which the poem is shaped to represent the topic (a flower poem is shaped like a flower, for example). For an excellent resource, look for Milton Klonsky's *Speaking About Pictures: A Gallery of Pictorial Poetry from the Sixteenth Century to the Present* (New York: Harmony Books, 1975). It reveals a number of sophisticated art/word combinations. Lavonne Mueller of DeKalb, Illinois, took concrete poetry a step further and had students create a three-dimensional "word museum" for the school library (*The English Journal,* May 1974). The students studied examples of visual language—pictographs, hieroglyphs, etc.—then created three-dimensional word renderings. *Wax* was created from chunks of candle wax, left in the sun to melt. *Boxed in* came as a series of Chinese boxes. Fun and games? Certainly. But Mueller reports that in the process, students' understanding of the relationship between symbol and object—word and thing—grew enormously.

Language and/in society

Beyond the sensitivity to language that can be gained by simply playing with words and letters, students need to explore how language functions in the world around them. We've had good success having students keep a journal or notebook of *Gleanings* (a concept and term we got from Leslie Pratt at Delta College in Michigan). Students comb newspapers and magazines for uses of language that strike them as interesting, clever, deceptive, important, imaginative. As a term or semester goes along, they become sensitive to new forms of the word in the world. We shift the focus of *Gleanings* from time to time, so that students look one week for samples of advertising language, another for humor, a third for political language.

The language of advertising

Someone has said that advertising language is the poetry of our time. Poets can't support themselves writing poetry, but an imaginative advertising writer can play with the language and make goodly bucks. Further, because so much money rests on advertising, writers tend to be very precise and careful in their research. In an advertising unit, you can have your students explore:

- Radio and television ads. With an audio or video recorder, they can capture good ads and analyze their content. What makes an ad effective? Who is the audience? What have the students purchased recently as a result of media ads? A guest speaker from the ad industry might give your students some inside stories. Also have your students create their own ads on tape.

- Billboards. Talk about them. What makes them eye-catching? How do they use words, color, and white space? Study the language carefully for cleverness and poetry. Look at the integration of art and language. Perhaps your students can create billboards (or at least posters) putting some of their knowledge into action to promote a school event or cause.

- Classified ads. Here is a gold mine of fascinating language, some of it effective, some of it not. Study the real estate ads. What does "needs work" mean as a house description? "Handyman special"? "Priced to sell"? "Price reduced"? Examine the language used to sell used cars.

What's being revealed and hidden by the language? What's going on in the personals? Under pets?

- Jingles. What advertising songs or jingles do the students have lodged in their brains? Have they ever gotten stuck singing or reciting one over and over? How many slogans and jingles can they list on the board? How does this use of language help to sell goods and services?

- Magazine ads. Look especially for clever uses of language:

  o "Ever wonder what your panties say behind your back?" (Pantyhose)

  o "The quickest way to a man's heart is through his feet." (Slippers)

  o "Who could make light of themselves better?" (Low-tar cigarette)

- Truth in advertising. Have your students read the fine print and check out the claims of advertisers. What does it mean to say that Chevy is "the heartbeat of America"? What's going on in those Ford/Chevy truck comparisons? What do advertisers promise? What don't they promise? Students can do especially fruitful analyses of advertising disclaimers: "Batteries not included." "Don't do this with your own automobile."

- Waffle words. Many ads use words that seem to make a claim but do not. Thus to say "No toothpaste gets teeth whiter than Bright-O" implies actually states that this product is no better than any other. Words like *new, improved, whiter,* and *better* leave out comparisons that would make realistic assessment possible. By collecting waffle words, students can become more sensitive to the abuse of language, not only in advertising, but in other kinds of language use as well.

Languages of the mass media

This topic is a book unto itself, especially given the role of television in young people's lives. Any contemporary medium—newspaper, film, radio, magazines, television—can provide material for many weeks of study, indeed should be an underlying problem for analysis from September to June. Some questions to ask about any mass medium:

- Who pays the bills? What is the relationship between the interests of the bill payers and the audience?

- What does this medium do especially well (e.g., report current events, comment on long-range trends, entertain, inform)? What does it do less well?

- What are the best uses of this medium today? Have your students create their own awards for the medium you are investigating, designing categories for awards, then finding winners.

- What point of view does a particular medium present? Can you detect bias in the perspective being offered by, say, a particular radio station or newspaper?

- How does people's behavior change as a result of exposure to this medium?

- How could the quality of the medium be improved?

- What are the dangers of mind control implicit in the medium? (Have your students write a consumers' guide to television, radio, or news-papers.)

If possible, get the owner/manager/program director/editor of a local medium outlet to come to your class to talk with the students about his or her perception of the influence of that medium on young people and adults today.

Language and mind control

Some antidoublespeak activities for your classroom:

- Let kids write doublespeak, the most abominable, two-faced, misleading prose they can manage. This activity is *not* meant to justify the use of doublespeak, but to help students understand it through actual use. Encourage the students to see what happens when they use long words where short ones would do (consult the thesaurus for possibilities), when they avoid calling things by their customary terminology, preferring to employ or utilize euphemistic synonymetrics. The ground rules for writing (or not writing) doublespeak were supplied by Orwell himself in "Politics and the English Language" (the essay is often anthologized in college language textbooks).

- In election years collect statements from politicians. Have students analyze precisely what is being promised, what *seems* to be promised, what is mere puffery. (Save those clippings for use in nonelection years.) Turn off the sound on political television commercials and read the candidate's lips and visual imagery. What's being said through body language and graphics that is not being said in words? For an exercise in the political process, have your students invite a candidate to an open forum at the school to answer their questions.

- Have students write essays arguing opposite sides of an issue. After-ward, have them describe what happened in their minds as they argued the cause in which they didn't necessarily believe. If they're experience is common, they may have found themselves employing language in the heat of battle that they would customarily find inap-propriate and even deceitful.

- Collect newspaper articles and political columns. Analyze their use of rhetoric and persuasive language. What flaws and oversimplifica-tions do the students detect? Have them write their replies in the form of letters to the editor.

- Encourage your students to identify a cause or problem around the school or your community that requires action. Then have them develop proposals, editorials, and letters urging people in power to adopt their ideas. Along the way have them look carefully at their own efforts to shape people's minds. Have them analyze replies from the people in power as well.

- Conduct a unit on "big ideas." What are the major ideas that have shaped society in the past five or ten years? Then have the students read some of the materials that helped promote those ideas. Good topics for examination would be the women's movement, environ-mental consciousness, the latest war or "skirmish" or "military incur-sion."

- Study trends, fads, and ideas popular among young people the stu-dents' own age. Where do these ideas come from? Who persuades young people that these are good things to do? What sorts of mass marketing or mass persuasion techniques are employed? What are the major ways in which people with ideas reach school age young-sters?

- Conduct a unit on "Issues for a Better Tomorrow." Have students think carefully about what they see as the most important problems for their generation to solve. Who is going to do the solving? What role do your students see for themselves in controlling their destiny? What role will their *language* play in acting out that scenario?

The meaning of meaning

It's important for students of all ages to engage in the analysis of language in daily use—collecting examples of doublespeak, assessing the media, analyzing ads, and so forth. But to place our "curriculum for George" on a solid foundation, one needs to go further, helping students gain an understanding of the nature of language and how it is shaped by human thought. Some classroom activities:

- Let students play with the difficult task of defining *language*. What is language? Where does it come from? How does language mean? How do words mean? What does *meaning* mean? Have students choose any common word, (possibly a word from their own slang or lingo) and define it as fully as possible. How did this word acquire its consensual meaning?

- Have kids speculate about how the world would change if communication changed. What if there were no face-to-face conversation and we had to communicate by writing? Or what if there were no writing, only talk? Only TV and no telephone? No telephone, only the old-fashioned telegraph? The new-fashioned fax? What if we communicated only by gestures, not words? Or if we communicated directly, omniscient mind to omniscient mind? You can do this activity in several ways, including having students write science fiction, role-play, or even try to solve actual problems using one medium of communication rather than another.

- Ask your students to keep a one- or several-day log of their encounters with language. What language forms (speech, writing, media) do they encounter most frequently? What ideas and information enter through those various sources? What means of "languaging" do they choose to use most frequently?

- Assign the task of expressing a strong opinion without using words. Students may use images (drawn or photographed), gesture, or music to get across the idea. In what ways, if any, does composing in a nonverbal medium *enhance* our ability to communicate? How does wordless communication slow us down?

- Explain how lexicographers gather *citations* of words in actual use in order to create their definitions. Then have students choose a common word—*walk, run, sleep, car*—and collect citations for a week or more. Pool all these examples and then create a definition based solely on these particular examples. How, if at all, does their definition differ from that of the dictionary?

- As part of a journal writing assignment, have students explore one of their strong biases or prejudices. Where did this come from? What words do they associate with it?

- Have students collect words that are used to demean racial and ethnic minorities: *nigger, wop, spic, dago, kike*. How do these words distort perceptions? Have the students track down the origins of these terms in a good dictionary.

- As a class project, have the students create a new mystery word, say, calling a hamburger a *snurfburn.* Then have your class use the word, without telling others what it means. What is the response of outsiders? How long is it before other people pick up on the mystery word and start to use it themselves?

Chapter Thirteen

Language Across the Curriculum

n Chapter 11 we take up the specifics of teaching grammar and correctness. In Chapter 12 we enlarge our view of "language" to include a range of linguistic adventures and inquiry, giving students a full understanding of language and its functions in their lives. Here we want to expand the perspective once again to show that "language" is not only a unifying concept for the teaching of English, but offers a way to view the whole school curriculum coherently.

Of course, each discipline has the potential to offer such coherence. Ask a scientist/science teacher what's the most important subject in the curriculum and you'll quite likely hear, "Science: because it deals with the central processes of coming to know and understand the world around us. What could be more fundamental than that?" Ask a history person and you'll hear, "History: because without it, people have no sense of the past, present, or future." A humanities/social science teacher might make the case for *people* and their *values* and *culture* as the center of the curriculum, while a mathematician might argue that *number* and processes of *computation* underlie virtually all human activities. We understand and value such claims and visions; in fact, we would like to see more mathematics-across-the-curriculum, more science in every classroom, increased attention to history and people in other studies.

But the fact remains that school studies are largely fragmented along disciplinary lines, kindergarten through college. And we believe that language has the greatest potential for providing unity and synthesis, for language is arguably the most important as well as the most common of the disciplinary common denominators.

Language already *is* in every classroom in the world, whether that classroom is presently concerned with numbers, dates, or science and technology. We note that in recent years the idea of competence in various fields has been linked to ours, so that one hears of the need for increased scientific *literacy*, mathematical *literacy*, historical *literacy*, and so on. To explore competence in their fields, subject-area teachers draw on ours, asking students to speak or write about what they know.

But enough of the disciplinary provinciality, ours and theirs.

A history lesson: about two decades ago, the "language across the curriculum" movement emerged as a cry for help from English/language arts teachers. We realized that students needed to do more reading and writing (as opposed to more study of grammar). They couldn't get enough practice in their elementary language arts block or their secondary English period. Do more writing in the disciplines, we pleaded, so students will get the practice they need. Do more reading across the curriculum so students will see there is more to books than the stories and plays they read in language arts.

To this cry, many teachers replied, "No thanks. I've got to cover material of my own." But in the 1970s a few people made deliberate efforts to increase the amount of language use in their math, science, social studies, health, geography, and physical education lessons, and they discovered an astonishing thing: when students read and write imaginatively in other disciplines, their learning in those disciplines increases dramatically.

As a result, we in English have broadened our claim. Instead of simply asking for support, we make a bold assertion: Pay attention to language; teach it in your classes; and your students will learn *more*. Further, we have come to discover the value of including the disciplines in our own classes. It turns out that allowing students to read and write about science, math, history, health, and physical education in the English/language arts block also increases students' appreciation of our field. From this symbiotic relationship, then, has grown what we call the *interdisciplinizing of English*. We've discovered that *whole language* really means *whole learning*, that *writing from experience* can include the experience of a science experiment or of devouring a history book, that *personal reading* can include a computer handbook as well as an adolescent novel.

English/language arts teachers have thus become leaders in a movement that seems to be taking place in all disciplines: a push toward breaking down the barriers, toward merging disciplinary concerns and issues.

As we write, the future of interdisciplinary language arts and language across the curriculum is up in the air. On the one hand, we see great progress in many elementary classrooms toward whole language/ whole learning approaches; we see an extraordinarily strong push toward interdisciplinary studies taking place at the middle school level; and we see pockets of interdisciplinary, language-centered teaching in the high schools and colleges. On the other hand, the dominance of disciplinary learning is very powerful and we see "whole language" elementary schools where kids still drag home deadly dull social studies texts with stupefying study questions; we see middle schools that really yearn to be "junior" high schools, focusing on disciplinary learning rather than the needs and interests of adolescents; and for every team of secondary/college teachers crossing disciplinary boundaries, we see many more individual faculty hanging on to discipline-centered teaching, with language reduced to a mere tool for testing rather than employed as a mode of learning.

The English/language arts teacher who likes the sound of language across the curriculum must be prepared to teach flexibly. To begin with, we should continue to focus on ways of interdisciplinizing our own classes: by including interdisciplinary readings in the language arts library, by letting students explore topics in many fields and disciplines, by helping them learn to write successfully about their knowing and learning in any field. At the same time, we need to seek opportunities to cross disciplinary lines: to merge social studies, geography, and language arts units in the elementary grades; to form connections and collaborations with colleagues at the higher grades.

Our teaching ideas in this chapter are designed to be used both ways and at many different levels. They provide a sampler of possibilities that we hope you will find useful in extending your own teaching across the curriculum.

Science

Like using language, science is a matter of observing, synthesizing, and describing the world. Make connections between science and language arts by helping students discover the role that language plays in learning and communicating about the natural world. Students can:

- Keep science logs, recording observations about the natural world, commenting on them, synthesizing their understanding. Opportunities for such observation and writing happen every day in every classroom. What are those specks of dust floating in sunlight? Why is bubble gum so difficult to get off your shoe or out of your hair? How do pencils work?

- Measure the arrival of a season and record its onset in a class notebook or scrapbook with measurements, observations, and even artifacts such as a fallen leaf or a spring flower.

- Prepare scripts for a series of scientific demonstrations for the class on, say, gravity or buoyancy.

- Collect newspaper articles showing modern science at work, mount them on posterboard or construction paper, and write explanations of the scientific principles and processes involved.

- Watch *Mr. Wizard* or similar science demonstration shows on television and discuss or reproduce some of the experiments.
- Watch science documentary programs on public or educational television channels and use these as the starting points for individual study or research.
- Participate in a "Science Soapbox," featuring minidebates (oral or written) on the moral and human implications of problems like nuclear power, environmental protection, or genetic engineering.
- Design inventions to make people's lives better, publishing a *Book of Needed Inventions* as a final project.
- Develop better written components for school science fair projects, writing explanations, not just labels.
- Investigate and write an explanation of why something *doesn't* work right: the kitchen blender, hot water heater, automobile engine.
- Interview a magician, learn some of the secrets behind magic's illusions, and present findings on how magicians seem to defy the laws of science.
- Research and write science fact sheets for younger students, or start a "Science Facts" column in the school newspaper or newsletter.
- Read and write about the history of current technology, say, from pencil to word processor, from door latch to voice identification lock.
- Research and write about careers in science; study colleges that have strong science programs.
- Write imaginary letters to the legendary figures of science: Curie, Pasteur, Galileo; or write scripts about great moments in their careers; or role-play visits of those people to class.

Mathematics

In math, as in language, people translate their perceptions of the world into symbols. In some ways we envy the world of math, where symbols hold constant meanings, where $2 + 2 = 4$ is a more precise statement than Noun + Verb = Sentence. Nevertheless, math students must use real words and our wonderfully idiosyncratic language in order to understand and communicate concepts. Your students can:

- Write explanations of difficult math concepts so others can understand them. (Surprise! Your students can write more user-friendly explanations than the authors of the adopted math text.)

- Interview local business people about how mathematics works in their area: the auto shop, the bakery, the insurance company. Have students write a book of *Real World Math.*

- Write a recipe book, including necessary measurements and calculations.

- Prepare a booklet of *Fun and Games with Math,* including puzzles, problems, perplexities, and conundrums; or, write a column with that title for the school newspaper or parent/teacher newsletter.

- Design their own story problems, much more imaginative than the dull ones in their textbook, and write up answers. (See Cathy's caloric calculations in Figure 13–1 for an example.)

- Read about the internal workings of calculators and computers and write an explanation.

- Research home computers and prepare a consumer buying guide.

- Investigate the role of mathematics in a career they might pursue, whether fire fighting or singing in a rock'n'roll band.

- Invent a better monetary system and put it into operation in a class or school simulation.

- Research and update school sports records or keep a sports statistics book.

- Perform a talk show with the giants of mathematics: Euclid, Pythagoras, Leibnitz, Newton.

- Write limericks about those worthies: "A math man named Euclid was grumpy. . . . "

Figure 13–1 ○ "Cathy" (9/7/87), by Cathy Guisewite

Social studies

This area (which includes history, economics, government, and civics) offers perhaps the most natural connection with English/language arts studies, for it's rich in writing and reading topics of interest to students of any age or interest level. Many of the early attempts to link the disciplines centered on "core" language arts/social studies programs. Your students can:

- Read, read, read: fiction, poetry, drama, nonfiction on issues in government, society, human affairs. (What work of literature *isn't*, in some way, a social science treatise?) Using literature can engage students in firsthand understanding of ideas and issues in ways far more complex and rich than your schoolyard-variety social studies book.

- Write, write, write: fiction, poetry, drama, nonfiction on the problems and circumstances of human affairs.

- Keep logs and journals instead of conventional notebooks, recording their responses and reactions to historical ideas and events.

- Launch letter-writing campaigns to elected officials expressing well-researched opinions on current events and problems. (Be sure to proofread.)

- Investigate the judicial system and write an explanation for younger learners.

- Study the history and present and future prospects for their community, neighborhood, or school.

- Start a cable news network for the school or community public access system, presenting a capsule of school, local, or world news.

- Read and write to participate in simulation games: the colonialization of America, the oil supply, international economics. Or, study an issue or problem and create a board or simulation game that represents it.

- Research their family tree, which could involve correspondence with relatives, interviews, analysis of family documents.

- Research, discuss, and write about any current local issue, and forward the results to the appropriate governmental officials.

Art and music

As Susanne Langer (1957) eloquently reminds us, human beings are *symbol makers,* and that includes symbols other than words. The fine arts clearly offer avenues for expression of some of the same human ideas, experiences, and emotions that are covered by English/language arts. Students in these areas can:

- Keep response journals about the art they view and the music they hear, recording reactions before moving on to analysis and history. In the fine arts as well as English, perhaps too much time has been spent teaching about form and technique, too little in helping students explore their own assessments and evaluations.

- Research and write about modes and techniques of expression in art: painting, sculpture, folk art and craft. What does each medium permit in the way of self- and artistic expression? What are the limitations of each? Students might conclude by writing illustrated how-to books for newcomers to an art form.

- Write a guide to old and/or obsolete musical instruments. What every happened to the glass harmonica or the shawm?

- Explore electronic art and its capabilities: the synthesizer, computer art. Students might even compose music on the computer, then show their creations to the class. Further, many computers now have multimedia capabilities that allow students to link image, music, and words in creative ways.

- Write a descriptive essay exploring representations of visual experiences in another medium—for example, word paintings, sound paintings. What can be portrayed in words that cannot be shown in graphic art or music? What can be included in a painting or musical composition that cannot be "talked about"?

- Read biographies of major artists and composers.

- Create an arts billboard for the school or local closed circuit television system, with announcements of coming attractions, reviews of those past.

- Find pieces of art and music to accompany their favorite pieces of literature; compile multimedia anthologies of literature and art; create scripts to enact the great ideas of music and art; draw and paint to illustrate their own writing.

Foreign language

The connection between foreign languages and English study runs far deeper than merely mastering the grammar of one language or another. Foreign language study deepens the understanding and appreciation of language in general and helps students understand linguistic and cultural differences. Students can:

- Keep journals in the foreign language—a record of day-to-day experiences. Such a journal should *not* be graded for grammatical correctness; rather it serves as a way of increasing fluency, n'est ce pas?
- Create a foreign language joke or riddle book.
- Study words in English derived from the foreign language and prepare a display.
- Translate some of their own (short) writing into the target language. (Such a practice encourages them to learn, in the language, the words and phrases and structures they most commonly use in their native tongue.)
- Correspond with a pen pal using the foreign language.
- Study the debate over bilingual instruction and English Only. Where do they stand?
- Read foreign language newspapers and prepare summaries (in the language) for posting on the board.
- Write in English (or the target language) about the customs, life, and culture in the home country of the language.
- Do improvisations in the language, very simple at first, moving toward full fluency.
- Prepare language lessons for younger children; tutor young learners; read aloud to them and translate.

Health and physical recreation

Yes, jocks, there is a connection between language and sports. You can ask students to:

- Write rule books for popular sports.
- Develop how-to books for newcomers to a sport.
- Conduct surveys of coaches or team members about the projected success of Little League, Pony League, or high school teams.
- Report on athletic contests for the school newspaper—not just the usual score-plus-exciting-moments gruel, but carefully crafted essays analyzing the game and its outcome.
- Write a *Brown Bag Lunch Book* including interesting and nutritious alternatives to PB&J.
- Study food systems management—the school cafeteria, home, a local restaurant. How does food get from field to table?

- Study the human heart, both scientifically and metaphorically, in essay, poem, song, or story.
- Investigate and prepare reports on drugs, alcohol, rest, exercise, nutrition.
- Design and illustrate a lifelong exercise/nutrition plan.
- Read sports biographies, autobiographies, fiction, nonfiction.
- Write critical reviews of fad diets.
- Investigate and report on science and sports: sports medicine, the physics and biology of sports, sports psychology, and scientific training methods.
- Study the language of sports in the locker room and in the daily newspaper.

Applied arts

The so-called practical fields of schooling are ideal for interdisciplinary language arts work. Language is an underlying element in fields as diverse as home economics, driver education, industrial arts, and business. Using contemporary techniques of language arts instruction, teachers can make such courses genuinely engaging. Students can:

- Write a book of rules of the road for other students coming into driver education, or prepare posters and displays of automotive concepts.
- Read the business page and follow up on current trends reported in the newspapers.
- Visit local businesses to see how reading and writing play a role. Visit government offices for the same purpose.
- Design and play a simulation game based on a problem in business and industry.
- Study new materials being used in industry and speculate how new plastics and alloys may be used in the future.
- Research technological developments in industrial fields and explain how industry is changing in our time.
- Research specific careers and write introductory guides on how to prepare for the career of your choice.
- Compile a guide to good writing in the area or field.

- Design and implement things: woodworking projects, school government, field trips, a new school newspaper or literary magazine, a statue or memorial for the foyer.

- Write how-to books on all manner of topics: cooking, sewing, using power tools, taking pictures, making maps, developing photographs.

Potpourri

Here are some ideas for the self-contained or interdisciplinary classroom or for any teacher who might find them useful. Have students:

- Listen to speakers brought to school because of their particular knowledge across the disciplines.

- Foray into the library and browse the stacks, looking for topics they'd like to know more about.

- Write plays dramatizing important moments in intellectual history. (What *did* George Washington's daddy say about that felled tree?)

- Visit community institutions that can shed interdisciplinary light on a topic: universities, museums, libraries, businesses and industries, possibly even garage sales.

- Devise scientific experiments to explore areas where their book learning leaves them in doubt.

- Read and write prophesies and predictions.

- Read and write about a community problem; propose solutions.

- Investigate the ecology of their town, its natural and human ecologies.

- Research a decade—the Gay Nineties, the Roaring Twenties, the Radical Sixties—noting its contributions across the disciplines: art, music, sport, literature, history, economics.

- Write a letter a week (or month) to a real person: political leader, newsmaker, hero or heroine, rock or film star, scientist.

- Write biographies of prominent citizens.

We rest our case for the English/language arts as the core discipline or field from which extraordinarily exciting curriculum-wide teaching can develop.

Summary and Troubleshooting

Four Sentence Diagrams From Nightmare Abbey

From time to time we dream about professional matters, and such dreamy nights often give us pause for reflection the following day. Following the advice of dream psychologists who advocate self-analysis, we keep pencil and paper on the nightstand and write down dreams that powerfully affect us.

About the time we were finishing work on this section of the *Handbook*, we had a particularly restless night, with creatures from the darkside dashing around in the corners of our mind. In the course of one nightmare, there were revealed to us four sentence diagrams that raise important issues about the teaching of language. We present them here as we recalled them by dawn's early light, along with our commentary and analysis.

Diagram 1

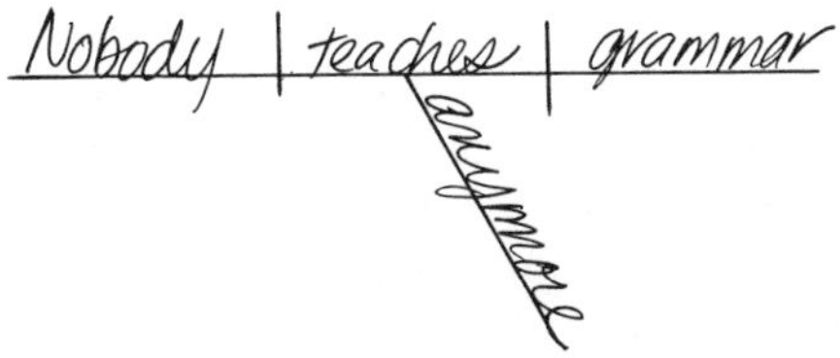

Nobody teaches grammar anymore.

This diagram reflects a common misperception among parents, newspaper editorialists, and even some teachers. Of course grammar is taught (and learned), as every native speaker of English intuitively knows. But *grammar* in this context means more than simply learning how to understand the language (a monumental accomplishment in its own right). It is a stand-in for the broad feeling that the schools are failing, the economy is falling apart, and language is in decay. (Don't we wish that grammar study could turn around a falling stock market?)

The trick for teachers who have studied the nature of language is to persuade their various audiences that newer approaches to English/language arts teach grammar in all sorts of ways: through reading, writing, listening, speaking.

Should we teach formal grammar on top of that? Our feeling is that a little grammar and maybe even a little sentence diagramming is not fatal. But does it bring about the changes in language that it has traditionally promised? Most native users of the language know the answer to that one, too.

Diagram 2

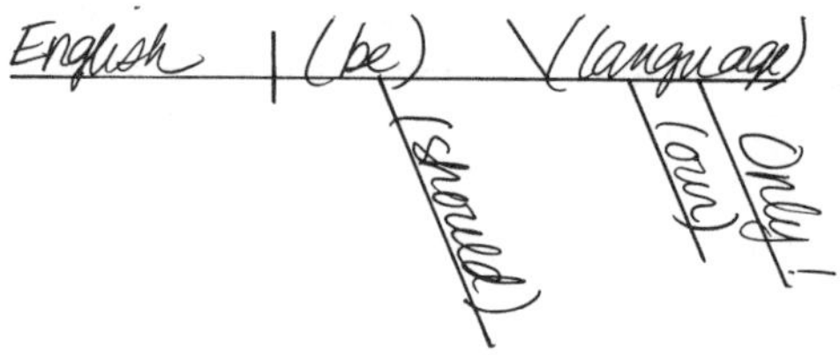

English Only!

The English Only movement, designed to establish English as the legislated "official" language, is certainly a nightmarish one, having achieved enormous support in almost half the states in the union. We can be confident that the laws about official language will not influence the languages people use (unless, of course, the nightmare of a linguistic police state comes about). But English Only is having the effect of limiting bilingual programs that give nonnative speakers a fighting chance to learn core subject matter in their own language even as they master their new or target language. Further, the English Only movement strikes us as being xenophobic and foolishly nationalistic. Despite denials by the advocates of English Only, there is strong evidence of racism in their motives as well.

What can we do about it? For one thing, we can be politically active, supporting such groups as the National Council of Teachers of English and its subgroup Support for the Learning and Teaching of English

(SLATE) in their efforts to fight English Only laws. One can also join in the countermovement, English Plus, which argues that every child has the right to learn to speak more than one language successfully.

Less dramatic, but more important, perhaps, is for us to make our own classrooms truly multinational and multicultural in the literature we use and to treat nonnative speakers as a resource rather than a pedagogical nuisance.

Diagram 3

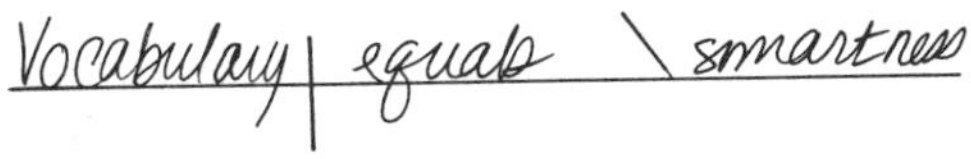

Vocabulary | equals \ smartness

Knowing lots of words makes one intelligent.

The lure of vocabulary teaching is great, and one sees "vocab" units in virtually all commercial textbooks and a great many school curriculum guides. We're not "against" vocabulary and recognize that there probably is a modest correlation between the number of words we know and our "smartness" or knowledge base.

But in the schools we often get the equation turned around, so we teach words out of context, in isolation, thinking that if kids master the vocabulary list, their grasp of the world will be improved. At its most extreme, we can see this equation reversal in E. D. Hirsch's concept of "cultural literacy." His five thousand bits of information that every American "should know" are essentially vocabulary items, and cultural literacy advocates operate under the delusion that teaching list mastery will enculturate young people.

How, then, do we build vocabulary? How do kids master the cultural literacy lexicon?

We argue that they must acquire the language through their own experiences in the world, including the world of reading and writing. Knowledge, smartness, and education should, at best, come about as students engage with their world and their community. Vocabulary emerges as an enabling tool that allows students to employ their language in the processes of knowing and understanding.

Diagram 4

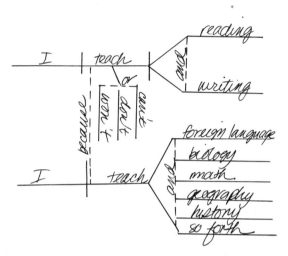

I won't, don't, or can't teach reading and writing,
because I teach another discipline.

The language-across-the-curriculum movement has certainly been a frustrating one for teachers of English/language arts, especially at the college and high school levels where departmentalization dominates.

For years, English teachers implicitly offered a view that language and content and idea were three separate things, that (for example) you could study word lists to learn a subject, you could display language in sentence diagrams without regard to the content, you could pass laws that make people change the way they talk.

If there's any single message to be delivered in this section of the *Handbook,* it's that language growth, development, and usage are naturalistic and inseparable from the content of human experience.

Teachers of other disciplines *do* "teach" language, whether or not they say they can or will. The only question is whether they're going to do it well or badly. Or to rephrase that, whether they're going to use language as a tool and ally or as an obstacle to learning.

The best way we know to help the unwilling or the doubting is to get them doing some writing and reading about their own subject matter, keeping journals about what goes on in their classes, and writing articles and reading essays about issues in the field that matter to them. As teachers of history, science, and mathematics read and write for real, they come to see the potential for language use in their own classes.

In this general area, we expect progress to be slow; we expect our nightmare to recur. In the meantime, we're having a wonderful time teaching language across the curriculum in our own self-contained English classes, inviting students to bring in and read and write about concerns in the worlds of science, business, politics, sports, computer science, medicine, law, education, and the like. When colleagues from other fields accuse us of poaching on their discipline, we invite them to poach on ours by becoming interdisciplinary teachers of reading and writing.

f · i · v · e

The Profession of Teaching

his final section of *The English/Language Arts Handbook* contains just one chapter (plus a letter). Yet it focuses on one of the most important and elusive concepts in education: *professionalism.* We describe some of the "peripherals" (to borrow from computer terminology) that connect with our day-to-day teaching. Like computer add-ons, many of these have the potential to contribute to our work and to our students' learning, but like computer add-ons that don't match your system, they can also lead to serious complications and malfunctions.

Chapter Fourteen

Colleagues, Collaborators, and Contraries

etting along in a school or school district is no easy task, whether you're a student teacher coming in for the first time or a grizzled veteran of twenty years or more. Like any institution, a school system is made up of people, and those people aren't cogs in a machine that always perform predictably (then again, the cogs in our aging family car don't always perform predictably, either). People have special interests, deeply held convictions, personal needs, and these don't always correspond ideally with those of fellow teachers along the corridor. People were hired into the system at different times and for different purposes. The length of time they plan to remain with the school will vary widely and affect their day-to-day performance.

In this chapter we discuss the difficult topic of *human* and *personal relationships* for the English/language arts teacher. We do this, not by offering advice on how to get along with your neighbor, but by discussing three major groups (other than students) with whom the teacher needs to work: administrators, parents, and colleagues. In each case we focus on the positive: steps and strategies that you can initiate to maximize your effectiveness as a teacher within a human institution.

Working with school boards and administrators

In our teaching lifetime, we've seen a dramatic shift in the relations between teachers and the people who hire them and oversee their work: the board and its administrators. As recently as twenty-five years ago, the relationship was one of *community.* The principal of the school served as a schoolhouse mother or father, overseeing day-to-day operations and serving as an intermediary between the teachers and the school board, the latter a cordial group of "family relations." That admittedly idealized relationship has changed, so that today school boards are often suspicious of teachers and their motives, and the principal is more likely to be seen as a middle manager of a business enterprise than as a pedagogical *pater-* or *materfamilias*.

The reasons for this shift are sociologically and economically complex, but two trends stand out in our minds:

1. *Teachers engaged in collective bargaining.* When we first entered teaching in the 1960s, teachers' unions were rare and were, in fact, regarded as unprofessional by many teachers and community members. Unions were something that construction workers and coal miners and truck drivers belonged to. Yet, as many perceptive educators noted, for teachers to act as if they were members of a kindly and supportive family was not paying off: salaries and teaching conditions were bad, and "the family" wasn't doing anything to change the status quo. Unionized school districts made important gains for their teacher/union members, but along the way, the board of education became the opposition. Familial chat between teachers and board members became difficult, because each side had its list of negotiable and nonnegotiable items; each decision became a precedent for future decisions; each concession by either group became locked into a contract. Principals could no longer afford to be our pals, because they were part of management, not labor, and sat on the opposite side of the negotiating table from the teacher reps. On the whole, we think the gains earned by the unions far outweigh the losses, but it's important to note that one major loss has been the ease of communication between teachers, administrators, and the board.

2. *The American people began to doubt the effectiveness of their school system.* Actually, they began to doubt a great deal more than that, including their ability to compete on the international industrial scene, their ability to fight and win a moral war, the strength of their economic system, and the ethics of their national leaders. Much of their frustration became focused on the schools, so we have experienced a twenty-year period in which the public has increasingly felt that its schools (and its teachers) aren't getting the job done. Teachers work in an atmosphere of distrust and, increasingly, in a system where their performance is likely to be judged through legislatively mandated tests, curriculum guidelines, and minimum standards of performance.

These shifts in relationships have been especially difficult for English/ language arts teachers, for ours is the subjective discipline, the *human/ humane* discipline, whose aims, goals, and dimensions are difficult to describe and assess. Sure, we could write a curriculum based on grammar terminology, spelling lists, literary names and dates, and correctness in writing, and such a curriculum would be accountable to and testable by local, state, and even national examinations. But we also know that such a program would not, in the long run, produce the highly literate citizens that teachers and parents want. There is, then, a built-in communications gap between what teachers want and what the people who elect and stand to serve on the school board want.

To avoid painting too gloomy a picture, we add that positive trends have taken place over the same period of time. In general, school boards are less benign than they were in the good old days, and they think closely and carefully about what they want to have happen in their system (never mind that sometimes the thinking is driven more by fear of lawsuits than desire for quality learning). In addition, patterns for curriculum reform and development have become clarified so there is potential for a more clear and orderly creation of new programs than there was in the old days, when curriculums were often little more than gentleperson's agreements on who taught what class or level based on whatever books the school had available in class sets.

The following ideas are designed for individual teachers but they will more likely be put into practice by groups of teachers working in concert. Ways of developing that "concert" will be described later.

- Develop a program to inform school boards and administrators of new developments in English/language arts. Routinely invite board members to participate in workshops, conferences, young author conferences, and the like. (In a survey he conducted for the National Association for Curriculum Development, Stephen [Tchudi, 1990] learned that among schools that had been the most successful in developing exemplary English programs, many had routinely followed this practice.)

- Create a newsletter for parents and administrators that describes and illustrates the aims and new directions of the language arts program.

- Ask the board to establish literacy as a priority for the school district, then use that declaration to work for needed support for new programs.

- Engage the board in textbook selection processes. In particular, educate the board and administrators to possibilities for English/language arts teaching that do not require the costly adoption of texts.

- Lobby with the board for increased materials for literacy instruction. Make comparisons between district allocations for computers, footballs, and reading materials.

- Ask for an in-class library for every language arts classroom in the district.
- Educate the board and administrators about the successes and failures of the current literacy programs. Write to the National Council of Teachers of English and obtain the names of schools and districts that have received awards for excellent programs and/or curriculum guides. Prepare point-by-point comparisons with your school district and draw these to the attention of board members and administrators.
- Take the issue of class size for language arts teachers to the board. Review the current research and resolutions of the National Council of Teachers of English concerning ideal numbers of pupils for English/language arts teachers. Whether or not you achieve smaller class size, use this occasion to enlighten the board about modern teaching practices.
- Enlist the aid of the school administration in seeking outside funding for English/language arts programs. In these days of tight fiscal constraints, school boards are likely to help programs that show signs of helping themselves.
- Get the board to establish awards for student excellence in English/language arts: good readers, good writers, good speakers.

Parents and community members

The board members *do* represent the community, and in our experience, school board members generally do raise the same sorts of problems and questions as those of community members. Thus, many of the projects suggested in the previous section are intended to engage the community on the side of English/language arts instruction. Beyond those, try some of the following:

- Sponsor articulation meetings where parents are invited to learn more about what is happening in the English/language arts program. (Alas, often only a small number of parents will come to such sessions, with the parents who could profit most from the meeting not among those to be counted.)
- Therefore and alternatively, hone the *English/Language Arts Newsletter* to reach parents and tell them what they need to know. Among good questions for either articulation meetings or the newsletter are:

- ○ What are college entrance examinations like and what do scores mean?
- ○ Why don't language teachers mark every error like they did when I was a kid?
- ○ Whatever happened to grammar?
- ○ What books should my children be reading?
- ○ How dangerous are books?

- Find ways to involve community service groups in the literacy program. Ask the Rotarians, the Kiwanians, the Elks and Moose to adopt a classroom or a school and find ways to supply it with supplementary reading materials.

- Educate yourself about how to get news in the local paper. Learn the name of the education editor and send in information on your latest projects. Learn how to write press releases that will draw attention to your program and/or get you free advertising on local radio and television channels.

- Start a parent volunteer program, with lots of publicity accruing to parents and other citizens who contribute time as tutors, as teacher aides, or even as collectors and compilers of books or book lists.

- Create a no-fee writing workshop for parents, an authors' circle where parents can bring work in progress for supportive discussion. (You won't have a large turnout, but you will unleash some caged writers!)

- Identify community members who have specialties that bear on English/language arts. (What specialty doesn't, actually?) Bring a steady stream of speakers to your school to discuss the language aspects of their work, whether that be politics, advertising, manufacturing, retail, or public service.

- Send out a call for community members to contribute subscriptions to needed magazines for school or classroom libraries.

- Find out about the newspapers-in-education program of your local paper and arrange for a steady flow of newsprint into the school.

- Engage parents in the cause of literacy at home. Both the National Council of Teachers of English and the International Reading Association have pamphlets designed to help parents do a better job of supporting reading and writing at home. Obtain copies of those materials or (better) write your own list of ideas and send it home via the newsletter. Among ideas to recommend for parents:

- Create opportunities for open-ended conversation and discussion (the old-fashioned family dinner hour, for example).
- Play word games with kids.
- Read aloud to children; encourage them to read aloud to one another, older to younger or vice versa.
- Tell stories to children; develop a family core of oral yarns.
- Fill the home with reading material: newspapers, magazines, books, pamphlets.
- Encourage letter writing instead of long distance telephone calls.
- Provide appropriate help with reading and writing homework (with guidelines provided by teachers).
- Create a home reference library with almanacs, dictionaries, a one-volume encyclopedia, a usage/spelling guide.
- Help kids design study areas for reading, writing, and homework in general.
- Take kids to the library and help them find books to read for pleasure.
- Give books as gifts.
- Don't worry overmuch about grammar and correctness.
- Help children establish guidelines for television viewing. Discuss television programs with your children.
- Write a letter to the editor of the local newspaper; when it's published, show your children how writing can lead to public expression.
- Talk about the language requirements of your vocations and avocations.
- Volunteer as a parent tutor in a school or community literacy program.

Teacherly colleagues

The day Steve began his student teaching in a Chicago city high school, a fellow teacher verbally attacked him because his alma mater, Northwestern University, was removing sand dunes from Indiana in order to build a campus extension into Lake Michigan. Such was not an auspicious beginning to collegiality.

Yet, we've discovered over the years the extraordinary value of colleagues, even those with whom we disagree over matters as major or minor as teaching sentence diagramming or mining the Indiana dunes. As we said in the Introduction, the ideas we present here are not all original with us. We've shared our problems with other faculty members and gotten helpful solutions; we also think we've contributed our fair share of possible solutions to others' classroom dilemmas. There's no substitute, in our minds, for the day-to-day learning that goes on in the schoolhouse as dedicated teachers offer ideas to one another in a community of learners.

But, as we said earlier, faculties are not uniform in interest and commitment. Most of the old pros in teaching are agreed that you have to select your close colleagues carefully, that you can't work with (or reform) everybody in the building. Thus, in our own work, we've done our best to be cordial to everyone, to listen to what every colleague has to say, but to design projects and activities that encourage, even *force* us to collaborate with people who have things to teach us.

Some suggestions for developing the faculty community and professionalism:

- Use departmental meetings for more than business; hold them in noncrisis times to:
  - Propose new ideas, programs, classes, and units.
  - Forge collaborative relationships among faculty members.
  - Develop strategies to strengthen relationships with the school board, administrators, and community members.
- Create a shared file of teaching units (identified with appropriate restrictions to prevent people from "scooping" one another's best ideas).
- Develop a newsletter for parents and community members.
- Develop a proposal for a weekly or monthly page of student writing in the local or neighborhood newspaper.
- Launch a campaign for more literacy materials in every classroom.
- At the secondary level, invite colleagues from other subject areas to attend language arts meetings and to present the problems they encounter with literacy; at the elementary level, set aside time at faculty meetings to hear, in depth, about what people are doing in their classrooms.
- Create a faculty writing circle where people can bring drafts of any kind of writing, from professional journal submissions to a family history.

- Create a faculty reading circle where you discuss a book a month, preferably something read for pleasure, not for professional reasons.
- Establish a used paperback exchange in the faculty lounge.
- Throw out month-old magazines in the faculty lounge; this is not a dentist's office.
- Make certain the school has subscriptions to major periodicals in English education and related fields (some are listed under Professional Resources). Assign individual faculty members the responsibility of scanning one journal a month and recommending good articles to the others; we are obviously too busy to read everything we should.
- Build up a faculty library with important books in English/language arts. (Our Bibliography includes not only the books we've referred to in the text, but books we believe ought to be available to all teachers of English.)
- Ask for funds to refurbish the teachers' lounge and/or the English office. If that fails, at least redecorate with posters, book jackets, kids' writing, or photographs of classes.
- Create a buddy system for new teachers, student teachers, teacher aides. Don't leave newcomers feeling as if they are outsiders. Give them more than a guide to the book room when they first show up. (At the same time, spare them your personal opinions about the faculty ogres; let them form their own opinions.)
- Start a volleyball team, basketball team, softball team. At the very least, hold a faculty croquet match.
- Fight for funds to support travel to professional conferences. Make certain the union keeps this as an item in negotiations.
- Ask for funds to bring good consultants to your school, from good teachers in the next town to national specialists in an area that interests your faculty. Consultants should not be expected to supply the last word or easy solutions to your problems; at best they will prod and poke at your thinking and assumptions and encourage you to stretch out in new directions.
- With or without funds, join and support local, state, and national organizations of teachers. Get on committees. Attend and help plan for conventions, conferences, and meetings.
- Become a teacher/researcher. Whenever you start a new class or course, jot down a few basic research questions about your curriculum, your students, your methods. Systematically collect data all term long, and when the dust has settled and grades have gone in,

spend the necessary time to study and write up your findings. Type up your conclusions on a page or so and share them with colleagues.

- Write for professional journals. It's not as difficult to get published as many teachers think. In fact, many teaching journals actually prefer solid teacher narratives and reports of teacher research to the customary academic gobbledygook.

- And don't forget kids-as-colleagues. By this we do not mean that you should become buddy-buddy with the kids. But your students are, after all, your best resource for learning about teaching. They are the final test you must pass. With the kinds of methods we have described in this book, it's easier than it used to be to *enjoy* kids, to *appreciate* them as human beings and as writers and readers. Granted, they will drive you everywhere from up the wall to stark raving crazy, but as a teacher of young people you (and we) are in a wonderful position to study, appreciate, learn from, and teach a great bunch of minds.

Summary and Troubleshooting

Letter to a "Young" Teacher

n 1932, Virginia Woolf published *A Letter to a Young Poet,* a book whose lead essay shared Woolf's views on contemporary poetry with a would-be poet. The letter that follows is in that tradition.

Dear "Young" Teacher,

Let's begin by saying what we mean by *young.* Age has nothing to do with it.

A few years back we wrote a book called *The Young Writer's Handbook,* which we designed for "young" writers aged eight to eighty, give or take a few years at either end. That book, like *The English/Language Arts Handbook,* was dedicated to people who are young in spirit, not necessarily in age or experience.

You are a young teacher because, one way or another, you find it possible to approach teaching afresh each day—or more realistically, four days out of five. You would rather not teach this year's students by the tried-and-true (or tried-and-wanting) methods and strategies of last year or fifty years ago. You assess students initially and finally on their personal growth, not on stereotypes or clichés.

It's not easy to remain young in our business. As a student teacher or first-year teacher arriving on the scene, you are often told, "Ignore everything they taught you in college. You're in the real world now. You'll wise up when you see what this place is really like."

Add a wrinkle or two to your forehead.

You go to the principal and request funds for this or that: a new literary magazine for the writing club, more paperback books, a computer for the advanced composition class. The reply: "We respect your enthusiasm and think it's wonderful that you have all these innovative ideas, but we don't have the money and frankly don't see why you can't make do with the handbooks we bought you a few years ago."

Add a sprinkling of gray hairs to your scalp.

You have great ideas about developing a thematic interdisciplinary unit for your students and want to spend some extra time in the library digging out resources. Instead, you are called to a meeting to explain why your students didn't show improvement on Objective 9 of the state assessment.

Add more wrinkles and gray hairs, the latter surrounding a bald spot created by pulling your hair out.

Yet, young teachers are all around us. Just the other day we attended a writing project board meeting where teachers of all ages enthused about a writing magazine they were developing for school district kindergartners, an interdisciplinary physical education/writing course being offered for teachers, some explorations in interdisciplinary writing across the curriculum, and new ideas for making statewide assessment more useful for teachers and parents. How does it happen that beneath the increasing wrinkles, gray spots, and bald spots, some teachers remain young?

There aren't any formulas, of course, and what follows is a very short list of two suggestions. To the extent we've managed to remain young, we've operated under these two principles.

Remain experimental. In writing her "Letter to a Young Poet," Virginia Woolf advised:

> Write then, now that you are young, nonsense by the ream. Be silly, be sentimental, imitate Shelley, imitate Samuel Smiles [a nineteenth-century popular writer and journalist]; give rein to every impulse; commit every fault of style, grammar, taste, and syntax; pour out; tumble over; loose anger, love, satire, in whatever words you can catch, coerce or create, in whatever meter, prose, poetry or gibberish that comes to hand. Thus you will learn to write.

Now you can't afford to be quite so flamboyant in your teaching, if only because your "products" are kids, not scraps of writing that can be tossed away if the experiment fails. But the spirit of Woolf's remarks strikes us as right: try *anything* that seems appropriate, possible, desirable, interesting, and (we add) responsible. What is *not* known about teaching English/language arts is considerable, and the most crucial discoveries will be made by classroom teachers, not necessarily by university researchers.

Elsewhere we've written about the idea of the teacher/researcher, one of the most energizing, liberating ideas to come along in education in some time. As a teacher/researcher you will, like Woolf's young poet, try many new things, but you will also collect data and evidence to determine whether or not the experiments are yielding the kinds of growth you predicted. In this way, you will successfully combine youth *and* experience.

Be institutionally savvy. Institutions—public or private, non-profit or profit—are often bizarre places to work. Despite the human beings who make them go, institutions are inanimate and impersonal. You may have loved your college profs, but singing the college fight song is, in the end, like pledging allegiance to a brick wall. Institutions breed bureaucracy, regulations, layers of ineffectiveness (including the new breed of management specialists whose job is to simplify things).

At first glance, many schools seem to rule out possibilities for the sort of experimental teaching we've described in *The English/Language Arts Handbook.* But we've discovered through years of practice that there are ways individual teachers can work in, through, around, about, and ultimately *over* just about any school bureaucracy.

To begin with, the cliché remains true: "The classroom is your castle." This is not meant to imply that you should run your class as a private kingdom, but it does suggest that day in and day out, you're quite free to organize and structure the way you wish. Sure, there are standardized exams that have to be taken, grades that must be given, a curriculum that needs to be covered. But even within those constraints virtually no school system limits how you approach the task of teaching; and even in the most rigid of systems, there's no effort to control the essential dynamic of teaching: the teacher/student relationship.

Beyond that, because schools are chronically underfunded and English/language arts classes are further underfunded within that system, you need to become a specialist in what we call the dirt-cheap alternative. You can't get the school to fund an in-class library? The dirt-cheap alternatives include learning how better to use the resources of school or public libraries, getting kids to find books on their own, or bringing in supplies yourself. The district won't set up a computer laboratory for English students? Poems, plays, imitations of Shelley, satire, and gibberish can be composed with the dirt-cheap pencil—imagination, not hard disk capacity, is the limiting factor.

"Rules were meant to be broken," goes the cliché. We offer an alternative: "Rules were meant to be understood." Concretely, this means that when the district mandates the teaching of formal grammar, you as a savvy teacher figure out that what is wanted is not so much knowledge of parts of speech as kids who write and speak Standard English. Understanding that rule, you increase attention to editing in peer-group workshops and teach parts of speech as necessary to help kids master tough usage items. (Down the hall, your colleagues are either breaking the rule by doing nothing with grammar or following it slavishly, in neither case helping students very much.)

In short, institutions often provide far more latitude and opportunity than you might suppose, and we urge you to find the ways to achieve what you see as important despite institutional constraints.

Virginia Woolf closed her letter this way:

> So long as you and you and you, ancient representatives of Sappho, Shakespeare, and Shelley, are aged precisely twenty-three and propose—O enviable lot!—to spend the next fifty years of your lives in writing poetry, I refuse to think that the art is dead.

Far from being dead, the art of teaching language is alive and well in the hands of you young teachers, who—O enviable lot!—have the power and potential to be the most successful practitioners in our profession the world has ever known.

Professional
Resources

 hat follows is a list of major professional organizations and publications we think can be of help to the teacher of English/language arts. It makes no claim at comprehensiveness; however, each of these organizations and publications has proven helpful to us more than once in our careers as teachers.

Organizations

The National Council of Teachers of English, 1111 Kenyon Road, Urbana, IL, 61801.

NCTE can be somewhat baffling to a newcomer because of its Byzantine structure of sections, commissions, conferences, committees, and assemblies. Suffice it to say that one of the great virtues of NCTE is that it offers publications and study groups to suit almost any teacher's individual interest.

Upon joining NCTE, the new member also becomes a member of a section—elementary, secondary, or college—and receives a subscription to a journal, *Language Arts* (primarily for elementary teachers), *The English Journal* (for secondary teachers), or *College English.* For additional fees, one can subscribe to more than one journal or to one or several of the Council's other publications such as *English Education* (principally for college English education teachers and school supervisors), *College Composition and Communication, Research in the Teaching of English,* and *Teaching English in the Two Year College.* (A particularly good buy is NCTE's comprehensive membership, which includes subscriptions to *all* those journals plus a copy of books published by the Council during the membership year.)

Probing further into NCTE, one finds assemblies, including several that might be especially interesting to readers of this book:

The Assembly on Literature for Adolescents

Assembly on Science and Humanities

Children's Literature Assembly
English as a Second Language Assembly
Junior High/Middle School Assembly
Whole Language Assembly

Most assemblies have low dues and depend very much on the vigor and enthusiasm of individual members.

State and Regional Affiliates of NCTE

By writing NCTE, you can also make contact with your state, regional, or even local affiliate. These organizations vary greatly in size but are at the very heart of English education activity nationwide. Area affiliates usually have modest dues, hold one or more annual meetings, and provide numerous committees and activity groups for the professionally minded.

Other National Organizations

Many nations other than the United States have vigorous national organizations, in particular:

Canadian Council of Teachers of English
National Association for the Teaching of English (U.K.)
Australian Association for the Teaching of English
New Zealand Association for the Teaching of English

These organizations, along with the National Council of Teachers of English, are members of the International Federation for the Teaching of English, which promotes exchanges of information among the member nations and their national organizations. U.S. teachers who are interested in international English studies should also consider joining the International Assembly of NCTE, which has close ties with, but is not identical to, the International Federation.

National Writing Project, School of Education, University of California, Berkeley, CA, 94720.

The NWP is not something that teachers join directly; you become involved by participating in summer and year-round programs sponsored by local NWP sites, now numbering over 150 in the United States and worldwide. You can write to Berkeley or ask around to learn of activities in your region. In addition, some states have independent writing projects; these include the Michigan Writing Project, the Iowa Writing Project, the Illinois Writing Project, and the New Jersey Writing Project.

The International Reading Association, 800 Barksdale Road, P. O. Box 8139, Newark, DE, 19714.

IRA publishes *The Reading Teacher* for those interested in reading at the preschool and elementary levels, and *The Journal of Reading* for those at the secondary level. Like the National Council of Teachers of English, it also publishes a wide range of books and monographs on various aspects of its field, which, in recent years, has broadened to include writing and oral language as well as reading. IRA has a particularly strong network of affiliates or local reading "councils" that allow for direct involvement in your immediate area.

Institute for Democracy in Education, 119 McCracken Hall, Ohio University, Athens, OH, 45701.

This group looks beyond the friendly confines of the English/language arts classroom to discuss learning across the disciplines. It is particularly dedicated to student and teacher empowerment, encouraging both to be decision makers within the institution.

National Association for Core Curriculum, 404 White Hall, Kent State University, Kent, OH, 44242.

"Core" curriculums, frequently a blending of history/social studies/ English, have been around for almost half a century. This organization is not only concerned with these kinds of interdisciplinary programs, but with the concept of core or general education learnings as well.

National Association for Science, Technology, and Society, 117 Willard Building, University Park, PA, 16802.

NASTS is a vigorous interdisciplinary group dedicated to getting more concern for values into math/science curriculums and for making connections between math, science, and the humanities. English/language arts teachers interested in this area should also consider joining the Assembly on Science and Humanities of NCTE, a group that is also affiliated with NASTS, thus promoting language as a fulcrum for reducing the distance between the two cultures.

Publications

Agora, P. O. Box 10975, Raleigh, NC, 27605.

An outstanding interdisciplinary magazine designed for high-ability junior and senior high school students, combining literature, science, and the arts through interdisciplinary perspectives.

Holistic Education Review, Box 1476, Greenfield, MA, 01302.

An impressive professional journal with an emphasis on integrated, holistic teaching and learning.

The Horn Book, 14 Beacon Street, Boston, MA, 02108.

This journal focuses on books for children, with articles by writers on their own work, author and illustrator profiles, and information on how to use the books in the classroom. The annual July issue features profiles on the Newbery and Caldecott award winners.

Instructor, P. O. Box 2039, Mahopac, NY, 10541.

A general, hands-on, nuts-and-bolts magazine with lots of practical teaching ideas, sometimes more gimmicky than substantial. It's not enough to keep you going September to June, but it certainly helps out with good what-shall-I-do-now ideas.

Learning, Box 2589, Boulder, CO, 80321.

Another general magazine with a focus on elementary and lower secondary school. It includes teaching ideas, research studies in plain language, trends and issues in education, teacher opinion surveys, and discussions of social issues and problems affecting the schools.

Bibliography

ABBS, PETER. *English Within the Arts.* London: Hodder and Stoughton, 1982.

ADAMS, MARILYN JAGER. *Beginning to Read: Thinking and Learning About Print.* Cambridge, MA: MIT Press, 1990.

ANDRASICK, KATHLEEN. *Opening Texts: Using Writing to Teach Literature.* Portsmouth, NH: Heinemann, 1990.

APPLEBEE, ARTHUR. *Tradition and Reform in Teaching English.* Urbana, IL: National Council of Teachers of English, 1974.

ASHTON-WARNER, SYLVIA. *Teacher.* New York: Simon and Schuster, 1963.

ATWELL, NANCIE. *In the Middle.* Portsmouth, NH: Boynton/Cook, 1987.

BARNES, DOUGLAS, et al. *Language, the Learner, and the School.* Portsmouth, NH: Boynton/Cook, 1989.

BARR, MARY, PAT D'ARCY, and MARY K. HEALY. *What's Going On? Language/ Learning Episodes in British and American Classrooms, Grades 4–13.* Portsmouth, NH: Boynton/Cook, 1982.

BASKWILL, JANE, and PAULETTE WHITMAN. *A Guide to Classroom Publishing.* Toronto: Scholastic, 1986.

BAILEY, RICHARD and ROBIN FOSHEIM, eds. *Literacy for Life.* New York: Modern Language Association, 1983.

BAYER, ANN. *Collaborative-Apprenticeship Learning: Language and Thinking Across the Curriculum, K-12.* Mountain View, CA: Mayfield, 1990.

BERTHOFF, ANN E. *Forming/Thinking/Writing,* 2nd Ed. Portsmouth, NH: Boynton/Cook, 1988.

———, ed. *Reclaiming the Imagination: Philosophical Perspectives for Writers.* Portsmouth, NH: Boynton/Cook, 1984.

BERLIN, JAMES. *Rhetoric and Reality.* Carbondale, IL: Southern Illinois University Press, 1987.

———. *Writing Instruction in Nineteenth-Century American Colleges.* Carbondale, IL: Southern Illinois University Press, 1984.

BISSEX, GLENDA. *GNYS at Work: A Child Learns to Read and Write.* Cambridge, MA: Harvard University Press, 1980.

BISSEX, GLENDA and RICHARD BULLOCK, eds. *Seeing for Ourselves: Case Study Research by Teachers of Writing.* Portsmouth, NH: Heinemann, 1987.

227

BOOMER, GARTH. *Fair Dinkum Teaching and Learning*. Portsmouth, NH:
Boynton/Cook, 1985.
———. *Metaphors and Meanings*. Hawthorn, Victoria, Australia: Australian Asso-
ciation for the Teaching of English, 1988.
———. *Negotiating the Curriculum*. Sydney: Ashton Scholastic, 1985.
BRADDOCK, RICHARD, et al. *Research in Written Composition*. Urbana, IL:
National Council of Teachers of English, 1963.
BRANNON, LIL, et al. *Writers Writing*. Portsmouth, NH: Boynton/Cook, 1982.
BRITTON, JAMES, et al. *The Development of Writing Abilities, 11–18*. London:
Macmillan Education, 1975.
BRITTON, JAMES, ROBERT SHAFER, and KEN WATSON, eds. *Teaching and
Learning English Worldwide*. Multilingual Matters, Ltd., available through
the National Council of Teachers of English, Urbana, Illinois. 1990.
BUSCHING, BEVERLY A., and JUDITH I. SCHWARTZ, eds. *Integrating the Lan-
guage Arts in the Elementary School*. Urbana, IL: National Council of Teach-
ers of English, 1983.
BYRON, KEN. *Drama in the English Classroom*. New York: Methuen, 1986.

CALKINS, LUCY. *The Art of Teaching Writing*. Portsmouth, NH: Heinemann, 1986.
CAMBOURNE, BRIAN. *The Whole Story: Natural Learning and the Acquisition
of Literacy in the Classroom*. Auckland: Scholastic, 1988.
CHATER, PAULINE. *Marking and Assessment in English*. New York: Methuen,
1984.
CHOMSKY, NOAM. *Language and Mind*. Orlando, FL: Harcourt Brace
Jovanovich, 1972.
CHUKOVSKII, KORNEI. *From Two to Five*. Berkeley, CA: University of California
Press, 1963.
CLARK, ROY PETER. *Free to Write: A Journalist Teaches Young Writers*.
Portsmouth, NH: Heinemann, 1987.
CLEGG, A. B., ed. *The Excitement of Writing*. New York: Schocken Books, 1972.
CORCORAN, WILLIAM, and EMRYS EVANS, eds. *Readers, Texts, Teachers*.
Portsmouth, NH: Boynton/Cook, 1987.
COOPER, CHARLES. *The Nature and Measurement of Competency in English*.
Urbana, IL: National Council of Teachers of English, 1981.
COOPER, CHARLES, and LEE ODELL. *Evaluating Writing: Describing, Measur-
ing, Judging*. Urbana, IL: National Council of Teachers of English, 1977.
COPPERUD, ROY. *American Usage and Style: The Consensus*. New York: Van
Nostrand Reinhold, 1980.
CREBER, J. W. PATRICK. *Sense and Sensitivity in Teaching English*. London:
University of London, 1965. Reprinted by the Exeter Curriculum Study Cen-
tre, St Luke's, College of Education, Exeter, U.K.

DANIELS, HARVEY A., ed. *Not Only English: Affirming America's Multilingual
Heritage*. Urbana, IL: National Council of Teachers of English, 1990.
DANIELS, HARVEY, and STEVEN ZEMELMAN. *A Writing Project: Training Teachers of Writing from Kindergarten to College*. Portsmouth, NH: Heinemann,
1985.

D'ARCY, PAT. *Making Sense, Shaping Meaning: Writing in the Context of a Capacity-Based Approach to Learning*. Portsmouth, NH: Boynton/Cook, 1989.

DAVIS, JAMES, and JAMES D. MARSHALL, eds. *Ways of Knowing*. Iowa City, IA: Iowa Council of Teachers of English, 1988.

DEWEY, JOHN. *The School and Society*. Chicago: University of Chicago Press, 1956.

DIAS, PATRICK. "A Literary Response Perspective on Teaching Reading Comprehension," in Deanne Bogdan and Stanley Straw, eds. *Beyond Communication: Reading Comprehension and Criticism*. Portsmouth, NH: Boynton/Cook, 1990.

DIEDERICH, PAUL B. *Measuring Growth in English*. Urbana, IL: National Council of Teachers of English, 1974.

DILLARD, J. L. *Black English: Its History and Usage in the United States*. New York: Random House, 1972.

DIXON, JOHN. *Growth Through English*. Urbana, IL: NCTE/NATE, 1968. London: Oxford University Press (2nd edition), 1976.

DONALDSON, MARGARET. *Children's Minds*. New York: Norton, 1978.

DONOVAN, TIMOTHY R., and BEN W. MCCLELLAND, eds. *Eight Approaches to Teaching Composition*. Urbana, IL: National Council of Teachers of English, 1980.

DOUGLAS, WALLACE. *An Introduction to Some Basic Processes in Composition*. Evanston, IL: Northwestern University Curriculum Center in English, 1963.

DUKE, CHARLES. *Creative Dramatics and English Teaching*. Urbana, IL: National Council of Teachers of English, 1974.

DYSON, ANNE HAAS. *Collaboration Through Reading and Writing: Exploring Possibilities*. Urbana, IL: National Council of Teachers of English, 1989.

EAGLETON, TERRY. *Literary Theory: An Introduction*. Minneapolis: University of Minnesota Press, 1983.

ELBOW, PETER. *Writing with Power: Techniques for Mastering the Writing Process*. New York: Oxford, 1981.

ELBOW, PETER, and PAT BELANOFF. *A Community of Writers*. New York: Random House, 1989.

EMIG, JANET. *The Composing Processes of Twelfth Graders*. Urbana, IL: National Council of Teachers of English, 1971.

FADER, DANIEL, and ELTON MCNEIL. *Hooked on Books: Program and Proof*. New York: Putnam, 1968.

FARMER, MARJORIE, ed. *Consensus and Dissent: Teaching English Past, Present, and Future*. Urbana, IL: National Council of Teachers of English, 1986.

FARR, MARCIA, and HARVEY DANIELS, eds. *Language Diversity and Writing Instruction*. Urbana, IL: NCTE/ERIC, 1986.

FARRELL, EDMUND J., and JAMES R. SQUIRE, eds. *Transactions with Literature: A Fifty-Year Perspective*. Urbana, IL: National Council of Teachers of English, 1990.

FARRELL, PAMELA B., ed. *The High School Writing Center: Establishing and Maintaining One.* Urbana, IL: National Council of Teachers of English, 1989.

FREEDMAN, SARAH WARSHAUER, ed. *Response to Student Writing.* Urbana, IL: National Council of Teachers of English, 1987.

FREIRE, PAULO. *The Pedagogy of the Oppressed.* New York: Continuum, 1988.

———. *The Politics of Education.* South Hadley, MA: Bergen, 1985.

FOX, MEM. *Teaching Drama to Young Children.* Portsmouth, NH: Heinemann, 1986.

GALVIN, KATHLEEN, and CASSANDRA BOOK. *Person to Person in Speech Communication.* Skokie, IL: National Textbook Company, 1986.

GARDNER, HOWARD. *Frames of Mind: The Theory of Multiple Intelligences.* New York: Basic Books, 1983.

GENISTI, CELIA, and ANNE HAAS DYSON. *Language Assessment in the Early Years.* Norwood, NJ: Ablex, 1984.

GERE, ANNE. *Writing Groups.* Carbondale, IL: Southern Illinois University Press, 1987.

GOODMAN, KENNETH, et al. *Language and Thinking in School: A Whole-Language Curriculum.* New York: Richard Owen, 1987.

GOODMAN, KENNETH, YETTA GOODMAN, and WENDY J. HOOD, eds. *The Whole Language Evaluation Book.* Portsmouth, NH: Heinemann, 1988.

GOSWAMI, DIXIE, and PETER STILLMAN, eds. *Reclaiming the Classroom: Teacher Research as an Agency for Change.* Portsmouth, NH: Boynton/Cook, 1987.

GRAVES, DONALD. *Writing: Teachers and Children at Work.* Portsmouth, NH: Boynton/Cook, 1983.

GRAVES, RICHARD, comp. *Rhetoric and Composition: A Sourcebook for Teachers and Writers.* 3rd edition. Portsmouth, NH: Boynton/Cook, 1990.

GILLES, CAROL, et. al. *Whole Language Strategies for Secondary Students.* New York: Richard Owen, 1988.

GRUGEON, ELIZABETH and PETER WALDEN, eds. *Literature and Learning.* London: Ward Lock/Open University, 1978.

HALPERN, JEANNE, and SARAH LIGGETT, eds. *Computers and Composing.* Carbondale, IL: Southern Illinois, 1984.

HANSEN, JANE. *When Writers Read.* Portsmouth, NH: Heinemann, 1987.

HARRIS, MURIEL. *Teaching One-to-One: The Writing Conference.* Urbana, IL: National Council of Teachers of English, 1986.

HARSTE, JEROME C., KATHY G. SHORT, with CAROLYN BURKE. *Creating Classrooms for Authors: The Reading-Writing Connection.* Portsmouth, NH: Heinemann, 1988.

HAYAKAWA, S. I. *Language in Thought and Action.* Orlando, FL: Harcourt Brace Jovanovich, 1990.

HAYNES, ELIZABETH F. "Using Research in Preparing to Teach Writing." *English Journal* 67 (January 1978): 76–84.

HAYS, JANICE, et al. eds. *The Writer's Mind: Writing as Mode of Thinking.* Urbana, IL: National Council of Teachers of English, 1983.

HEATH, SHIRLEY BRICE. *Ways with Words: Language, Life, and Work in Communities and Classrooms.* Cambridge, U.K.: Cambridge University Press, 1983.

HILLOCKS, GEORGE, JR. *Alternatives in English: A Critical Appraisal of Elective Programs.* Urbana, IL: NCTE/ERIC, 1972.

————. *Research on Written Composition: New Directions for Teaching.* Urbana, IL: National Council of Teachers of English, 1986.

HIRSCH, E.D. *Cultural Literacy: What Every American Needs to Know.* Boston: Houghton Mifflin, 1987.

HOLBROOK, DAVID. *Children's Writing.* Cambridge, U.K.: Cambridge University Press, 1967.

————. *English for the Rejected: Training for Literacy in the Lower Streams of the Secondary School.* New York and London: Cambridge University Press, 1964.

————. *The Exploring Word.* Cambridge, U.K.: Cambridge University Press, 1963.

HOLDAWAY, DON. *The Foundations of Literacy.* Portsmouth, NH: Heinemann, 1979.

COOPER, MARILYN, and MICHAEL HOLZMAN. *Writing as Social Action.* Portsmouth, NH: Boynton/Cook, 1989.

HYNDS, SUSAN, and DONALD L. RUBIN, eds. *Perspectives on Talk and Learning.* Urbana, IL: National Council of Teachers of English, 1990.

ILLICH, IVAN. *Deschooling Society.* New York: Harper & Row, 1971.

JACKSON, DAVID. *Continuity in Secondary English.* New York: Methuen, 1982.

JENSEN, JULIE, ed. *Composing and Comprehending.* Urbana, IL: NCTE/ERIC, 1984.

————. *Stories to Grow On: Demonstrations of Language Learning in K–8 Classrooms.* Portsmouth, NH: Heinemann, 1988.

JOHNSON, BRIAN. *Assessing English.* Sydney: St. Clair Press, 1983.

JOHNSON, LIZ, and CECILY O'NEILL, eds. *Dorothy Heathcote: Collected Writings on Education and Drama.* Portsmouth, NH: Heinemann, 1984.

KIRBY, DAN, and TOM LINER. *Inside Out.* 2nd edition. Portsmouth, NH: Boynton/Cook, 1988.

KNOWLES, MALCOLM S. *Using Learning Contracts.* San Francisco: Jossey-Bass, 1986.

KIRSCHENBAUM, HOWARD, SIDNEY B. SIMON, and RODNEY W. NAPIER. *Wad-Ja-Get: The Grading Game in American Education.* New York: Hart, 1971.

KOHL, HERBERT. *A Book of Puzzlements: Play and Invention with Language.* New York: Schocken Books, 1981.

KOZOL, JONATHAN. *Illiterate America.* Garden City, NY: Anchor/Doubleday, 1985.

KUHN, THOMAS S. *The Structure of Scientific Revolutions.* Chicago: University of Chicago Press, 1962.

LANGER, JUDITH A., and ARTHUR N. APPLEBEE. *How Writing Shapes Thinking: A Study of Teaching and Learning.* Urbana, IL: National Council of Teachers of English, 1987.

LANGER, SUSANNE. *Philosophy in a New Key: A Study in the Symbolism of Reason, Rite, and Art.* Cambridge, MA: Harvard University Press, 1957.

LEE, DORRIS, and ROACH VAN ALLEN. *Learning to Read Through Experience.* New York: Appleton-Century-Crofts, 1963.

LLOYD-JONES, RICHARD, and ANDREA A. LUNSFORD, eds. *The English Coalition Conference: Democracy Through Language.* Urbana, IL: National Council of Teachers of English, 1989.

LUTZ, WILLIAM, ed. *Beyond 1984: Doublespeak in a Post-Orwellian Age.* Urbana, IL: National Council of Teachers of English, 1989.

MACRORIE, KEN. *The I-Search Paper.* Portsmouth, NH: Boynton/Cook, 1988.

MANDEL, BARRET, ed. *Three Language Arts Curriculum Models: Pre-Kindergarten Through College.* Urbana, IL: National Council of Teachers of English, 1980.

MARSHALL, SYBIL. *An Experiment in Education.* Cambridge, U.K.: Cambridge University Press, 1963.

MASTERMAN, LEN. *Teaching About Television.* London: Macmillan Education, 1988.

MAYHER, JOHN S. *Uncommon Sense: Theoretical Practice in Language Education.* Portsmouth, NH: Boynton/Cook, 1989.

MAYHER, JOHN S., NANCY B. LESTER, and GORDON PRADL. *Learning to Write/ Writing to Learn.* Portsmouth, NH: Boynton/Cook, 1983.

MCCLELLAND, BEN, and T. R. DONOVAN. *Research and Scholarship in Composition.* New York: Modern Language Association, 1985.

MEDWAY, PETER. *Finding a Language.* London: Chameleon, 1980.

MILNER, JOSEPH O'BEIRRE, and LUCY FLOYD MILEOCK MILNER. *Passages to Literature: Essays on Teaching in Australia, Canada, England, the United States, and Wales.* Urbana, IL: National Council of Teachers of English, 1989.

MOFFETT, JAMES. *Teaching the Universe of Discourse.* Portsmouth, NH: Boynton/Cook, 1983.

MOFFETT, JAMES, and BETTY JANE WAGNER. *A Student-Centered Language Arts Curriculum, K–12.* 4th edition. Portsmouth, NH: Boynton/Cook, 1991.

MURRAY, DONALD. *A Writer Teaches Writing: A Practical Method of Teaching Composition.* Boston: Houghton Mifflin, 1968.

———. *Learning by Teaching: Selected Articles on Writing and Teaching.* Portsmouth, NH: Boynton/Cook, 1982.

MYERS, MILES. *The Teacher Researcher: How to Study Writing in the Classroom.* Urbana, IL: NCTE/ERIC, 1985.

NELMS, BEN F., ed. *Literature in the Classroom: Readers, Texts, and Contexts.* Urbana, IL: National Council of Teachers of English, 1988.

NEWMAN, JUDITH M. *Whole Language: Theory in Use.* Portsmouth, NH: Heinemann, 1985.

NORTH, STEPHEN M. *The Making of Knowledge in Composition: Portrait of an Emerging Field.* Portsmouth, NH: Boynton/Cook, 1987.

OHMANN, RICHARD. *English in America.* New York: Oxford University Press, 1976.
———, ed. *Writing: Voice and Thought.* Urbana, IL: National Council of Teachers of English, 1977.
ONG, WALTER. *Orality and Literacy: The Technologizing of the Word.* New York: Methuen, 1982.
ORWELL, GEORGE. "Politics and the English Language." In *Shooting an Elephant and Other Essays.* Orlando, FL: Harcourt Brace Jovanovich, 1946.

PATTISON, ROBERT. *On Literacy: The Politics of the Word from Homer to the Age of Rock.* New York: Oxford University Press, 1982.
PEETOOM, ADRIAN. *Shared Reading.* Toronto: Scholastic, 1986.
PETERS, WILLIAM, ed. *Effective English Teaching: Concept, Research, and Practice.* Urbana, IL: National Council of Teachers of English, 1987.
PETROSKY, A. R., and D. Bartholomae, eds. *The Teaching of Writing.* Part II of the 1986 NSSE Yearbook, V. 88. Chicago: National Society for the Study of Education, 1986.
PIAGET, JEAN. *The Language and Thought of the Child.* New York: New American Library, 1985.
PLIMPTON, GEORGE, ed. *Writers at Work: The Paris Review Interviews.* 2nd series. New York: Viking, 1962.
POLANYI, MICHAEL. *Personal Knowledge: Towards a Post-Critical Philosophy.* Chicago: University of Chicago Press, 1958.
POOLEY, ROBERT. *Understanding English Usage.* New York: Appleton, 1945.
PRADL, GORDON M., ed. *Prospect and Retrospect: Selected Essays of James Britton.* Portsmouth, NH: Boynton/Cook, 1982.
PROBST, ROBERT. *Response and Analysis: Teaching Literature in Junior and Senior High School.* Portsmouth, NH: Boynton/Cook, 1988.
PURVES, ALAN, THERESA ROGERS, and ANNA O. SOTER. *How Porcupines Make Love II.* New York: Longmans, 1990.

RIGG, PAT, and VIRGINIA C. ALLEN, eds. *When They Don't All Speak English.* Urbana, IL: National Council of Teachers of English, 1989.
ROMANO, TOM. *Clearing the Way: Working with Teenage Writers.* Portsmouth, NH: Heinemann, 1987.
RODRIGUES, DAWN, and RAYMOND J. RODRIGUES. *Teaching Writing with a Word Processor: Grades 7–13.* Urbana, IL: NCTE/ERIC, 1986.
ROSENBLATT, LOUISE. *Literature as Exploration.* New York: Modern Language Association, 1983.
———. *The Reader, the Text and the Poem: The Transactional Theory of the Literary Work.* Carbondale, IL: Southern Illinois University Press, 1978.
ROSE, MIKE. *Writer's Block: The Cognitive Dimension.* Carbondale, IL: Southern Illinois University Press, 1984.

ROUSE, JOHN. *The Completed Gesture.* New Jersey: Skyline Books, 1978.

ROUSSEAU, J. J. *Émile, ou, de l'Éducation.* Paris: Garnier, 1961.

SHOR, IRA, ed. *Freire for the Classroom: A Sourcebook for Laboratory Teaching.* Portsmouth, NH: Boynton/Cook, 1987.

SELFE, CYNTHIA, et al. *Computers in English and the Language Arts: The Challenge of Teacher Education.* Urbana, IL: National Council of Teachers of English, 1989.

SHANNON, PATRICK. *The Struggle to Continue: Progressive Reading Instruction in the United States.* Portsmouth, NH: Heinemann, 1990.

SHAUGHNESSY, MINA. *Errors and Expectations: A Guide for the Teacher of Basic Writing.* New York: Oxford University Press, 1977.

SHUMAN, R. BAIRD, and DENNY WOLFE. *Teaching English Through the Arts.* Urbana, IL: National Council of Teachers of English, 1990.

SHUY, ROGER. *Discovering American Dialects.* Urbana, IL: National Council of Teachers of English, 1974.

SIMONS, ELIZABETH RADIN. *Student Worlds, Student Words: Teaching Writing Through Folklore.* Portsmouth, NH: Boynton/Cook, 1990.

SMITH, FRANK. *Joining the Literacy Club: Further Essays into Education.* Portsmouth, NH: Heinemann, 1988.

SMITH, FRANK. *Reading Without Nonsense.* New York: Teachers College Press, 1985.

SMITH, FRANK. *Understanding Reading: A Psycholinguistic Analysis of Reading and Learning to Read.* New York: Holt, Rinehart, and Winston, 1971.

SMITHERMAN, GENEVA. *Talkin and Testifyin: The Language of Black America.* Boston: Houghton Mifflin, 1977.

SNOW, C. P. *The Two Cultures.* Cambridge, U.K.: The University Press, 1964.

SOMERFIELD, MURIEL, MIKE TORBE, and COLIN WARD. *A Framework for Reading: Creating a Policy in the Elementary School.* Portsmouth, NH: Heinemann, 1985.

STASHOWER, DANIEL. "A Dreamer Who Made Us Fall in Love with the Future." *Smithsonian* 21 (August 1990): 44–57.

SUHOR, CHARLES and CHRISTOPHER THAISS, eds. *Speaking and Writing K–12.* Urbana, IL: National Council of Teachers of English, 1984.

SUMMERFIELD, GEOFFREY. *Topics in English.* London: Batsford, 1965.

STIBBS, ANDREW. *Assessing Children's Language.* London: National Association for the Teaching of English, 1979.

TAYLOR, DENNY. *Family Literacy: Young Children Learning to Read and Write.* Portsmouth, NH: Heinemann, 1983.

TAYLOR, RUTH. "Linguistic Experiment in the English Class." *English Journal* 65 (December 1976): 45–51.

TCHUDI, STEPHEN. *The Burg-O-Rama Man.* New York: Delacorte, 1984.

———. *Travels Through the Curriculum.* Toronto: Scholastic, 1991.

———, ed. *English Teachers at Work: Ideas and Strategies from Five Countries.* Portsmouth, NH: Boynton/Cook, 1986.

————. *Language, Schooling, and Society*. Portsmouth, NH: Boynton/Cook, 1985.

————. "What Makes a Good Curriculum." *English Journal* 79 (October 1990): 13–31.

TCHUDI, STEPHEN, with LILLIAN HASSLER, BETTY SWIGGETT, JAN LOVELESS, and CAROL KUYKENDALL. *The English Language Arts Curriculum: A Guide to Planning and Assessment*. Alexandria, Virginia: Association for Supervision and Curriculum Development, 1991.

TCHUDI, STEPHEN, MARGIE HUERTA, JOANNE YATES, and SUSAN TCHUDI. *Teaching Writing in the Content Areas*. 4 vols. Washington, DC: National Education Association, 1984, 1986.

TCHUDI, STEPHEN, and DIANA MITCHELL. *Explorations in the Teaching of English*. 3rd edition. New York: Harper/Collins, 1989.

TCHUDI, STEPHEN, and SUSAN TCHUDI. *The Young Writer's Handbook*. New York: Scribner's, 1984.

TCHUDI, SUSAN, and STEPHEN TCHUDI. *Gifts of Writing*. New York: Scribner's, 1980.

VAN ALLEN, ROACH. *Language Experiences in Communication*. Boston: Houghton Mifflin, 1976.

VYGOTSKY, LEV. *Thought and Language*. Cambridge, MA: MIT Press, 1962.

WALSHE, R. D., ed. *Writing and Learning in Australia*. Melbourne: Oxford/Dellasta, 1986.

WALSHE, R. D. and PAUL MARCH, eds. *Teaching Writing K–12*. Melbourne: Dellasta, 1988.

WARD, GEOFF. *I've Got a Project On . . .* Rozelle, New South Wales: Primary English Teaching Association of New South Wales, 1988 and Portsmouth, NH: Heinemann, 1989.

WEAVER, CONSTANCE. *Understanding Whole Language: From Principles to Practice*. Portsmouth, NH: Heinemann, 1990.

WELLS, GORDON. *The Meaning Makers: Children Learning Language and Using Language to Learn*. Portsmouth, NH: Heinemann, 1986.

WHITEHEAD, ALFRED NORTH. *The Aims of Education*. New York: Macmillan, 1929.

WRESCH, WILLIAM, ed. *The Computer in Composition Instruction*. Urbana, IL: National Council of Teachers of English, 1984.

ZEMELMAN, STEVEN, and HARVEY DANIELS. *A Community of Writers: Teaching Writing in the Junior and Senior High School*. Portsmouth, NH: Heinemann, 1988.

Index